The Space of Disappearance

SUNY series in Latin American and Iberian Thought and Culture
———————
Rosemary G. Feal, editor
Jorge J. E. Gracia, founding editor

The Space of Disappearance
A Narrative Commons
in the Ruins of Argentine State Terror

Karen Elizabeth Bishop

Ferrari, León (1920–2013)
Untitled. 1962. Ink on paper, 40 × 28⅝" (101.6 × 72.7 cm).
Copyright: FALFAA–CELS Agreement
Digital Image © The Museum of Modern Art/Licensed by SCALA / Art Resource, NY

Published by State University of New York Press, Albany

© 2020 State University of New York

All rights reserved

No part of this book may be used or reproduced in any manner whatsoever without written permission. No part of this book may be stored in a retrieval system or transmitted in any form or by any means including electronic, electrostatic, magnetic tape, mechanical, photocopying, recording, or otherwise without the prior permission in writing of the publisher.

For information, contact State University of New York Press, Albany, NY
www.sunypress.edu

Library of Congress Cataloging-in-Publication Data

Names: Bishop, Karen Elizabeth, 1972– author.
Title: The space of disappearance : a narrative commons in the ruins of Argentine state terror / Karen Elizabeth Bishop.
Description: Albany : State University of New York Press, 2020. | Series: SUNY series in Latin American and Iberian thought and culture | Based on the author's dissertation (doctoral)—University of California, Santa Barbara, 2008. | Includes bibliographical references and index. |
Identifiers: LCCN 2019042440 (print) | LCCN 2019042441 (ebook) | ISBN 9781438478517 (hardcover : alk. paper) | ISBN 9781438478524 (pbk. : alk. paper) | ISBN 9781438478531 (ebook)
Subjects: LCSH: Argentine fiction—20th century—History and criticism. | Disappeared persons in literature. | Political persecution in literature. | Literature and society—Argentina.
Classification: LCC PQ7707.D58 B57 2020 (print) | LCC PQ7707.D58 (ebook) | DDC 863/.640935882064—dc23
LC record available at https://lccn.loc.gov/2019042440
LC ebook record available at https://lccn.loc.gov/2019042441

10 9 8 7 6 5 4 3 2 1

for my mother, Helen,
and
my sons, Theo and Julian,
for teaching me to see otherwise

What is there, with the absolute calm of something that has found its place, does not, however, succeed in being convincingly here. Death suspends the relation to place, even though the deceased rests heavily in his spot as if upon the only basis that is left him. To be precise, this basis lacks, the place is missing, the corpse is not in its place. Where is it? It is not here, and yet it is not anywhere else. Nowhere? But then nowhere is here.

—Maurice Blanchot, *The Space of Literature*

History isn't done yet with turning itself into stories.

—Jacques Rancière, *Figures of History*

Contents

Illustrations — ix

Acknowledgments — xi

Introduction — 1
The Space of Disappearance: Knowledge, Form, Rights
  Historical Distortions 4 | Modes of Disappearance 10 | Refraction and Resistance 15 | Literary Form and Human Rights 21 | At the Limits of the Literary 27 | The Book to Come 31

Chapter One
Mimesis by Other Means: The Aesthetics of Disappearance in Rodolfo Walsh's "Variaciones en rojo" — 39
  Operation True Crime 42 | In the Beginning 46 | Variations in Red 50 | Privileged Sight 54 | The Framing and Unframing of Art 60 | Bloody Dawn 68

Chapter Two
Double Exposure: The Hermeneutics of Catastrophe in Julio Cortázar's *Fantomas contra los vampiros multinacionales* — 71
  A Fellowship of Exile 73 | On Gaining Political Purchase 79 | Smokescreen 88 | Catastrophe and Consciousness 94 | Double Vision 105 | Force of Form 111

Chapter Three
In Abeyance: Strategies of Suspension in Tomás Eloy Martínez's *La novela de Perón* — 119
  Other Logics 119 | A Deliberate Gap 123 | Dead Center 131 | What World Is This? 140 | Where in the World? 145 | Anticipatory Fictions 154

Chapter Four
Errant Metonymy: The Embodiment of Disappearance in
Tomás Eloy Martínez's *Santa Evita*   159
    Liquid Sun 160 | Null Intersection 165 | Simulacra, Site,
    and the Superabundant 171 | Burial Plots in the Bardo 178 |
    Aesthetic Justice 188

Conclusion
The Disappearance of Literature   191

Notes   203

Works Cited   227

Index   237

Illustrations

1.1 Diego Velázquez, *Las Meninas*. 53

1.2 Blueprint of Peruzzi's studio. Rodolfo Walsh, *Variaciones en rojo*. 57

1.3 Daniel's hypothesis. Rodolfo Walsh, *Variaciones en rojo*. 65

2.1 Cover of Julio Cortázar's *Fantomas contra los vampiros multinacionales*, by Oswaldo for Excélsior Cia. 81

2.2 Cortázar on the phone with Fantomas in "Inteligencia en llamas." Julio Cortázar, *Fantomas*. 91

2.3 Metropolitan skyline. Julio Cortázar, *Fantomas*. 99

2.4 Buñuel reinterpreted. Julio Cortázar, *Fantomas*. 107

2.5 Exposures. Julio Cortázar, *Fantomas*. 109

Acknowledgments

This book is the product of many conversations, collaborations, and generosities, for which I'm grateful to many. At Rutgers, my colleagues in both the Department of Spanish and Portuguese and the Program of Comparative Literature have been an important source of camaraderie and intellectual motivation. I am particularly indebted to Marcy Schwartz for many lively and incisive exchanges about the evolution of this project and her support throughout; to Andy Parker for his unwavering support and the generosity of his counsel; to Tom Stephens for sharing with me what he knows; and to Camilla Stevens, Susan Martin-Márquez, Carlos Narváez, Dámaris Otero-Torres, Miguel Jiménez, Anjali Nerlekar, Janet Walker, Michael Levine, Jeff Lawrence, and Rhiannon Noel Welch for their collegiality and encouragement of my work. A bit further beyond Seminary Place, friendships with Michelle Van Noy, Hilit Surowitz-Israel, Azzan Israel, and Jamie Pietruska and her family have all sustained me while at Rutgers. The years I spent before moving to New Jersey on the faculty of History and Literature at Harvard were among my happiest. There I taught with and wrote alongside some of the most curious, creative, and talented scholars I know. I am grateful to Jeanne Follansbee for her unrivaled direction and continued friendship. And among my many esteemed colleagues who made the basement of the Barker Center home, Penny Sinanoglou, Teresa Villa-Ignacio, Anna Deeny Morales, and Patrick Pritchett continue to be dynamic collaborators and dear friends.

The idea for this project first took root in the form of a now-distant doctoral dissertation in the Program of Comparative Literature at UC Santa Barbara. I remain indebted to my dissertation committee—Ellen McCracken, Shirley Geok-lin Lim, and Suzanne Jill Levine—for their kind and rigorous engagement, and the many conversations that helped shape my early thinking on this work. Thanks also to Swati Chattopadhyay for her intellectual solidarity and generosity throughout, and to Susan Derwin, Elisabeth Weber, Catherine Nesci, Enda Duffy, and the late Timothy McGovern for their always-open doors. This book has also been informed and improved by many keen questions and conversations, in class and beyond, from students at both Harvard and Rutgers. My particular thanks to the students in my seminars on the Legacies of Torture, Lives of the Dead, Human Rights and Latin American Literature, and Writing Torture in the Southern Cone, as well as to the very talented doctoral students and senior thesis writers with whom I've had the good fortune to work.

A number of friends and colleagues, in whose debt I remain, read and provided invaluable feedback on portions of the manuscript: David Kurnick, Marcy Schwartz, David Sherman, Penny Sinanoglou, Lisa Swanstrom, and Teresa Villa-Ignacio. Many thanks also to Christiane Ingenthron and Kathy Sherretts for help with images. My sincerest thanks to the two anonymous reviewers of this project's early manuscript, the integrity and depth of whose comments much improved the book and helped it find its final shape. Finally, warm thanks to this series' editors, Jorge J. E. Gracia and Rosemary Geisdorfer Feal, to Rebecca Colesworthy for her initial interest and enthusiastic support of the project throughout, to Dana Foote for her expert and generous assistance in preparing the final version of the book, and to Holly Day for preparing the index.

I am grateful for an American Council of Learned Societies New Faculty Fellowship, for a grant from the Rutgers Research Council, to Rutgers for a semester's sabbatical, and to the Escuela de Estudios Hispano-Americanos in Seville, which provided me with library space to work while abroad. I am also grateful to Julieta Zamorano and Anna Ferrari, as well as to Cecilia Ales from the Centro de Estudios Legales y Sociales in Buenos Aires, for their generous permission to use León Ferrari's artwork on the cover of this book. Many thanks also to Iara Freiberg from the Fundación Augusto y León Ferrari Arte y Acervo.

I am most thankful for the generosities of my wide and cherished community of friends, variously near and far as I have moved from one corner of the world to the next. This book would not have reached its conclusion without the support, afforded in many different ways, of Lisa Swanstrom, Eliza Zingesser, Stacey Van Dahm, Yanoula Athanassakis, Anne Marcoline, and Christiane Ingenthron. Rachel Hart, Jennifer Fregeolle, and Terry Besch provided welcome drinks and warm conversation when most needed. In Seville, I am thankful for old friends who have seen me through this project from the beginning and new friends, particularly los de la Huerta, who have seen me through the end of it with many unforgettable kindnesses.

My family has entertained my desire to read and write about books long past the point when they might have expected my enthusiasm to diminish. My deepest thanks to all the kids at Serendipity House, and also to my parents, Helen Humphries Bishop, Susan Scott Grider, and Bruce Bernard Bishop, for their unflagging support. Gracias a Mario Ángel Fanjul Villa and Amparo Campos Grafía por su apoyo y cariño. But my greatest debt is to Luis, Theo, and Julian Fanjul, whose constant encouragement and daily support on multiple continents allowed this book to reach its conclusion. Thank you for giving form, and meaning, to my life.

—KEB
March 2019, Seville

Introduction

The Space of Disappearance

Knowledge, Form, Rights

34° 32,3660 S / 58° 26,2575 W. At these coordinates, against the blank eastern sky and amid the gray waves of the Río de la Plata, stands the *Reconstrucción del retrato de Pablo Míguez* (Reconstruction of the portrait of Pablo Míguez). The boy's figure faces out to sea, toward the horizon, his back to the city of Buenos Aires and the Parque de la Memoria that abuts the shore. His right hand clutches the elbow of his left arm behind his back, one leg steps out just slightly, the water hides his ankles. It is a casual, if pensive, stance that belies the significance of his body in the water. For this water once received other bodies, the river a water-tomb to the men and women sunken in its depths so that their bodies would not be recovered. The sculpture stands as memorial to these enforced disappearances and moves in and out of sight, artist Claudia Fontes explains, as its "polished surface reflects its surroundings and makes the image more or less visible in the landscape depending on the weather conditions and the moment of the day."[1] When it takes on the gray of the water, the sculpture seems to disappear into the river; at other moments the light allows us to follow the curve of the young boy's back, the sinking line of his shoulders, the angle of his jaw. But we do not from the overlook on the shoreline see his face, reconstructed from surviving photos of the fourteen-year-old boy disappeared with his mother into the tortuous network of Argentina's detention and torture centers during the country's last military dictatorship. That we cannot make out his face allows the boy to represent the disappeared at large, to serve as a kind of universal figure while turning both toward the mass grave at his feet and away from the horrors he has lived. Fontes asks us, in tandem with her own meticulous efforts, to participate in the reconstruction of Pablo Míguez as we attempt to give a face to the boy and to the history of disappearance that he represents.² The memorial sculpture, product of the competing attentions of water, light, and our efforts to see that which is concealed, gives a form to absence that we can engage with. The force of this form is undeniably overwhelming, even as we may not immediately or wholly understand what it communicates.

Fontes's sculpture illustrates, in the incorruptibility of steel, the subject of this book: the forms that disappearance acquires, the spaces it takes up, and the oblique reading practices it compels. These are, despite the fact that Argentina returned to democratic rule more than three decades ago, still vital concerns. On August 10, 2016, for example, newly elected Argentine president Mauricio Macri told an interviewer from the foreign press that he did not know how many people had been forcibly disappeared by his country's most recent military dictatorship: "I have no idea. That's a debate I'm not going to enter, whether they were 9,000 or 30,000."³ Macri's public refusal to recognize the more than thirty thousand victims disappeared by state terrorism—a number long recognized by historians, the United Nations, and human rights organizations and governments around the world—signals the historical distortions that still haunt Argentine political and civil society forty years after the coup d'état that ushered in eight years of state-sponsored genocide against alleged political dissidents.⁴ These chasms, however, are more than deep divides in a national consciousness that has splintered into conflicting interpretations of historical fact and competing opinions about how to move a country forward under the heavy weight of memory and impunity. They are also evidence of a larger network of gaps, holes, rifts, and fissures that is the complicated legacy of systematic disappearance. Breaches in knowledge, subjectivity, and identity emerge as constitutive of the state, its democratic apparatus, and wider cultural and aesthetic efforts then tasked with assimilating, responding, and making something new out of the chasms that enforced disappearance leaves behind.

This book is about these absences, the new spaces they forge, and the strategies and structures that late twentieth-century Argentine novelists have used to make art from disappearance. It is a study of disappearance as a formal literary phenomenon that evolves in tandem with significant historical breaches in a state's protection of human rights and dignity. But while the history of enforced disappearance and the representation of the disappeared help shape the core of this work and inform its scope, I do not directly attend to the politics and ethics of the disappeared's material absence. Nor do I parse the crucial details of the political battles over how to recover their bodies and the genetic material of the dead, how to locate and repurpose the detention and torture centers that systematically manufactured disappearance, or how to bring the perpetrators of genocide to justice. Instead the chapters that follow propose that the structures and strategies proper to storytelling acknowledge and help us care for, mourn, and memorialize the absent dead by serving as an aesthetic index that transforms how we engage with and what we know of disappearance, as well as its future history. Rather than attending to the disappeared body, then, this work attends to disappearance as a body of work. Where art and the lived world exert equal pressures on each other, it may be that these are inseparable tasks.

Disappearance emerges in late twentieth-century Argentine fiction, I propose, as a literary device and narrative mode that responds to or intersects with the country's use of enforced disappearance as a mechanism of state terror during the military dictatorship. As it takes shape in fiction as a salient formal force—from the cusp of the coup d'état in 1976 through the decades of postdictatorship in the 1980s and 1990s—disappearance becomes a catalyst for the production of new forms of historical knowledge, knowledge production, and organizing knowledge, particularly where fiction serves as a viable primary source of alternate histories. Furthermore, and of particular significance to how we understand the legacies of disappearance, the literary strategies and structures that it takes on come to function as the ethically charged fundament of a new narrative commons that confirms the many and urgent reciprocities of the political and the aesthetic. This book engages a postmodern literary corpus particular to the twentieth century, but this commons opens up to new generations of writers from Argentina and indeed the rest of the Southern Cone who continue to craft narrative from disappearance on the far side of the millennial divide.

The literary turn to disappearance in the last quarter of the twentieth century also evidences the ways in which absence drives contemporary literary history more generally. For forms of absence show up in Western literature as conspicuous narrative devices at about the same time that midcentury hermeneutics and deconstruction offer up the possibility that what is most fully and properly literary enacts its own kind of disappearance on our given aesthetic horizons. Here disappearance as narrative technique reveals itself to be both evidence and harbinger of a Blanchotesque "disappearance of literature," an always present future condition in which literature becomes most itself, most properly art. The narrative mode of disappearance that appears in late twentieth-century Argentine literature contributes, even half a century later, to this state of art still becoming.

The Space of Disappearance studies the ways in which disappearance shows up as literary preoccupation, device, and mode in relation to the legacies of concealment, disavowal, and withholding of knowledge that enable enforced disappearance to work as a tool of state terror. Each of these strategies of dissimulation produces the epistemological aporia that make systematic disappearance possible, endow it with a perverse negative logic, and ensure that its effects are felt long into the future. I look at how three prominent Argentine authors—Rodolfo Walsh, Julio Cortázar, and Tomás Eloy Martínez—turn these gaps in knowledge that facilitate enforced disappearance into a productive aesthetic strategy. The epistemology of disappearance that emerges asks us—here where art responds to terror—to access knowledge in new, oblique modalities and to understand and engage with fiction in innovative, participatory ways amid the ruins of dictatorship.

The modes of disappearance that serve as the central axes of this book—dissimulation, doubling and displacement, suspension, and embodiment—are specific, dynamic manifestations of absence in which moments, things, ideas, knowledge, and historical possibilities that are withheld, recede, or go missing are recast as vital agents in the shaping of narrative form and both literary and lived worlds. They allow us to see the processes and techniques by which absence takes shape, takes place, and functions as a constitutive part of both storytelling and world-building. Read in the historic context of a dictatorial regime whose central strategy of repression was to fabricate invisibility, this aesthetic phenomenon abuts, resists, and repurposes disappearance in ways that have not been formally acknowledged or analyzed in literary study. The narrative spaces that an aesthetics of disappearance occupies allows disappearance to be seen, studied, and situated historically such that literary space—this the space of the book's title—verifies lived experience, validates historical reality, and becomes an agent of potential political and social engagement. The chapters that follow, in a series of engaged and contextualized close readings, examine how these spaces are provided for and function, and what they might signify both within the immediate context of their production and today, decades later, in a new literary atmosphere still trying to come to terms with the complicated legacies of disappearance.

Historical Distortions

Approximately thirty thousand people were forcibly disappeared under the military dictatorships that governed Argentina from 1976 to 1983.[5] As strategies of state terrorism, the Argentine government organized, armed, and greenlighted paramilitary police forces that carried out the dirty work of disappearance on the streets and set up a network of over five hundred clandestine torture and detention centers and concentration camps around the country to house the disappeared until their likely murder or, less likely, eventual release under the guise of social rehabilitation.[6] But in order for disappearance to function on a large scale, the military juntas—especially that of General Jorge Videla, responsible for the initial coup that ousted Isabel Perón—also enacted certain social and legal distortions that worked to normalize disappearance and cement the state of exception under which the country operated until its return to democracy in early 1984. These included 1) an official disavowal both at home and abroad that anything out of the ordinary was happening in Argentina; 2) implementing a systematic withholding of knowledge aimed to mask the crime of disappearance, disorient and destabilize society at large, and inhibit acts of individual and collective agency; and 3) altering and naturalizing perceptions of personhood by positing a future anterior state that excluded alleged "subversives," a high proportion of which were young people, from the national body.

The Videla government, in particular, took great pains to mask the work of its paramilitary police forces and the existence of its clandestine torture and detention centers. It denied domestic accusations and international suspicion that it had implemented a program of systematic disappearance—comprised of illegal detention, torture, murder, and the clandestine disposal of a body—that targeted specific populations in Argentina considered either "subversive" or sympathetic to subversive agendas. Videla's nascent military dictatorship took cover behind the state's ongoing conflict with the weakly armed Left, whose most prominent group were the Montoneros, a Peronist guerilla organization responsible for a series of urban bombings, assassinations, and ransomed kidnappings. Since their formation in the early 1970s, the Montoneros trained their eye largely on police or military units and collaborating business executives; the eradication of this smaller allied opposition was a likely rationale for the war against subversion that the Videla junta would claim. Whereas the junta would allege, however, that the number of subversives in the country totaled twenty-five thousand, Marguerite Feitlowitz documents in her landmark study of the dictatorship, *A Lexicon of Terror: Argentina and the Legacies of Torture*, that "at their height in 1974–5, these leftist groups totaled no more than 2,000 individuals of whom only 400 had arms."[7] The Videla government grossly exaggerated the numbers and capacity of the leftist insurgency in order to justify the construction and implementation of the so-called Proceso de Reorganización National, or Process of National Reorganization, under whose aegis it implemented a widespread system of national cleansing the insidious effects of which continue to shape Argentine society and politics more than forty years later.

In June 1978, two years into the dictatorship, the World Soccer Championships were held in Buenos Aires, which produced enormous national fervor when Argentina won the cup. But members of the foreign press took advantage of their access to the country during the three-weeks-long games to investigate international reports of human rights abuses, including torture and disappearance and clandestine concentration camps. The Videla government seemed to take an a priori defensive position to the rumors, however, by plastering Buenos Aires in advance of the games with the slogan "Los argentinos somos derechos y humanos," or as Feitlowitz offers, "We Argentines are human, we Argentines are right."[8] The information gathered by foreign journalists during that summer helped in part to fuel the visit in September 1979 by the Inter-American Commission on Human Rights of the Organization of American States (OAS), who organized the trip to investigate the increasingly widespread rumors of human rights abuses in the country. Throughout both the World Cup and the subsequent visit by the OAS, the junta and the national news press worked to simultaneously discredit the human rights organizations active in the country, most notably the Madres de Plaza de Mayo, and to build widely disseminated pro-Argentina advertising campaigns promoting the social and economic well-being of the country.[9] These efforts, detailed and deconstructed at length by Feitlowitz, worked to actively obscure both at home and abroad the realities of the campaign of social cleansing that was taking place across Argentina. Constructing and promoting the appearance of normalcy was paramount to the success of the regime; a carefully devised campaign of normalcy allowed enforced disappearance to take place in plain sight, broad daylight, and next door without causing undue attention.

Official response to reports of disappearance began with local police forces that alleged they had no information regarding a missing person and local judges who routinely denied requests of habeas corpus. Civil institutions, including religious organizations such as the Catholic Church and the Delegation of Argentine Jewish Associations, were also complicit in fostering or covering up the illegal work of the regime;[10] the history of civil complicity during the dictatorship is complex and difficult, but not necessarily extraordinary to life under an authoritarian state. The installation of a system of state terror might have been fashioned by Videla's government, but it was bolstered and cemented by national, regional, and local police forces and civil organizations who claimed to not know anything, see anything, or have any information that might help people looking for loved ones who had been disappeared.

This state-sponsored network of carefully crafted denial and disavowal worked to sow in the country a kind of widespread social schizophrenia. This allowed Argentine citizens to carry out the tasks of daily life while either ignoring or not seeing (or some psychologically difficult combination of the two) the violent work of the regime on the ground. Diana Taylor identifies this kind of social blinding—either ideologically willful or a strategy for survival under an authoritarian regime—as a "percepticide" capable of crippling the country's ability to see and make sense of the widespread systematization of disappearance, even despite its very often public spectacles.[11] Percepticide allowed paramilitary police forces to carry out violent detentions in public places without raising alarm; torture and detention centers to be built into lived urban spaces, such as churches, schools, and shopping malls; and the Madres de Plaza de Mayo to demand every week before the Casa Rosada the whereabouts of their children without interrupting the daily life of the city. This large-scale social blinding drafted, Taylor proposes, the "good" citizens of Argentina into an insidious power structure that allowed them to knowingly witness what the state crafted as the "given-to-be-seen" and not to see its inverse, the "given-to-be-invisible."[12] This new kind of selective sight fomented by the very public machinations of the military dictatorship allowed people not to "know" what was going on around them. Taylor writes:

> The military spectacle made people pull back in fear, denial, and tacit complicity from the show of force. Therein lay its power. The military violence could have been relatively invisible, as the term *disappearance* suggests. The fact that it wasn't indicates that the population as a whole was the intended target, positioned by means of the spectacle. People had to deny what they saw and, by turning away, collude with the violence around them.[13]

In crippling a citizenry's capacity to witness, the dictatorship secured its battle lines. People could see what the government wanted them to see and not more or, if given to "dangerous seeing," become the target of the new government's program of violence. The policing of sight is also the policing of knowledge; when witnessing becomes itself a crime or a life-threatening act of rebellion, the production of knowledge is severely truncated. Knowledge under the dictatorship—especially during its early years, which were the most violent—was suspect and made its owner suspicious in the logic of the regime. Unknowing, or better, not knowing in the first place, became a means of preservation. At the same time it protected the individual, however, it also protected the military regime.

The dictatorship sought to cultivate a widespread unseeing and lack of knowledge in the daily lives of its citizens, but it also wielded a denial of knowledge when confronted about its extralegal activities. When relatives of the disappeared went to the police to register their loved ones as missing or to inquire about their whereabouts, these requests were met with a carefully crafted ignorance that denied knowing anything about a person's arrest. Families were offered alternate explanations for a loved ones' absence, including the possibility that they had assumed false identities—presumably in order to facilitate the execution of subversive acts against the state—or had gone to live abroad.[14] This official rhetoric was mirrored in a larger social imaginary that willfully denied the existence of the disappeared. Feitlowitz cites a passage from a leading magazine of the time, *Para Tí*, that rebuked the populism and false patriotism of the "missing" while demanding that they show themselves for the good of the country: "A los que *se borraron*, que se vuelvan, que den la cara si es que sus conciencias se lo permiten" (To those who *disappeared themselves*, return and show your face if your conscience permits).[15] This more popular denial of the fact of disappearance—indeed the suggestion that the disappeared had willingly "erased themselves" from larger Argentine society—rearticulated in a public sphere the individual conversations held between families and the police officers, lawyers, and judges who actively withheld information and disavowed any knowledge of the crime. At both the level of the law and in a public arena, disappearance was a fiction the possibility of which was propagated by gaps in knowledge and the prohibition against knowledge collection.

Disappearance as a tool of state repression was also facilitated by a critical alteration in the perception of national subjecthood, as Taylor describes. She explains:

> Entry into or expulsion from the judiciary and cultural system came to depend on the performance of nationness. If there is no subject *before* the law, if subjects are produced by the very systems that claim human subjectivity as their basis (law, culture), then the disappeared, as the military leaders said all along, do not exist. . . . All those considered subjects, "authentic" Argentineans (as opposed to other Argentineans), were subjects before the law, that is, had legal rights. The others, the so-called

subversives, lacked humanity and subjectivity according to the military government and thus had no legal status or rights. They fell outside or beyond the law. . . . As General Ramón Camps said, "It wasn't people that disappeared, but subversives."[16]

The logic of the regime excluded in its conception and rhetoric the national subjecthood of the subversive. Being a "good" Argentine—again here the patriarchal vision of the *patria* offers up a binary, nonpermeable, and fixed structure of national worth that must be performed—means inclusion in the state, whereas subversion is left out avant la lettre. Taylor here identifies an Argentine subjecthood worked out *before* the law in which "before" indicates a spatial position in front of, for example, a judge—rendering the widespread denial of habeas corpus a staple of authoritarian policy—but also a temporal position taken up in advance of the conception or enacting of the law. Reconceived by the junta, in a series of official proclamations and reports that Feitlowitz in her turn deftly studies, the juridical and cultural systems that produce human subjectivity reject a priori forms of national belonging seen as subversive. This exclusion from a national body allowed the regime, per its logic as Camps cites, to disappear not people but subversives.

The junta also, by withholding the fact of death from family members searching for their loved ones, denied the disappeared inclusion in a larger human collective. Judith Butler identifies precariousness as constitutive of human life and fundamental to how we apprehend this life. That life might be apprehended—grasped, learned—depends on social and political frames that set us up to see or not see and to value or not value certain lives. For Butler, this apprehension also signals a certain vulnerability or precariousness inherent in human life marked by grief or mourning. She writes, "Precisely because a living being may die, it is necessary to care for that being so that it may live. Only under conditions in which the loss would matter does the value of life appear. Thus, grievability is a presupposition for the life that matters."[17] Grievability points to precariousness, the precarious life, and in this scenario, confirms that a life matters. The precariousness of human life is marked, Butler proposes, by the promise of grief that functions as a future anterior condition before a life has even been lived. In denying knowledge of the death of the disappeared, in withholding that information from their loved ones, the junta negated the very precariousness, and thus the human worth, of the disappeared. It foreclosed upon the possibility of grief, placed mourning in abeyance, by rejecting death where death had already occurred.[18] In the logic of the military dictatorship, and of enforced disappearance, no crime against humanity occurs because there is already no humanity in play; by denying mourning, the junta denied a priori the definition of a human life lived. The effects of this logic last for generations as family members, particularly children of the disappeared, continue to search for answers to their loved ones' deaths and reclaim within the justice system the precariousness on which their lives depended.

Knowledge under Argentina's military dictatorship was carefully curated, withheld, disavowed, and denied both under and before the law. The knowledge that the regime fought violently to suppress was the knowledge that the systematic and orchestrated absence manufactured by enforced disappearance formed its foundation. The military dictatorship produced bodily and social absence in order to confirm and rationalize the possibility of its own presence, but the propagation of its power depended on the rejection of this absence. This negation of negation provided for a false positive that allowed the regime to continue to function even as evidence of state-sponsored disappearance emerged both nationally and internationally. The holes in the power structure of the regime, and the gaps that it worked to produce, have long been located. But their effects—on individuals, families, on Argentine society writ large—are still felt more than thirty years after a return to democracy. This book looks at how these spaces manifest in literature as narrative device and form and defining epistemological agent as fiction responds to, supplements, and reworks knowledge withheld. Narrative modes of disappearance serve as new forms of knowledge production in response to the dictatorship and provide for new structures of knowledge that are transportable to other social and artistic contexts. The resulting epistemologies of disappearance instruct us in seeing and reading otherwise, accessing knowledge in new ways and often encoded forms, and understanding the absent as a dynamic agent capable of effecting change both on and off the page. These epistemologies work counter to the historical distortions, knowledge withheld and denied, and grief foreclosed upon that the dictatorship systematically generated.

Modes of Disappearance

The narrative work that this book examines responds to, directly and indirectly, the withholding of knowledge and the states of epistemological suspension propagated by disappearance. The novels of Cortázar and Martínez, published between 1975 and 1995, intersect with or reply to their immediate historical circumstances or take up the longer effects of years of disavowed knowledge and impunity in the Argentine government. The trilogy of short stories by Walsh, published a full twenty-three years before the coup of 1976, serves as precursor to the later work of his friends and contemporaries, offering up an early model of how disappearance functions as epistemological and literary preoccupation. These works intersect with the historical background of the military dictatorships and serve as a response to the withholding of knowledge that facilitated systematic disappearance, but their most significant engagement with the tensions of their historical present is in their use of disappearance as a literary technique and mode. The authors gathered together in this study offer up disappearance as more than historical fact, new social reality, or catalyst for mourning by employing it rather as a device and mode of narration. This adaptation of disappearance into textual form, structure, and method means that it is written *into*, becomes a constitutive part of, these narrative works and worlds at the moment when it is being disavowed or while the legacies of that long disavowal are still materializing. So here fiction offers up a counternarrative that more closely reflects a lived reality unable to safely and openly engage with its own epistemological constraints. It provides for alternate worlds not only capable of representing what is otherwise unrepresentable, but built out of the empty spaces, abysmal logic, conflicting accounts, divided and refracted ontologies, and states of suspension that are all also proper to disappearance.

Disappearance becomes a narrative device and strategic mode in these works of fiction and indeed in the larger corpus of modern Argentine literature, if not also of the Southern Cone as a whole. Disappearance as narrative device takes up room on the page and in the reading process in the same ways as other literary devices by providing for new cognitive and imaginative spaces through operations of displacement, substitution, supplementation, and representation. In the same way that human speech, writing, and art are encoded by metaphor, metonymy, and allegory—and here I am indebted to the late Angus Fletcher's and Idelber Avelar's elegant studies of this last[19]—perhaps it is worth considering disappearance as a fundamental rhetorical figure only limited in its expression because of its necessarily receding form. Disappearance often relies on contiguous literary devices to fully take shape, but absence and things receding are a constitutive part of our speech acts and discursive endeavors. All figurative devices work otherwise, work to name things in other ways, serve as hinges or apertures to deeper, lateral, or even superscript readings of a textual surface structure. Disappearance asks us to perform the same cognitive processes with the same ethical endpoint in mind—to think, to know, to engage otherwise—but banks on the materialization of a critical rupture to make this happen. Absence and disappearance on or from the page have the same technical agility and capacity to shape text and world as related figurative devices that we study in more concrete form.

The twentieth-century evolution of these operations has been well rehearsed in the linguistic, literary, and historical theory of Mikhail Bakhtin, Roman Jakobson, Jacques Derrida, Paul de Man, Barbara Johnson, Paul Ricoeur, and Hayden White, among others. My study of aesthetic disappearance draws from this body of thought and is aligned, if within a political context, with its largely deconstructive tendencies and commitment to extended close and rigorous reading practices. I seek to locate and emphasize in my own close readings and attention to narratological experiment the ways in which disappearance appears as linguistic and aesthetic fulcrum that opens up new spaces and provides for an extension of narrative and then also lived worlds.

As a mode, disappearance functions as a way, manner, and means of telling a story; is both a technique and method of narration; and becomes a constitutive component of form and narrative structure. Modes of disappearance find a place, or make a place, for disappearance as not only a political reality to which fiction responds, but as a critical means of seeing the world and then, by way of narrative, reconstructing that world and the systems of knowledge production upon which gross human rights abuses have acted. The larger social world here works upon literature, but this fiction is in turn also poised to work upon the world as it offers up new tools, structures, and forms by which to recognize, take into account, and account for what is not present, particularly in the context of Argentina's transition to democracy in the postdictatorship. These narrative modes of disappearance mean that disappearance is no longer denied; they function instead as markers of a Jamesian political unconscious to participate in the construction of a new hermeneutic that might return the world, necessarily transformed, to itself.

Put another way, literary studies has acknowledged since Abrams that works of art do not merely mirror reality but also illuminate it through an author's subjective expression of his interior life. Through this study I demonstrate that the aesthetic strategy of disappearance goes even further in this direction. Just as the viewers of the *Reconstruction of the Portrait of Pablo Míguez* must bring their own specificity to the figure's face—positioned purposefully to remain unseen—the authors I examine use blank spaces, elided histories, and obfuscated surfaces to imagine a different world. Art becomes not merely a lamp to illuminate what is already present but something far more potent: a tool to illuminate both what has been systematically obscured and new forms of meaning-making that emerge from the darkness of state terror. Here disappearance, by way of the most fundamental techniques of narrative, tells a story and models a means of world-building in which that which is gone, receded, vanished, or absented is a dynamic and vital force capable of exerting pressure on a corresponding lived and known world.

The four modes of disappearance I identify at work in the narrative of Walsh, Cortázar, and Martínez each perform a specific function that helps shape the text or what it aims to communicate such that disappearance becomes fundamental to how we read and what we read for. In Walsh, dissimulation manifests as key to properly reading and interpreting art, Cortázar uses techniques of doubling and displacement to catalyze historical consciousness in the face of catastrophe, suspension serves in Martínez's *La novela de Perón* as narrative infrastructure and fulcrum for parsing the relationship between history and fiction in the postdictatorship, and *Santa Evita* gives us the embodiment of disappearance as metonymic and superabundant remainder in Eva Perón's errant corpse. While each chapter distinguishes a principal mode in the work it analyzes, these four modes, in various combination, also overlap, intersect, or dialogue with each other. What appears in one work as a principal mode appears in another as a supplementary mode or at work in the background in some way. Together these four modes of disappearance function as fundamental strategies of narrative and world-building in this literary corpus. As such, they also allow for a recuperation, if partial or oblique, of the component mechanisms of enforced disappearance. Dissimulation, doubling and displacement, suspension, and remaindered embodiment are all techniques that aided in Argentina's platform of state terror. Here manifest as literary modes, they allow disappearance to do another kind of work that asks us to reevaluate our structures of knowledge, many of which participated in the construction of state terror in the first place.

The etymological history of *mode* sustains this move toward recuperation or recalibration. Where *mode* is "a manner" or "way" or "means," it comes to us from Latin's *modus*, evolved from the Proto-Indo-European root *med*, "to take appropriate measures." The root splits into various linguistic directions that appear in words such as *modern, model, accommodation, meditation, mediation, remedy, modify, mood, empty,* and *mold*. This last appears by way of Old French to signify "a hollow space" that coincides with the root's manifestation as something empty at the same time that it acts to mediate, modify, or remedy. A narrative mode, then, is a way and a means that signals in its very appearance both empty space and the capacity for modification and remediation. The modes of disappearance at work in fiction activate these affordances in narrative mode that already deal in open spaces, space hollowed out, and in the possibility that these might perform some kind of mediating function at a moment invested in its own newness. They appear as ways to represent or narrate by way of things gone or going, a narrative means that allows us to see how disappearance takes shape, takes form, takes up space, and functions to mean otherwise.

Dissimulation, doubling and displacement, suspension, and embodiment are constitutive to how the works of Walsh, Cortázar, and Martínez function, how they construct, shape, and communicate a particular narrative and world. Together they make up an important fundament for the motivation, arc, and horizon of storytelling at the same time as they participate actively in these narrative impetuses. This is to say, disappearance and the modes in which it appears in the works I study function as both base and means in the construction of new narrative, and by extension, also new possible social realities that will again in turn manifest in literature. Disappearance is at once a technique and method of narration and a constitutive part of form and narrative structure. It operates by way of specific and recurring rhetorical designs, functions in ways that can be understood together as a type of narrative movement or hermeneutics, and actively works to shape the ways in which fiction presents new worlds and engages and informs the lived world with which it interacts.

The recognition and reading of holes, gaps, and absences in literature became, under the careful lenses of post-structuralist theorists, an important aesthetic and political endeavor whose own evolution occurs in tandem to the production of the literary corpus this book identifies. Cortázar and Martínez—and alongside them Ricardo Piglia, Juan José Saer, Aída Bortnik, Griselda Gambaro, Tununa Mercado, and Liliana Heker, among others—wrote many of their works within the context of this post-structuralist moment, so that as deconstructionists noted absence as an active hermeneutic agent at work in literature, these writers were offering up works that made pointed use of gaps, holes, states of suspension, withholding, and things no longer present as a fundamental part of narrative construction and a way to engage a social reality they could not otherwise. They belong to a particular moment in literary history that identified an ethics—if often complicated and sometimes troubled—of reading what is not present, what remains, the trace, the meaningful open spaces that literature proffers. But this endeavor takes on new significance when understood as a project that evolves in tandem with, or in response to, the real-world production of absence. Literature here is not by any means a mirror image of the lived social realities of the Argentine dictatorships. To the contrary, it is a kind of *contre-écriture* or counterwriting that allows a readership to better parse the ways in which knowledge is withheld or produced; history lived, constructed, and archived; and in which art engages with and amplifies the human condition. While the stakes here are not fatal, they are mortal. For this corpus of Argentine fiction instructs us in modes of disappearance that allow us to understand how absence and the knowledge of that absence is produced, fabricated, planned, and provided for so that we move better armed through a history that wields disappearance as a tool of silencing, oppression, and dirty warfare.

Refraction and Resistance

The intimations of disappearance—blank space, gaps, deferral, the withheld—that emerge as crucial components of late twentieth-century thought and experience give way to a refracted literature troubled with its own capacity and limits of representation. Genette warns us of this as early as 1966, when he writes:

> It is as if literature had exhausted or overflowed the resources of its representative mode, and wanted to fold back into the indefinite murmur of its own discourse. Perhaps the novel, after poetry, is about to emerge definitively from the age of representation. Perhaps narrative . . . is already for us, as art was for Hegel, *a thing of the past*, which we must hurry to consider as it retreats, before it has completely disappeared from our horizon.[20]

In Genette's estimation—offered the same year as Derrida delivers up the dislocated, shifting structural center that ushers in post-structuralism—contemporary narrative folds back in on its own means of representation to reveal a troubled and imperfect artifice. "The only imitation is an imperfect one," Genette tells us, "*Mimesis* is *diegesis*."[21] Here imitation cannot help but *tell* a story, and that narrative is inherently imperfect. When the limits of narrative are violated by discursive technique, however, the text speaks for itself in ways that lay bare its artifice, reveal the unsteady subject position of the author and narrative subject, and trouble the borders between text and world. The represented world struggles against the means of its own material depiction. But as the scaffolding of representation comes asunder, where the possibility of representing the world falls short, here world construction begins toward the end of the twentieth century. What we have come to know as postmodern literature freely admits its failure to represent the world wholesale, indeed uses that failure to its aesthetic advantage to replace the effort of incongruous or imperfect representation with one of world-building. If we look back through the various theoretical efforts to describe how that world construction occurs, we find it cut through with the possibility of things disappearing, with the possibility that the very worlds that narrative seeks to build up are already precariously balanced upon certain hermeneutic vanishing points.

These acts of textual disappearance belong to what Brian McHale identifies as the ontological nature of the postmodern text: a text that self-reflexively investigates the worlds it creates, the nature of these possible worlds, and the "modes of existence" and structures of the worlds it offers up.[22] McHale provides a detailed reading of the narrative techniques and strategies that postmodern literature makes use of in its world-building efforts, many of which employ forms of disappearance or end in some kind of vanishing world. But McHale stops short of dealing explicitly with disappearance; he does not name it as such or, in his work so keenly focused on the inner workings of fiction, address the possibility that literary ontologies under erasure have a counterpart in real sociopolitical landscapes. I build on the work McHale begins by investigating the formal qualities of disappearance that make it a literary technique in its own right, the ways in which narrative strategies of disappearance respond to the formally disavowed realities of political disappearance, and the possibility that together this work of disappearance signals a shift in how we think about the work of literature—its form, engagement, and future—writ large.

McHale proposes that the ontological emerges as the defining characteristic of postmodern fiction in the same way that the epistemological became the dominant tendency in modernist literature. Postmodernism's preoccupation with literary ontologies replaces the modernist epistemological concerns that, in McHale's estimation, ask not what world is this, but "How can I interpret this world of which I am a part? And what am I in it? . . . What is there to be known?; Who knows it?"[23] Where postmodernist literature multiplies the worlds we might know, modernist literature investigates and pushes back against how we know, how that knowledge is transferred and changes over time, and "the limits of the knowable."[24] McHale acknowledges that these tendencies are inextricably interconnected, that there is no world-building without knowledge of the world and the self in it. But the evolution from the epistemological to the ontological over the course of the twentieth century allows McHale to ground the possibility of new worlds and world-making in prior structures of knowledge and knowledge production that then become in postmodern literature more questions than structures.

If postmodern literature exhibits an essential refractory quality in which it turns in on itself, back toward itself, enters into meditations upon or interferes with its own narrative structure in its efforts to advance, then whatever ontological preoccupations it displays necessarily fold back in on themselves and in so doing trap the reader within the hermeneutic circuitry of the text. A narrator or reader who finds herself caught up in the machinations of the text may well ask: Where am I? What world is this? What makes this world possible? But these questions return to the epistemological as soon as our reader wonders: Where does this world intersect with the world I already know? How do I perceive possible differences between these worlds? What are the limits of this apperception and how do I grasp these limits? The ontological returns us to the epistemological, even if just to ask us to experiment with how we engage with the new spaces we inhabit. I would propose—from the vantage of thirty years after the publication of McHale's work and more than fifty years after Genette observed narrative's nascent impulse to fold back into the "indefinite murmur of its own discourse"—that new epistemological concerns and forms of knowledge are produced when new worlds turn in on themselves, violate their perceived structural or discursive limits, or multiply in unexpected ways.

The chapters that follow examine the new knowledge and structures of knowledge that appear as the necessary consequence of worlds narratively refracted. This knowledge is intimately bound up with the construction of new fictional worlds and understands these worlds as potential blueprints for future lived political and social realities. So where McHale observes a modernist epistemological tendency followed by a dominant postmodern ontology, I see also a new epistemological framework that emerges to make sense of these new postmodern worlds and states of being. These worlds give way to knowledge as much as modernist epistemologies might have provided for the possibility, indeed the necessity, of the new multiple, dynamic, and refracting ontologies that have come to define the postmodern experience. *The Space of Disappearance* is concerned with what kind of knowledge is required, produced, or motivated by these worlds—lived and textual—when cut through with disappearance. The narrative that this work analyses foregrounds disappearance as a literary technique or narrative mode that signals a concern with how to know and how to document or represent the knowledge that the new world construction proper to postmodern fiction demands. An aesthetics of disappearance emerges, as becomes evident in the work of Walsh, Cortázar, and Martínez, as constitutive of a larger postmodern engagement.

The postmodernism that these authors participated in is a very different project from the postmodernism that we are living today. The refracted narrative worlds—and the pages that follow will look closely at examples of this refraction and its politicization—that populated Western literature from the late 1960s to the 1990s hit up against new modes of lived experience at the turn of the millennium, including multiple and dynamic cyber and virtual realities, the complex networks forged by transnationalism, the precarity and arbitrariness of war on terror, and linguistic differences at once leveled and multiplied in new media and their translation and consumption around the globe. Our current postmodern condition is not quite postmodern any longer, but perhaps rather modern again in ways that better rival the experiences of newness, shock, war, and experimentation that our early twentieth-century counterparts lived a hundred years ago.[25] It is from the perspective of this new modernism that this book looks back on the significance of disappearance in twentieth-century postmodernism and then, at its close, at its legacies evidenced in the literature being produced by a new generation of writers from Argentina today. For, at least from this vantage in the early years of the new millennium, a preoccupation with disappearance—things going or gone, receding or vanished or missing—turns out to be a lasting contribution to postmodern thought and literary technique, fundamental to the aesthetic expressions and experiences that have ushered in the new, as yet unnamed, millennial modernism we currently inhabit.

The modes of narrative disappearance seen in Argentine fiction are as much evidence and product of this fully mature modern condition as they are response to the ethical breach of state-sponsored terror at a particular historical moment. The latter works in concert with the former so that postmodern Argentine fiction does not give us disappearance as one half of a binary in which the seen, known, and constructed world is the other half. Rather it substantiates disappearance as constitutive of how and what we see, know, and build of this modern world; aperture to new kinds of visibility and presence; and as catalyst for new forms of historical, political, and cultural engagement. Dealing in disappearance follows a different logic, fulfills different narrative requirements and expectations than when building a narrative world out of what is present and tangible. It requires a giving in to the trace, the artfulness of the oblique, and a command of disconcealment. It entails making space for intimation and approximation, a deftness for navigating blank space and receding borders, and a propensity for the strategies of spatial reconstruction even when an aesthetic field is not entirely visible. These tasks—this art—works outside any binate logic, such as that promulgated by the military dictatorship that divided Argentine society into "good Argentines" or subversives. Instead, it works as part of a larger system of meaning-making that seeks not only to dismantle the knowledge structures established by dictatorship—although this act of resistance is a first step—but to construct new aesthetic forms and forms of engagement that privilege the oblique, contingent, incidental, paradoxical, fragmentary, interstitial, negated, overheard, discarded, ephemeral, and rhizomatic.

Nelly Richard describes an aesthetics that works outside of binary systems of representation in the context of the Chilean postdictatorship, whose resonances with Argentina's own dictatorship are many:

> In order critically to twist the ideological linearity of that "standpoint of the vanquished," it was necessary to be able—just as Adorno himself had proposed in his essay on Benjamin—"to address . . . things which were not embraced by this dynamic, which fell by the wayside—what might be called the waste products and blind spots that have escaped the dialectic." Blind spots that demand an aesthetic of diffuse lighting, so that their forms acquire the indirect meaning of what is shown obliquely, of that which circulates along the narrow paths of recollection, filtered by barely discernible fissures of consciousness.[26]

Richard turns here to Adorno's reading of Benjamin in *Minima Moralia* in order to describe the possibility of creating art that operates outside the dialectic of oppressor/vanquished or perpetrator/survivor.[27] Where Benjamin works to craft an alternate history out of the remnants and ruins of nineteenth-century Paris, Richard sees her contemporaries—perhaps especially the neo-avant-garde art group CADA (Art Actions Collective)—working with the materials and means that fall outside the purview of the binaries that buttress the possibility of dictatorship in the first place and that support, in many ways, the mainstream social reconstruction of the postdictatorship. There is an alternative way of moving forward that operates according to a more communitarian, paradoxical, and rhizomatic ethics than to a system of political logic that includes some at the expense of others.[28] But of particular interest in the preceding passage from Adorno and Richard is the possibility that blind spots, in assimilating and refracting the neglected, forgotten, and barely seen, demand a new aesthetics that channels new ways of understanding a recent historical past and subsequent social structures. Here art works upon historiography such that a historical future is rewritten by way of what we do not see, see well, or wholly see. Where a blind spot is what we do not discern, willfully or unwittingly, when we proceed according to prescribed or familiar means of apperception, it both falls outside our field of sight and makes possible what we think we know.[29] But this obfuscation gives way to new modes of seeing—as evidenced in the fiction that follows, variously oblique, doubled, suspended, or remaindered—that demand as consequence other forms of historical engagement that serve not only to reinterpret the present but to chart how to know differently future histories or coming catastrophes.

Disappearance functions, both on the ground and in art, as its own kind of aporetic blind spot and makes a similar epistemological claim: gaps, holes, elisions, and obfuscations actualize our received and perceived knowledge. But this book asks what happens when what we are missing or what has receded from view is activated as a narrative force. What happens to the form of the novel, in particular, but also to modes of historiography when our blind spots become, in De Man's words, "a phenomenon in [their] own right"?[30] How do our reading strategies change, or how must we change them, when absence takes shape and works upon the text before us? How do these strategies then mobilize alternative interpretations of historical event and opportunities for renewed historical consciousness? In the works of fiction this study attends to our blind spots are activated in the form of dissimulation, doubling and displacement, suspension, and embodiment. Seeing, apprehending, grasping, and understanding these forms and the pressures they exert upon literature and history requires that we adopt obliquity as an interpretive method. In so doing, obliquity becomes a reading of resistance, a new historiographical method capable of responding to coming crises and their aftermath, and a means of addressing some of the paradoxes and blind spots inherent to human rights discourse and their aesthetic representation.

Literary Form and Human Rights

One of the central motivations of this book is to examine the connections between literary device and form and human rights. The complexities of the relationship between human rights and the humanities has emerged since 9/11—which is also to say, not unimportantly, since the turn of the millennium—as a critical conversation in academic scholarship. Some of the most important conversations on where, how, to what end, and with what complications human rights and the humanities intersect and inform one another are being carried out in collective, comparative contexts that allow for work that crosses disciplinary boundaries or otherwise capitalizes on diverse intellectual traditions, positions, and methodologies.[31] The wide analytical and theoretical views being taken here in the first decades of the twenty-first century are crucial in determining how the many generalities at work in human rights theory—Enlightenment universalities, a Kantian categorical imperative, Western legal definitions—are variously upheld, reified, compromised, or contested in specific historical circumstances or examples of human rights abuses, whether real or fictional. Untangling the complex relationship between the general and the specific—as well as the theoretical and the actual—in human rights discourse[32] has become a project of critical interest to the humanities, and a project critical to the future of the humanities. For in play are definitions of the human, questions about protecting that humanness, and the social, political, and aesthetic means and consequences of representing human dignity and life; the larger project of the humanities cannot *not* attend to these concerns without vacating its own purpose in the civil world.

The Space of Disappearance, for its part, aims to explicate the ways in which literary device and literary form—each of which functions as both transferable generality and specific intervention—serve as evidence of human rights at work in the novel or the novel at work on human rights. Disappearance appears as literary device or product of source devices that feature prominently in the novels at hand, such as metalepsis, metonymy, and allegory, and of narrative techniques such as intercalation, multiple diegetic planes, and recursive ontologies. It thus takes up textual space through expansion, extension, and excavation, all fundaments of world-building; manifests new hermeneutic spaces that require an active and self-reflexive reader; and provides for new literary and ethical common places in narrative structures to which we can return amid the ruins of state terror. The dynamic relationship between device as a means to represent otherwise, and to therein open up spaces within a text, and the larger ethical demands of the novel comes here into focus. More specifically, I look to the very smallest and most fundamental components of literature as important interveners in the construction of human rights discourse. For in their most basic incarnations, the literary devices I am concerned with here strive to represent something in another way, as something else, as something other than what it initially purports to be. They diminish, amplify, reconfigure, reconstruct, and transform themselves into some other expression, thereby both extending their life on the page and ceding their place to something else. The cognitive and hermeneutic processes at work here make up space, clear the way for their own passage from one moment in a text to the next. These are spaces of cognitive abstraction but also the instantiation of world construction as one thing named becomes another thing meant or vice versa, and so a textual world and a reader's world are extended, amplified, or built up. This speaking otherwise, imagining otherly, offering something up by way of what it is not quite or what it might yet be enacts an outward expansion and a move toward organic or constructed kinship that reveals an ethical capacity inherent to literary device.

At the end of his study of Southern Cone postdictatorship fiction, for example, Idelber Avelar proposes that speaking otherwise is an inherent function of allegory. He writes:

> If the historical defeat to the dictatorships also implied a defeat for literary writing, the task of allos-agoreuein, speaking otherwise, imposes itself. "Speaking otherwise" should not only be understood as a mere search for alternative forms of speech but also as speaking *of* the other (in the double sense of the genitive) and, first and foremost, as speaking *to* the other, of answering the call of the other. Postdictatorial literatures speaks (the) other(wise).[33]

This speaking otherwise in the ruins of dictatorship requires new forms of enunciation and writing capable of housing the striving of human expression in the literary and its mimetic purpose sacrificed at the hands of state terror. These new forms respond to the abiding call and challenge to aesthetics that Adorno proposes in his well-known dictum about writing poetry in the aftermath of mass genocide by speaking, in writing, even where both will certainly fall short of what they want to express.[34] In Avelar's study, allegory makes this ethical move toward the other, to speak of and to the other. The narrative device and modes of disappearance that this book proposes also inhabit and mobilize this aporetic space such that speaking otherwise, in tandem with the reading otherwise that disappearance demands, becomes an alternative historical model and methodology.

There are connections to be made between the moves toward otherness that function at the level of narrative device and similar gestures toward the other that form the basis of ethical platforms that attempt to make sense of human rights both abstractly and at work in the world. Hannah Arendt's proposition, for example, that a human being is possessed of human rights only if and when she is *other* than human makes use of similar structures of being, of being human, by way of otherness that we see at work in the literary devices we use to construct new and other worlds and new and other selves to inhabit these alternate worlds. Jean-François Lyotard further explicates Arendt: "if [man] is to be other than a human being, he must in addition become an *other* human being. Then 'the others' can treat him as their fellow human being. What makes human beings alike is the fact that every human being carries within him the figure of the other."[35] Lyotard finds in Arendt an otherness that is a necessary precursor to and active constituent of human community, self-definition, and the right and moral requirement to protect both. The mode of becoming other or of otherness at work in Arendt's understanding of human rights mirrors the work of deferral, displacement, substitution, and potential transformation that literary devices perform. This book endeavors to expose the intricacies and common roots of these parallels moves so that we might understand literary device as an important agent of human rights work.

Literary form is perhaps more diffuse than narrative device, more abstract and difficult to define. But form emerges as one of the lynchpins in the relationship between aesthetics and human rights discourse. The shapes that texts take, the scaffolding of a story, its patterns and designs, the structures that authors build within and out of works of literature, and the categories by which we classify art, both reflect and work on larger cultural-historical norms that shape how we understand and construct human rights. As Sophia McClennen and Joseph Slaughter insist, "we cannot talk about human rights without talking about the forms in which we talk about human rights."[36] While legal or historical documents will most readily appear as the sources that inform the construction of human rights, my thinking is aligned with McClennen and Slaughter when they posit cultural and aesthetic forms as also "regulatory: they make it possible to frame and transmit some thoughts and themes and to disable others."[37] Literary form regulates, reports on, and shapes sociocultural experience and expectation as much as it serves as archive of the world around it. This book examines how form—understood variously as structure, movement, network, and genre—proper to the late twentieth-century novel in particular responds to the sociopolitical realities of enforced disappearance during the last Argentine military dictatorship, as well as offers up new ways for a reading public to face, engage with, and remember disappearance. The epistemology of disappearance that emerges in part from the forms this body of literature takes, allows for the crystallization of new forms of thought that shape how we understand Argentina's immediate history as well as its ongoing cultural and judicial battles in the long aftermath of the dictatorship. Here, for example, lived realities become divided and multiple, cultural engagement is refracted with the political, and justice becomes an exercise in multifold forms of suspension; form both responds to and shapes public knowledge up against state-sponsored structures of knowledge predicated on constructing holes in what is known and how it is known. Literary form becomes doubly important in the face of social and political deformation in that it can lay down new channels, systems, and structures of thought.

In her book *Forms: Whole, Rhythm, Hierarchy, Network*, Caroline Levine makes similar claims to a "new formalist method" that understands form not just from the limited hermeneutics of New Criticism, but as a mutable, transferrable sociopolitical agent that not only represents and signals changes in thought and cultural structures but is also capable of effecting change within these always temporary orders.[38] Levine takes a broad view of form to include "all shapes and configurations, all ordering principles, all patterns of repetition and difference."[39] She insists—and I agree—that the stakes of this expansive definition are high, for, she writes, "it is the work of form to make order."[40] It is Levine's work to make sense of how form performs on the page and beyond, but also how the spatial and social arrangements that form takes up organizes our thought and, in particular, our political worlds. Form here applies pressure to art, politics, epistemes, and ethics by way of the space it takes up and provides for, such that formalism becomes a concern proper to the studies of space and place that shape the Geohumanities. *The Space of Disappearance* understands form with the same flexibility and sense of urgency that Levine does. For form is what makes disappearance—as literary preoccupation, but also political condition—visible, legible, decipherable, and then also transformable.

Levine offers up her study of form as a kind of recuperation from recent scholarly focus on "indeterminate spaces and identities . . . liminality, borders, migration, hybridity, and passing. This work has been compelling and politically important, without any doubt, and it will surely continue to be productive to analyze formal failures, incompletion, and indefinability . . . [But] too strong an emphasis on forms' dissolution has prevented us from attending to the complex ways that power operates in a world dense with functioning forms."[41] Levine's study of form is an important one, and it has certainly informed the present project; but here I think Levine's estimation of incompletion, indeterminacy, flux, and dissolution overlooks the possibility that these conditions might also themselves take form. Disappearance is a force, a condition, a state that would surely fit comfortably in the list she offers of things indefinable or vanishing. But all of these abstractions, perhaps particularly forms' dissolution, also take shape in and exert force upon literary texts, an aesthetic and political capacity that Levine emphasizes as one of form's most salient. The formal force and qualities of things undone, absent, and mutable are a rich and ethically charged site of hermeneutic investigation; I aim to confirm the urgency inherent in understanding how these more abstract conditions take shape in literature. In the case of disappearance, the patterns, structures, and spatial arrangements that materialize in textual forms bring it into relief against murky backgrounds of censorship, historical obfuscation, and, if on a different analytic plane, postmodern experimentation. And, following Levine's incisive study, those forms that intervene in the lived world help craft a more accurate and ethical history of enforced bodily disappearance in Argentina capable of withstanding and standing up to the ongoing machinations in the judiciary, media, and national and local politics.[42]

This kind of new formalism, and other iterations of new formalist methodologies, intersect in important ways with inquiries into the reciprocal and fundamental relationship between literary form and human rights. In *Human Rights, Inc.: The World Novel, Narrative Form, and International Law*, Slaughter proposes that the *Bildungsroman* supplements and naturalizes the evolution of international human rights law, more ably communicating in narrative grammar remote legal conceptions of human individuality. In the introduction to their special issue of *Comparative Literature Studies*, "Introducing Human Rights and Literary Forms," McClennen and Slaughter ask how vocabularies serve as a vehicle for human rights discourse while their collaborators take on innovative studies in the ways, for example, in which the form of the Anglophone novel promotes human dignity as a "salient form of resistance" or the complex relationship between the novel and the human rights report, including the possibility that fiction offers up "novel truths" that truth commissions cannot.⁴³ In his recent *The Novel of Human Rights*, James Dawes analyzes the formal features of the contemporary US human rights novel, which he proposes functions as its own genre in American literature, "a form that affects both reader and writer expectations" and in turn "adds an aesthetic and conceptual depth to our readings not fully provided by the human rights interpretive method."⁴⁴ These investigations, as well as others undertaken in both comparative and numerous national-language contexts, serve as examples of the kind of work that asks how and where human rights discourse is informed by literary form. These projects are not limited by genre, and both lyrical poetry and drama also prove rich sites of inquiry into the relationship between form and human rights. But I agree with Levine when she estimates that narrative lends itself particularly well to the study of what she calls "colliding forms," or different forms that exert some kind of pressure on each other, insomuch as, "What narrative form affords is a careful attention to the ways in which forms come together, and to what happens when and after they meet."⁴⁵ While Levine's focus here is on the literary representation of social form, what she espies in narrative form holds more generally. Narrative provides for the propagation of time and space on the page and the laying bare of the complex interrelation between competing and colliding aesthetic and social forms. This is to say, narrative allows us the space and time enough to see how forms play out, change over time, and take hold in unexpected ways and places. Narrative form functions here as both constraint and liberating force and, in the spaces it offers up, allows us to keenly parse its complex and changing points of intersection with human rights discourse, ideologies, and protections.

Disappearance functions in Argentine fiction as both literary technique and narrative form. It shows itself by way of literary devices that allow it to take shape as something that should be there and is not, something missing, absent, or gone. Disappearance also *takes form* over time in the narrative works that follow and, in so doing, takes up space and *takes place*. This is a wholly ethical enterprise deeply connected to the inherent capacity of fiction to produce empathy, forge or strengthen democratic communities, and to model new strategies of knowledge collection or production. The ways in which disappearance takes form in the works this book takes up, the modes it inhabits that exert pressure on narrative content, shape, and meaning, allow us to see disappearance at work on the page, in the imagination, and, if tangentially, on the ground.

At the Limits of the Literary

One of the arguments that frames this book is that both as mode and formal aesthetic preoccupation, disappearance functions to construct a narrative commons—a shared space, a common place, grounds for community—in late twentieth-century Argentine literature.[46] It works to open, at a moment of ethical ruin, narrative spaces that might house the historical experiences actively denied by the state and lend narrative form to trauma and memory that necessarily defy coherent articulation. The disappearance that shows up here in novel form also functions as a kind of productive displacement that allows readers to engage with it not only as a lived political condition but also as a structural and philosophical concern that propagates new obligations of aesthetic analysis and interpretation. The reading public that shares in these works is compelled to inhabit a commons that gives space to disappearance and that understands disappearance to be a narrative and ethical agent in its own right. This common place allows disappearance, much like White's trope,[47] to show up as a tool or device in other forms of discourse, perhaps most notably historical or aesthetic modes. In this scenario, disappearance becomes an epistemological category with its own purpose and parameters, a mode of knowledge production that can be studied, applied, and transferred and that informs other ways of knowing. The narrative commons of disappearance is, then, a rich ethical common ground: at once a graveyard for those denied one, a textual meeting place, and a staging ground for new ways into text, world, and how we know.

The community that emerges from this commons founded on rupture, disappearance, and absence embodies in its construction Jacques Rancière's proposition, borrowed from Mallarmé, that "separés, on est ensemble," or "apart, we are together." While the sense is muted in translation, in its original formulation Mallarmé's "we" already takes the form of an ensemble in the collective singular third-person "on est." Here together many are one whose individuation or rupture is signaled grammatically only by the past plural form that introduces the subject pronoun. The resultant community is in Rancière's formulation political, democratic, and always contingent, brought together in the first instance by a rupture between the mimetic and its capacity to provoke an ethical response[48] and then sewn together by his "distribution of the sensible" (*le partage du sensible*), in which the principal concepts and material realities of a society operate by way of partition and position in time and space as they circulate and organize our daily lives and civil structures. This "dissensual community" is product of, to borrow from Jean-Luc Nancy and J. Hillis Miller, a *partage* that is both sharing and shearing.[49] It does not assimilate or work to overcome its originary break but rather builds on or by way of rupture, empty space, and productive disconnection and disruption.

While most pointedly concerned with the forms of knowledge it provides for, the narrative commons that I propose as a collective aesthetic and literary-historical space that crystallizes in postmodern Argentine fiction is similarly predicated on what is not or cannot any longer or in the future be present or whole. Both coming communities know "that there is no more any border separating what belongs to the realm of art and what belongs to the realm of everyday life,"[50] and that while this dissolution of boundaries does not imply a strict causal relationship between aesthetics and politics, it does allow for a porous and dynamic reciprocal movement in which each works upon the other to produce new art and "a new community between human beings, a new political people."[51] But art, for our purposes literature, functions here as a placeholder—at once present and evidence of something not materialized—for a yet-to-be-realized community. "The paradoxical relationship," writes Rancière, "between the 'apart' and the 'together' is also a paradoxical relationship between the present and the future. The artwork is the people to come and it is a monument to its expectation, a monument to its absence."[52] Literature stands in for the possibility of politics and a new human community, even as it commemorates in large its present absence. Here absence grounds both what we imagine and how we might live.

One of this book's minor arguments—it appears perhaps more at the edges of the following chapters than as a key point of engagement—is that this narrative commons is, in part, formed by the exigencies of exile. Disappearance is a particular, if here total, form of exile, of being forcibly banished by state power from a community, a nation, a home. So the narrative commons that emerges from the writing of disappearance is also a kind of exilic common space, and the community that it provides for is then necessarily concerned with how excision from a national imaginary works upon literature both formally and extratextually. Exile is first and foremost a spatial condition, an experience predicated on the desire to overcome space, to close an originary rift that confuses geographies, temporalities, and memories. But it also requires the construction and navigation of new spaces opened up by the inquiry, necessity, and inventiveness that the lived condition of exile requires. The narrative commons of disappearance that I propose here serves both as a proving ground for narrative techniques and modes that can be read against larger concerns with how exile functions in literature and as a literary common ground of authors who themselves write from within some experience of exile, be it, as in the cases of Walsh, Cortázar, and Martínez, internal exile, expatriatism turned exile, or enforced political exile turned transnationalism. Exile is not by any means a requirement for participation in this commons, but this book foregrounds its constitutive exilic nature and investigates the possible correlations between the need to represent new narrative spaces while navigating new lived ones, as do Cortázar and Martínez. The narrative commons of disappearance that emerges from their work signals a shared, if necessarily broken and fragmented, fellowship of exile.

This common space converges—in its potential to galvanize art, political action, and new forms of community at their limits—with the state of art that Maurice Blanchot identified in the mid-twentieth century as the "disappearance of literature." Where I am concerned throughout with the manifestation of disappearance as narrative device, form, and aesthetic preoccupation, this literary turn is also evidence and instantiation of the ways that absence, the missing, or the receding drive literary history and our contemporary engagement with literature more generally. Blanchot's proposition—offered in his 1955 *The Space of Literature* and in the short essays that close his 1959 *The Book to Come*—that twentieth-century literature writ large is moving steadfastly toward a dynamic essence of disappearance serves as a useful horizon for this discussion. For Blanchot, the disappearance of literature is literature's inward turn toward itself, toward what it most wants to express, which is in turn an always present future condition in which literature becomes most itself and most properly art. Disappearance for Blanchot is both a fully present site of aesthetic potential and a new aesthetic ethos that unfolds always toward the future in ways that preface Rancière's conception of the political. Literature here becomes a mode of becoming, the movement toward a new kind of "non-literature" that inhabits a space beyond what we know to be the work of art. The ethical stakes of what Blanchot teaches us about disappearance are high, for in the same way that here the work of literature's disappearance reveals the literary, the disappeared reveal, in their state of absence, what is most human. They become, after Arendt and Lyotard, more than human, an *other* human, wherein they are most properly human and the very fundament of the possibility of human community. Blanchot teaches us to read aesthetic disappearance differently, to understand it as a site of absolute humanness, the place where the figure of the other speaks for itself if only we learn how to move toward it.

Blanchot's estimation, or perhaps prognostication, about the state of literature innervates the literary and what we understand to be literary about a text and how it communicates to us. Far from obfuscating "necessary contradictions,"[53] he foregrounds these as a constitutive component of the dynamic of disappearance as it exerts a particular hermeneutic and ethical force upon the aesthetic and how we understand its present condition. Blanchot's proposition understands this last condition as a "form of experienced time [*durée*]"[54] that eschews the historical in favor of a future espied but not fulfilled. Here Blanchot enunciates what the late German historian Reinhart Koselleck will work out some decades later—and Koselleck will be important to my own reading of catastrophe and historical consciousness in this work's second chapter—namely, the possibility that we come to understand both the past and the present, as well as the crises that punctuate them, by way of how things turn out in the future. According to Koselleck, we are in no position to judge our past in the present but must gauge the course of human action, including how we perceive and respond to crisis, against an ever unmaterialized future. This "experienced time"—a felt, embodied time expansive enough to include Hölderlin's madness, Char's catastrophe, and Blanchot's own silence—is not ahistorical or "withdrawn from time" but rather "speaks to us in the intimacy of history." This history is one that can accommodate "the absence of time toward which the literary experience leads us,"[55] is a history made more expansive by aesthetics. Even, then, as Blanchot points us toward a literature that performs its own disappearance—an inverted but parallel movement to the performance of history that Cathy Caruth has proposed[56]—he understands this coming absence of the book to come as not unhistorical, not outside of time, but as indeed "a historical question" through which the literary might come fully into itself.

Disappearance here is a dynamic catalyst that propels literature to move beyond itself, to communicate something other, something essential but not essentialist. It becomes in Blanchot both site and mode that allows us to hear the literary speak for itself even as this enunciation is evidence of a particular sense of time and historicity. If these are "obscure problems"—a possibility that the author freely admits[57]—they are also wholly ethical concerns. When we read Blanchot in conjunction with the modes of disappearance that Walsh, Cortázar, and Martínez—representatives of the larger turn toward absence that becomes a defining feature of a generation of Argentine writers—enact in their fiction, these become form and expression of literature's very future. Here dissimulation, doubling and displacement, suspension, and embodiment emerge as harbingers of a more sweeping shift in literary ontology that itself evidences the possibility that we subjects of Western, late capitalist postmodernism know ourselves and our world by way of those processes, structures, instantiations, or incarnations of disappearance that, in their turn, make possible what is most materially present.

The Book to Come

Thinking about disappearance as narrative affordance that intersects and diverges in complicated ways from the legacy of dictatorship in Argentina requires a doubled reading strategy that perceives absence at once in its smallest literary iterations and as a larger aesthetic phenomenon that shapes a social and literary consciousness across the decades that open up on either side of the dictatorship. Both lenses—the specific and the more sweeping—of this stereoscopic vision compel new ways of thinking about the relationship between the literary and the ethical and their particular capacities to mobilize one another. They also ask us to focus our attention on one thing while at the same time seeing otherwise so that the scope of the aesthetic and historical potential of disappearance on and off the page is doubled and redoubled.

I engage this stereoscopic vision by way of a series of close readings that parse where and how disappearance shows up in the fiction that follows, the specific demands it makes upon the text and the reader, and the larger claims it makes on memory, lived history, and historiography. Close reading, the principal methodology of this book, seeks to reveal disappearance at work in three ways: 1) at the very smallest levels of literary production, device, and technique; 2) at the level of form, structure, and genre; and 3) as a defining aesthetic phenomenon that exerts force upon the larger social contexts in which it emerges. This kind of close reading animates the textual intimacies practiced by the New Critics while also attending to the sociohistorical particularities that render disappearance an urgent political condition.[58] Together, they reveal the work of narrative surrounding Argentina's last military dictatorship to be the site of a significant epistemological renovation wherein dissimulation, doubling and displacement, suspension, and the embodied remainder are vital modes of presencing, storytelling, and world-building otherwise. This "otherwise" is the obliquity that disappearance demands, the looking slightly askance, the capacity to value the agency in what is only diffusely outlined, shakily propped up, not wholly heard,[59] or receded from view. Close reading is here a form of ethical innervation that strives to attend to—to give heed to, wait upon, care for, be present for, but also in its deepest etymological incarnation, to stretch toward—the singularities of textual disappearance and the new imaginaries they provide for. This hermeneutic *stretching toward* is another way of reaching out for, apprehending, grasping, and attending to the realities of disappearance and the facts of terror and death that they attempt to veil.

Chapter 1, "Mimesis by Other Means," examines the aesthetics of disappearance that journalist Rodolfo Walsh cultivates in his early trilogy of detective fiction, *Variaciones en rojo* (Variations in red, 1953), as a precursor to the ways in which disappearance shows up as a narrative device and mode in later twentieth-century Argentine fiction. Throughout the collection, but particularly in the titular short story, Walsh deploys absence and disappearance as techniques of subterfuge in plain sight, and then dissimulation as a means to divert attention from the gaps they leave behind. Disappearance as a means to a crime in "Variaciones en rojo" is covered over by dissimulation, by covering up for what is not present and closing holes in knowledge. In order to perceive this absence—which ends up being critical to solving the murder at the center of the story—Walsh's young detective has to decipher the various acts of dissimulation that work to hide disappearance in the first place. The murderer closes, in this case, the aesthetic gap that disappearance leaves behind before enclosing the key to the crime in another work of art so that what is not present in each instance does not unmask his guilt. Here Walsh evidences the ways in which dissimulation, per Baudrillard the effort "to pretend not to have what one has,"[60] aids and abets the crime of disappearance. His murderer crafts aesthetic cohesion and completeness in order to cover over the excision and then blank space that signals the missing tool with which the murderer displaces the murder weapon, which he removes and then hides from view in another series of dissimulations. Disappearance here depends on the construction of an alternate viable story, the successful projection of the "given-to-be-seen," to cover over a central, mortal crime.

Absence, disappearance, or things receding all appear in or are signaled throughout Walsh's short story in paintings or art installations before they are exposed as clues to solving the mystery at hand. "Variaciones en rojo"—both the story itself and the eponymous painting rendered by its murderer—challenges how we read, interpret, and make sense of art, the forms it takes, and the spaces it occupies. These variations in aesthetic interpretation are many: in the first instance an artist's interpretation on canvas, then the detective's reading of visual works and an "ideal painting" rendered only in symbols that proves a red herring, and finally the reader's keen interpretation of both art and reason. In every instance, the reader must look otherwise if she is to solve the crime, but in doing so enters into a labyrinth of deduction and complicity that finds its counterpart in Foucault's interpretation of Velázquez's recursive masterpiece, *Las Meninas*. In the end, the crime—like any perfect crime—is not complicated. But this does not become clear, Walsh shows us, until we learn how to read both art and absence differently.

Walsh offers up things missing, removed, or disappeared from art as cipher and symptom of violence. He instructs us in the ways in which the dissimulation of disappearance encodes death, and also how to use art to unravel what it hides. This aesthetics of disappearance serves as basis and precursor to the emergence of disappearance as a narrative device and mode in later twentieth-century Argentine fiction. Where disappearance is not yet in Walsh's work a formal affair—it is proper to plot rather than modes of narration—it confirms the connection between oblique reading strategies, knowledge production, and the uses of art that will be crucial in Cortázar's and Martínez's work. Walsh would soon trade in his fiction for works of investigative journalism in which bodily disappearance—already used as a strategy of state-sanctioned repression in the decades leading up to Videla's military coup—features as the central crime. But his detective fiction, largely overlooked in scholarship, serves as a blueprint of the liaison between dissimulation and disappearance that would become lynchpin of his later work.

In chapter 2, "Double Exposure," I identify disappearance as a political preoccupation and burgeoning narrative mode manifested in the techniques of doubling and displacement that Julio Cortázar employs in his 1975 graphic novel, *Fantomas contra los vampiros multinacionales* (*Fantomas versus the Multinational Vampires*). Here the revelation of enforced disappearance as a symptom of US intervention in Latin America motivates both the production and content of the book. Cortázar wrote *Fantomas* to disseminate to a wide reading public the sentence of the Russell Tribunal II, convened from 1974 to 1976 to debate the effects of US political and economic imperialism in Latin America. He exposes enforced disappearance, particularly its widespread use across the Southern Cone, as one of the most insidious expressions of this intervention. But beyond calling attention to the use of disappearance as a tool of state repression, Cortázar reveals how it functions as index of a still larger network of violence sold, taught, and facilitated by North America to the southern continent. He narrates, by way of an embedded comic whose world soon merges with that of the protagonist—here the author's own alter ego—the mass, systematic disappearance of books from around the world's public and privately owned libraries. But this bibliocide turns out to be a smokescreen for the very real crimes against humanity testified to by survivors during the meetings of the Russell Tribunal II. Where the world of the comic laments the loss of human knowledge, the world of the author/narrator—which also becomes the reader's world—laments instead the loss of human life and dignity.

With the help of a pulp fiction version of the late nineteenth-century serial villain Fantomas, Cortázar details his investigation into the bibliocide that threatens the world. But these efforts soon give way to the real-world inquiries of the Russell Tribunal narrated in intercalated text and image, doubled narrative perspectives, plunging and ascending diegetic planes, and split metafictional ontologies. These techniques of doubling and displacement work in tandem to disclose the doubled function of disappearance and the stereoscopic vision required to espy historical catastrophe on the horizon. Together they innervate a certain historical consciousness on the part of the reader such that she might recognize catastrophe in the making and, in the best of worlds, construct alternate future histories. Catastrophe becomes here, per Reinhart Koselleck's theories of history, a future option instead of a historical necessity if only we learn to read otherwise and act accordingly.

The political efficacy of *Fantomas*—whether the implicit Latin American collective and call to action that Cortázar scripts translates into real-world change—has been a matter of scholarly debate whose complexities reflect a series of doubled extratextual stances. These include Cortázar's transition from expatriate to exile, his conflicted feelings about his own status as a writer of high or mass culture, and his hesitation to accept wholesale the capacity of literature to effect political change. *Fantomas* does more to further foment these tensions than resolve them, and both the political potency and the literary value of the book remain in question. The long overlooked book succeeds instead, I argue, on a historical front. It serves as historiographic intervention, provides for an abiding historical consciousness, and is a catalyst for the production of a new hermeneutics of catastrophe that is as vital today as it was on the eve of the incoming military dictatorship.

In chapter 3, "In Abeyance," disappearance emerges as a fully formed narrative mode in the early years of the postdictatorship when Tomás Eloy Martínez crafts his 1985 *La novela de Perón* from a series of states of suspension that render the work's subject and protagonist historically inaccessible. At the center of the novel is "the deliberate gap"[61] that occludes Perón's life from 1945, when Peronist masses called for the General's release from prison and returned him to power, until 1974 when he returned from an eighteen-year exile to assume the presidency of Argentina for the third and final time. Martínez leaves this almost-thirty-year gap a blank space in the middle of the novel so that he can attend to the events that led up to his rise in power and then his fall, and therein fill in the gaps that necessarily open up in any official history of Perón.[62] The historical Perón is here suspended so that we might know other versions of Perón that answer better to the logic of fiction, or verisimilitude that announces itself as such. Martínez set out to write a novel that both allowed him to supplement the biographical insufficiencies that remained after his publication in the early seventies of Perón's memoirs and to reanimate on a larger scale the slight historical distortions and elaborations that he had, in order to fill in the gaps that Perón had left in narrating his own life to Martínez, to commit when constructing the final draft of these now-canonical memoirs.[63] Suspension here makes room for and validates this technique of counterwriting that aims to neither supplement nor supplant history, rather to "reach the same truth that History reaches, but by other means, the path of that which maybe was but cannot be proven."[64]

While the sinkhole of Perón's rise and fall to power proves the absent center of the book, it is only the most notable of a much more complicated series of suspensions that Martínez effects throughout the novel. Perón is suspended for the length of the work on his flight out of exile, which is the only space in which we see and hear from him in real time. Embedded within this central infrastructure are descending diegetic levels that open onto recursive box worlds, simulacra and simulations, slippages between history and memory, spatial dissolution, and temporal interstices that all function to defer, withhold, substitute, remove, or vacate stable moments in the text. These strategies of suspension are a dynamic instrument of form that shapes the structure of the novel, its content, and the means by which we access the stories it gives us. Here syuzhet becomes fabula such that suspension becomes the raw material of the story, what Martínez gives us of Perón as historical agent and the fractured legacies of Peronism.

As a narrative mode of disappearance in which stable textual, biographical, and historical elements are held at a remove, stalled, or dissolved, suspension acts as a conduit for forms of knowledge that have been likewise withheld, discarded, or negated in official versions of history. Suspension no longer operates here, in the aftermath of the military dictatorship, as a technique of ideological suppression but as a means by which to access other aesthetic and historical possibilities that materialize obliquely on the page. Here literary form serves as site of resistance, and takes on both a recuperative and anticipatory function poised, if however incompletely, to exert pressure on systems of knowledge and social organization that privilege the total, immediate, and wholly substantiated.

If, in *La novela de Perón*, Martínez uses as the fundament of fiction verifiable historical information collected during his interviews with the General, *Santa Evita*, published ten years later, offers up in the form of documentary narrative a fictional account of the complicated afterlife of Eva Perón's corpse. In chapter 4, "Errant Metonymy," I examine the ways in which Martínez repurposes Evita's dead, embalmed, copied, and exiled body as a dynamic and ethically charged metonym for what has been absented or left out of Argentine history, most pointedly the dictatorship's disappeared. In this work, disappearance as narrative mode takes its most material shape yet when the empty signifier of Eva Perón's preserved body—here void, cipher, Paul Ricoeur's "null intersection"—is recast as metonymic structure that both expands in meaning as the novel progresses and functions as its driving narrative force. Here, if in a more visible and tangible version of what we see in *La novela de Perón*—sometimes satirical in execution, but deadly serious in purpose—the historically absented, excised, or left out become both subject of the novel and agent of its telling.

Via readings of Jakobson and Ricoeur, I look at the function of the metonym—and its expansion, transformation, and regeneration of the cognitive and literary space it takes up—as particularly poised to communicate fiction's ethical capacity. *Santa Evita* provides, in the preserved and unburied body of Eva Perón, a *topos*, both literary theme and physical place, that forms of absence might inhabit. In opposition to the fixity of the built memorial, however, Evita's literary body opens up—per Irigaray's conception of woman-as-place—as a female, fluid, and dynamic place that is in skin and womb "doubly engaged" and self-contained. I read the corpse's capacity to serve as itinerant memory site by way of Elizabeth Grosz's call for "architectures of excess" to house that which a sovereign body or nation has deemed excessive or superabundant. This new architecture, in Grosz's formulation, serves as site of new forms of community shaped from what has been remaindered. Evita's corpse—preserved, unburied, copied three times over in wax and fiberglass simulacra, manhandled, and disappeared by a new Argentine government—is this structure of excess.

Finally, I read the ways the superabundant—the corpse and the metonym—functions to drive the novel's narrative emplotment. *Santa Evita* is a burial plot twice over: in the first instance, the body serves as its own grave; in the second, the novel is the story of the failed attempts to bury the body and its copies and remove it from Argentina. Martínez, by way of his central metonym, asks us to consider what kind of stories the unburied dead require. The corpse resists burial at every turn and wreaks havoc wherever it goes—a political and postmodern adaptation of Faulkner's gothic epic—such that every plan and map fails to constrain what will not be contained: memory, myth, and metonym. I read the cartographical efforts that should stabilize the body but do not as reenactments of the impossible labyrinths that Borges proposes in his own detective fiction and as evidence that the body will not be emplotted, buried, or forgotten. This last novel embodies in full force the ethical stakes of a dynamic and abiding narrative mode of disappearance that works on both our memory and historical imaginations.

The book's conclusion, "The Disappearance of Literature," attends to the ways in which the narrative techniques studied in this work serve as evidence of both the state of contemporary literature according to Blanchot and as an aesthetico-ethical narrative commons that unites twentieth- and twenty-first-century authors of fiction that draft disappearance as the raw formal or thematic material of their projects. The always future state of becoming proper to this common place instantiates Blanchot's literary vision as well as models an example of the kinds of community that literature—across generations and particular historical moments—makes possible. By ending here, with an eye turned toward examples of more contemporary works that join in this commons, I argue that disappearance continues to function as an innovative force of form whose future is not yet decided.

The chapters that follow offer up disappearance as an aesthetic preoccupation that finds an outlet in narrative, with the subsequent potential to constitute or prompt historical intervention. They each evidence how disappearance works on the page, the role it plays in the larger structural organization of the work, and its participation in the construction of a narrative commons that signals the possibility of community—however necessarily precarious, mutable, incomplete—from amid the strategic contradiction, organized denial, and systematic loss of state terror. These examples of disappearance at work each reveal the complexities of dealing with absence, of engaging the oblique and its ancillary reading strategies, as well as the epistemological stakes of this effort. The narrative works that make up the central corpus of this study also serve as examples of a wider literary preoccupation with disappearance that opens up geographically across the Southern Cone to include Chile and Uruguay but also temporally to include both possible narrative precursors and a look forward to how a twenty-first-century literary aesthetics engages disappearance in innovative and urgent ways. By opening up the crux of this book in this way—if in an admittedly incomplete fashion—I hope to lay the groundwork for the possibility of a larger, more inclusive oeuvre of disappearance that crosses national boundaries and traditions and that, while here intimately connected to a particular historical moment, reveals disappearance to be a defining feature of a more expansive, more complicated modern condition that is not yet exhausted.

1

Mimesis by Other Means

The Aesthetics of Disappearance in Rodolfo Walsh's "Variaciones en rojo"

Todo crimen que deja indicios materiales es imperfecto.

—Rodolfo Walsh, *Mayoría* n° 61

The image should stand out from the frame.

—Michel Foucault, *The Order of Things*

The production of space is thus transformed into its opposite: the reproduction of things in space.

—Henri Lefebvre, *The Production of Space*

In March 1977, one year after Jorge Rafael Videla's anti-Peronist junta ousted Juan Domingo Perón's third wife as president of Argentina, Admiral Emilio Massera informed a task force that he wanted the journalist and revolutionary Rodolfo Walsh captured alive. The death squad, which included the notorious torturers Alfredo Astiz and Jorge Acosta, requested a "Free Zone"—an order that alerted local police forces to stay clear so that the State could carry out a clandestine arrest—in downtown Buenos Aires in order to set a trap for Walsh. The usually alert and cautious Walsh walked into the ambush. In preparation for this moment, the author carried with him both a cyanide pill and a small pistol that might provoke his captors to shoot him. He used the latter that day and was gunned down in the street. His body was put in the trunk of a car and taken to the Escuela Superior de Mecánica de la Armada, or the ESMA, then operating as a clandestine concentration camp on the shore of the Río de la Plata in Buenos Aires. Walsh's body was recognized by two friends when left overnight in a corridor, but it would be some years before they were released and could confirm the journalist's death to his family and friends. In the meantime, a habeas corpus writ filed on his behalf was denied, his family did not know if he was alive or dead, and his body was never recovered. Walsh's disappearance was condemned widely, including in an open letter to the junta published in *La Nación* on November 25, 1977, and signed by fellow writers Roland Barthes, Michel Foucault, and Italo Calvino.

Among the documents that Walsh's murderers found on his person was a map they deemed an important key to his clandestine revolutionary operation. Accompanied by a moveable disc, it was interpreted by the army to reveal the locations of upcoming attacks from the revolutionary left.[1] But they could not identify these locations or otherwise make sense of the chart. The meaning of the map was later revealed by his daughter Patricia as a chart of the night sky that Walsh drew up to teach his daughters to follow the progression of constellations throughout the year; the disc revealed not the future sites of guerilla attacks but rather the orbits of the planets around the sun.[2] The account evidences the shortsightedness of the dictatorship, but it also serves as a cautionary introduction to reading not only the investigative journalism for which Walsh is more widely recognized but also his detective fiction. For it reminds us that clues might not mean what they seem, that the key to a crime may reside in our reading practices, and spatial organization can be in its own right an important source of new knowledge. These analytic propositions prove fundamental to making sense of Walsh's early fiction and the model it offers up for later twentieth-century Argentine authors who will go on to draft disappearance as a particular narrative mode and device in response to the pressures of state terror.

This chapter examines how disappearance manifests as a significant literary trope and tool in the eponymous short story of Walsh's 1953 trilogy of detective fiction, *Variaciones en rojo* (Variations in red). Throughout the work, Walsh cultivates an aesthetics of disappearance in which the absent and then also the forms of dissimulation that cover up and over what is missing become particular modes of knowledge. Walsh constructs gaps, deferrals, and disappearances that are fundamental to the narrative structure of his fiction and to solving the crime at hand, but these become also critical to how we read art and its potential relationship to mortal crime. For disappearance, and the murderous attempt to use art to close the gaps it leaves behind, proves the clue that leads to the crime's resolution. Walsh's early detective fiction offers up the possibility that art and disappearance are intimately connected and instructs his reader in the oblique interpretive tools and practices that allow us to parse their relationship and the forms of knowledge and intimations of justice that emerge from it.

The more complex potential of this relationship will manifest decades later in Argentine fiction where doubling and displacement, suspension, and embodiment emerge as fully fledged narrative modes of disappearance. But Walsh's "Variaciones en rojo" offers up an early version in which techniques of deferral and dissimulation—the attempt to hide, mask, or deflect presence—point simultaneously to disappearance, art, and new knowledge. Here art is realized or read as mimetic intervention only after having served as a means of deflection such that deferral, referral, and displacement appear as constitutive components of imitation. Put simply, art deflects in order to reflect real, if narrative, life—which in this case involves murder—and the reader, viewer, and metadetective resists attending to what obliquity plainly reveals at her own risk. For there, Walsh's narrative universe reveals—in its complicated, recursive network of the visual, the missing, and the denied—resides the knowledge that we need to restore balance and justice in a world gone wrong.

Solving the crime, which is also solving for disappearance in this *relato de enigma*, requires we read the ways that art intersects with the lived world as much as reflects it. Walsh uses art to communicate what is not immediately visible so that the story's detective, and the reader alongside him, have to turn to art in order to make sense of the world before them. Navigating this circuitry of mimetic referral depends on both logic and the careful parsing of spatial organization. The close circumscription of space—not unimportantly also one of Poe's requirements for literary composition[3]—and of time are both traditional provisions of analytic detective fiction; a classical crime must occur within a bounded space and bracketed time period such that space has always had an important role to play in works of detective fiction. But in Walsh's work, the useful interpretation of physical space is only possible by understanding the function of disappearance and how it informs our reading of art.[4] Here the spaces that disappearance takes up, conquers, and opens in the overlapping lived and aesthetic worlds prove the key to solving the mortal crime at the heart of the story. In "Variaciones en rojo" Walsh tests the relationship of disappearance to both logic and art, and he crafts an aesthetics in which what is missing reveals what is before us. The possibility, while here still literary preoccupation, serves as precursor to the more urgent formal narrative interventions that disappearance will make decades later as a response to the realities of state terror. But Walsh confirms already art's capacity to house and make visible disappearance; he asks that we pay careful attention to the aesthetic forms and spaces it occupies and the pressure these exert on how we see and interpret the lived world.

Operation True Crime

Forty years after his death, Rodolfo Walsh is best remembered for his literary journalism or true crime narrative, particularly *Operación masacre* (1957), *Caso Satanowsky* (1958, 1973), and *¿Quién mató a Rosendo?* (1969), and for his final work, "Carta abierta de un escritor a la junta militar" (Open letter from a writer to the military junta, 1977), the document that surely sealed his death. These works, as well as a vast collection of journalistic pieces, short stories, posthumously published outlines for future work, and partially finished pieces, reflect the personal and professional transition that Walsh underwent from author of literature to literary journalist to purely political writer.[5] In hindsight, the transition makes sense. Early on in his career, while he was still writing detective fiction and submitting his work to municipal literary prizes, he worked as a proofreader and translator at Hachette in Buenos Aires, and as an editor, most notably of the first collection of Argentine crime fiction, *Diez cuentos policiales argentinos* (Ten Argentine police stories, 1953), in which he brought together works by Jorge Luis Borges, Jerónimo del Rey, Leopoldo Hurtado, and the pseudonymous H. Bustos Domecq (shared alter ego of Borges and Adolfo Bioy Casares). The last work in the anthology is his own, "Cuento para Tahúres" (A story for cheats). Walsh's world was largely a literary one at least until 1951, when he began to work as a journalist at the magazines *Leoplán* and *Vea y Lea* in Buenos Aires. He continued to dedicate himself to both literature and journalism throughout the fifties, but his definitive entry into the world of investigative political writing came in 1957, with the serial publication of his first work of literary journalism, what would later become *Operación masacre* (*Operation Massacre*).

Walsh's account—which precedes by nine years Truman Capote's *In Cold Blood* (1966), often cited as inaugurating the genre of true crime literature—details the José León Suárez massacre, the attempted execution of eleven alleged participants in a June 1956 Peronist uprising against then-president Aramburu.[6] Of the eleven men police attempted to execute in a wasteland next to a city dump, six survived by running beyond the scope of the police vehicle headlights and escaping into the dark or by playing dead. All of the survivors went into hiding and were presumed dead by the police. In December 1956, Walsh received a tip that there had been survivors to the execution, one of whom Walsh tracked down in the Bolivian embassy where he had taken refuge. This survivor related the night's events to Walsh, who subsequently put his own life on hold in order to investigate the police violence.[7] He published a final version of his account, "Massacre del barrio José León Suárez: un libro sin editorial" (Massacre in the José León Suárez district: a book without a publisher), in nine installments that ran from May to July 1957 in the magazine *Mayoría*; three different publishing houses came out with new editions in 1964, 1969, and 1972.

Shortly after beginning his investigation into the Aramburu government's illegal executions, Walsh wrote in a letter to his American friend, translator, and detective genre enthusiast Donald Yates, "I've had a hell of a time these three months. Most of it away from home. But I'm doing what I've always wanted to do, working on a *real case* and succeeding too. This thing grows more sensational every day."[8] After years of reading and writing detective fiction, Walsh was now putting his efforts toward investigating a real crime; the move was a logical one that in retrospect both solidifies the beginning of Walsh's career as a writer of political literature and makes manifest his belief that politics and art be contiguous projects. While Walsh continued to write literary fiction over the next twenty years, including the important collection of short stories *Los oficios terrestres* (1965), he increasingly devoted his efforts to political journalism, politicized fiction, and further true crime narrative. He took on two new investigative projects, *Caso Satanowsky* and *¿Quién mató a Rosendo?*, in which he detailed the cover-ups surrounding the political murders of a prominent judge and a union leader, both in Buenos Aires.

About this shift in his writing, he observed:

La desvalorización de la literatura tenía elementos sumamente positivos: no era posible seguir escribiendo obras altamente refinadas que únicamente podía consumir la intelligentzia burguesa, cuando el país empezaba a sacudirse por todas partes. Todo lo que escribiera debía sumergirse en el nuevo proceso, y serle útil, contribuir a su avance. Una vez más, el periodismo era aquí el arma adecuada.

The devaluation of literature had wholly positive elements: it wasn't possible to keep on writing highly refined works that only the bourgeois intelligentsia could consume when the whole country was starting to shake up. Everything I wrote had to immerse itself in the new process, and be useful, contribute to its advance. Once again, journalism was here the appropriate weapon.⁹

Walsh describes his turn to journalism as a response to the social and political demands of his time. But he doesn't ever see art and politics as entirely unconnected. Instead, he sees them as dynamic facilitators of each other's projects: politics as a valid literary preoccupation and literature as a crucial mechanism for political change.

In March 1970, in an interview with his friend Ricardo Piglia, Walsh confirmed what his writing had long espoused, a concerted commitment between aesthetics and politics:

> Hoy pienso que no sólo es posible un arte que esté relacionado directamente con la política, sino que como retrospectivamente me molesta mucho esa muletilla que hemos usado durante años, quisiera invertir la cosa y decir que no concibo hoy el arte si no está relacionado directamente con la política, con la situación del momento que se vive en un país dado, si no está eso, para mí le falta algo para poder ser arte. No es una cosa caprichosa, no es una cosa que yo simplemente la siento, sino que corresponde al desarrollo general de la conciencia en este momento, que incluye, por cierto, la conciencia de algunos escritores e intelectuales, y que realmente va a ser muy clara a medida que avancen los procesos sociales y políticos, porque es imposible hoy en la Argentina hacer literatura desvinculada de la política o hacer arte desvinculado de la política, es decir, si está desvinculado de la política por esa sola definición ya no va a ser arte ni va a ser política.¹⁰

> Today I think that not only is an art directly related to politics possible, but that also in hindsight, this catchphrase that we have used for years really bothers me; I'd like to invert it and say that today I cannot conceive of art that is not directly related to politics, to the current situation being lived in a given country. If that's not there, I think something is lacking for it to be art. This is not caprice, it isn't something that I simply feel, but rather that corresponds to the general evolution of conscience

right now. This indeed includes the conscience of some writers and intellectuals, and is really going to become very clear as social and political processes go forward. Because it is impossible today in Argentina to create literature disconnected from politics or to create art disconnected from politics. I mean, if it's disconnected from politics, for that reason alone it's already not going to be art nor is it going to be politics.

Walsh here responds to Piglia's questions about the relationship between the novel and the short story, about the type of fragmentary novel that Walsh constructs in his true crime narrative. Earlier in the interview, Walsh identifies the novel as a "bourgeois conception of literature" and posits that different moments in social history require different forms of representation; he feels that "fiction is likely coming to its splendid end" and that "new forms of production necessitate a new kind of more documentary art."[11] Walsh aims to create art that demonstrates something, an art founded on the idea that testimony (*testimonio*) and protest or criticism (*denuncia*) are artistic categories at least as worthwhile as fiction.[12] This brings him to his claim that art and literature are directly and inextricably related, a belief that responds to the political upheaval and social changes taking place in Argentina at the time. For Walsh, literary form must reflect a lived present; the novel, at least the traditional nineteenth-century novel that informed the novels produced in mid-twentieth-century Argentina, was either not capable of containing or not the appropriate sociopsychological container for the political history his country was constructing for itself. His espousal of the intimate relation between literature and politics, that one defines the other, is a call to rethink narrative form as much as a measure of his political commitment.[13] Thus Walsh joins the many Latin American writers who, faced with repressive economic and violent political changes in their countries in the second half of the twentieth century, transgressed traditional boundaries of literary form and genre as they sought to create politicized literature that mirrored the tumultuous times they were living.

Walsh's literary trajectory from *Variaciones en rojo* to his later documentary narrative is not at all a straight line,[14] but the work of deduction that he performs in his early detective fiction prepares him for the kind of investigative thinking he will need to do to expose the real-world crimes of state violence in his later work; he uses the same skills of logic, detection, and spatial analysis to investigate and report on real world political crimes that he does to construct his detective stories. He reminds his readers of this when he publishes works of journalism under the pseudonym Daniel Hernández, the name of the modest proofreader turned amateur detective who solves the crimes in the three works that make up *Variaciones en rojo*. Walsh first inserts himself into his literature, then extracts, borrows from, and gives back to himself from this body of work. Walsh would dedicate the majority of his career to exposing real crimes of state terror and impunity rather than constructing further fictional worlds; but this move was possible only after Walsh had spent time building, testing, and transgressing the limits of fiction. Walsh's detective fiction is not devoid, then, of political potential; rather, it serves as the testing ground for important real-world techniques of deduction and knowledge production that will work to make disappearance visible and legible both leading up to and during the early years of the military dictatorship. This potential can be parsed on its own terms, but it garners strength when read in relation to the future work it engenders. For the oblique strategies of interpretation—of both crime and art—in "Variaciones en rojo" serve as early example of the later reading practices compelled by the modes of disappearance that will soon take shape in Argentine narrative.

In the Beginning

When Walsh began writing detective fiction in the early 1950s, he was already well versed in the English and French traditions of the detective novel, as well as what had been until then, according to the author, the largely derivative and sporadic contributions to a Latin American detective genre. Exceptions to this would have included Borges's canonical metaphysical short stories, such as "La muerte y la brújula" ("Death and the Compass") and "El jardín de senderos que se bifurcan" ("The Garden of Forking Paths"); the urban crime narratives of Roberto Arlt; and the *relatos de enigma* of Uruguayan Horacio Quiroga. Walsh lamented the difficulty of establishing a uniquely Latin American genre of detective fiction; he identified as the major setback the fact that most Latin American authors set their detective stories in either Britain or the United States and that many also wrote under anglicized pseudonyms in order to fit into a more established body of work.[15] So when he wrote *Variaciones en rojo* in 1953—in, reportedly, one month—he set two of the trilogy's stories in Buenos Aires and published them under his own name with the publishing house Hachette where he worked. He anchored the stories, and the investigations, with descriptions of locations detailed enough to find on a map, timetables of real train routes, floor plans where appropriate, and sketches of maps that illuminate the settings of the crime. Walsh located his detective fiction in a real world in real time, making the settings familiar and identifiable to an Argentine audience. This specificity aided in putting Argentine detective fiction on an international literary map but the solidity of this emplacement also proved an important counterpart to the significance of disappearance in Walsh's first collection of detective stories.[16]

Variaciones en rojo is comprised of three short works of classical analytic detective fiction, "La Aventura de las pruebas de imprenta" (The galleys affair), "Variaciones en rojo" (Variations in red), and "Asesinato a distancia" (Murder from a distance). Walsh's early literary endeavor is a classic whodunit that depends upon a fairly simple formula. W. H. Auden, self-confessed addict of the detective genre, provides a useful summary of this formula: "A murder occurs; many are suspected; all but one suspect, who is the murderer, are eliminated; the murderer is arrested or dies."[17] While Walsh constructs a series of complicated and often innovative crimes, he relies throughout on this basic schemata of an initial murder that takes place before the story begins, a subsequent investigation undertaken by the formulaic and shortsighted local detective who relies on the acuity and intuition of his friend the proofreader-turned-amateur-detective, the proposal and rejection of various hypotheses to describe the events that led up to the crime and the murder itself, and finally the identification of the murderer by the police detective's amateur sidekick. The resolution of the case foregrounds the detective's skills of deduction enacted within a confined physical space, over a short period of time, and in relation to a limited number of people who are primarily family or friends. The general quest to restore a state of innocence to a temporarily ethically marred society prevails. That Walsh had adhered to this traditional prescription of the analytic detective story would later trouble him, but I see in its aesthetic imperatives an important precursor to the possibility of political action. And the young Walsh was not at all devoid of invention.

He prefaces his collection with a brief author's note in which he reflects, as convention seems to dictate, on the methodology and unavoidable shortcomings of his stories, yet he ends his prologue with a very much unformulaic challenge to his reader. Walsh begins by setting up a circular relation between himself and his protagonist, opening the work with:

> Sé que es un error—tal vez una injusticia—sacar a Daniel Hernández del sólido mundo de la realidad para reducirlo a personaje de ficción. Sé que al hacerlo contribuyo de algún modo a fijarlo en un destino que no quiso para sí y que le fue impuesto por la casualidad. Sin embargo, no veo cómo podría resistir la tentación de relatar—aun torpemente—algunos de los numerosos casos en que le ha tocado intervenir.[18]

> I know that it is an error—perhaps an injustice—to bring Daniel Hernández out of the solid world of reality in order to reduce him to a fictional character. I know that by doing this I am helping in some way to fix him to a fate he didn't want for himself and that was imposed upon him by coincidence. However, I don't see how I could resist the temptation to relate—if clumsily—some of the numerous cases in which he intervened.

Walsh here recalls the self-effacing introductions of his precursors Poe and Borges, as well as the tropic doubling of author-protagonist. But this latter is an important move, for herein Walsh begins with a confession and an injustice. He opens his book by confessing to an error, a rhetorical move that both reveals the necessary end of each story and implicates him, the author, in a parallel crime. Walsh presents himself from the outset as perpetrator of an authorial injustice, his crime being having reduced a real Daniel to a fictional character. The reader must question, then, before beginning the book, who Daniel Hernández might be in "the solid world of reality." Any avid reader of detective fiction will recognize Walsh's tactic as literary convention, but Walsh also has historical and generic pretensions here. In February 1954, Walsh published an article titled "Dos mil quinientos años de literatura policial" (Twenty-five hundred years of crime literature) in *La Nación*, in which he posits the biblical prophet Daniel, interpreter of dreams and courtly interrogator, as the first literary detective.[19] By naming his protagonist Daniel, Walsh inserts himself metatextually, as Daniel's real-life proofreader counterpart, and historically, as author, into a long history of crime fiction. This introduction also tells the reader that Daniel has intervened in numerous other crimes. The construction of a series of mirror-image identities recalls, in hindsight, Walsh's authorial sleight of hand, the many disguises that Walsh would later adopt in order to investigate real-world political crimes, and the porous boundaries between fiction and reality that will come in later years to take on critical ethical significance.

Walsh goes on to reflect on the professional and intellectual similarities between the proofreader and the detective. He writes:

> Seguramente todas las facultades que han servido a D.H. en la investigación de casos criminales eran facultades desarrolladas al máximo en el ejercicio diario de su trabajo: la observación, la minuciosidad, la fantasía (tan necesaria, vgr., para interpretar ciertas traducciones u obras originales) y, sobre todo, esa rara capacidad para situarse simultáneamente en planos distintos que ejerce el corrector avezado cuando va atendiendo, en la lectura, a la limpieza tipográfica, al sentido, a la bondad de la sintaxis y a la fidelidad de la versión.[20]

> Surely all of the faculties that aided D.H. in the investigation of criminal cases were skills refined to the fullest in the daily exercise of his work: observation, attention to detail, imagination (so central, e.g., in interpreting certain translations or works in the original) and, above all, that rare capacity to situate oneself simultaneously on distinct planes that the skilled proofreader exercises when he looks out, in his reading, for typographical cleanliness, sense, the felicity of syntax, and the faithfulness of the text.

Walsh pays homage to the occupation of the proofreader, yet he also provides his readers with a catalog of requirements they will need in order to be active and careful readers, which is to say, literary detectives. He cautions his readers to hone both their skills of observation and the strength of their imaginations. He warns them that in order to solve the crimes at hand, they will have to themselves be proofreaders—literally, readers of clues, evidence, proof—and cultivate the ability to simultaneously inhabit different temporal, physical, and intellectual realms. And the active reader—who he will later distinguish from the passive reader who only waits for the detective to present the solution of the crime—will look out for typographical abnormalities, sense, the felicities of time and order worked out on the page in the form of syntax, and faithfulness to the correct version of both text and event. Walsh provides his readers, if they are reading well, with a list of clues avant la lettre as to how to read the texts and thus solve the crimes that follow. Each of the proofreader's skills that Walsh mentions is a practical key to solving the crimes that he constructs. While they might together serve as general admonishment, the individual talents can also be rather cleanly divided between the stories: the attention the reader must pay to typographic cleanliness hints at where the clue to "La Aventura de las pruebas de imprenta" resides; dedication to aesthetic sense and geometric imagination will reveal the key to solving "Variaciones en rojo"; and a heightened awareness of how time takes place will prove an essential part of interpreting how the "Crimen a distancia" was committed. Walsh here commends the proofreader, the detective, and the active reader to each other as different versions of themselves. And as if, in the luxury of reading for leisure, this has not been clear enough, he ends his preface by issuing a private challenge to the reader. He tells us that in each story there comes a moment at which the reader has enough information to solve the crime for herself and provides the page number at which this synthesis occurs. The clues to the crime hide here in plain sight, obfuscated only by the complicated variations in dissimulation the author performs to test how we read art, space, and the world we inhabit.

Variations in Red

The Players
Carla de Velde: the deceased; Giardino's wife; Peruzzi's lover
Duilio Peruzzi: internationally renowned artist; Carla de Velde's lover
Hans Baldung: Peruzzi's assistant; escaped Nazi war criminal
Count Romolo Giardino: Carla de Velde's husband
Carmen Sandoval: cleaning lady
Chief Jiménez: police chief of Buenos Aires
Daniel Hernández: proofreader; amateur detective; friend of police chief

The Crime Scene
Duilio Peruzzi's apartment in Buenos Aires. Carmen Sandoval arrives, as usual, at 6:00 a.m. to clean the artist's studio; he works at night, and finishes by the time she gets there. This morning, Sandoval finds the key to the studio outside in the lock, which is unusual, as she has her own key to open the door. She turns the key in the lock, opens the door, and finds Carla de Velde dead, laid out on the studio floor. A sculpture of a head stands on a pedestal, a mask with a monstrous open mouth hangs from the ceiling. In a corner of the room crouches a wide-eyed Duilio Peruzzi. The whole room is bathed in a wild red light that flows from the ceiling and the walls and across the room's red

> curtains. Carla is dressed in a scarlet dress, her red hair falling around her bare shoulders; from a tiny hole in the center of her chest pours forth a steady stream of blood. The whole scene is disproportionate, fantastic, grotesque. Red.

In the titular work of *Variaciones en rojo*, Walsh constructs *a relato de enigma* predicated upon an aesthetics of disappearance that calls into question the material necessities of art and its interpretation. The crime committed is, in the final analysis, a crime against art and traditional reading practices, for Carla de Velde's murderer conscripts art in an attempt both to commit and cover up his crime. But the latent ideological undertones of the tale as well as its possible political ramifications are significant, especially given the context of Peronism in which Walsh was working and the series of violent insurgencies that would come to define Argentine politics for at least the next thirty years. Disappearance, in "Variaciones en rojo," is both the failed facilitator of violence and the hermeneutic crux of the case.

Walsh hides the key to the "Case of the Scarlet Room," as Chief Jiménez calls it, when he presents his erroneous hypothesis in a visual and philosophical mise en abyme that forms the framework of the narrative structure of the story.[21] The investigation and its resolution hinge upon the role that seven works of art play in the mystery:

1. the portrait that Peruzzi is drawing of de Velde, the execution of which drew her to the artist's studio;
2. the scene of the crime, including the plaster head and gaping mask that adorn it;
3. Baldung's miniature cityscape portraying large velvet bats hanging above skyscrapers and, to the right, a crane digging into the floor of fresh dirt decorated with tiny white crosses;
4. Peruzzi's sketch of his assistant's cityscape prototype;
5. a painting by Peruzzi of humanity on an abyss, which Daniel studies in the artist's gallery across from his studio;
6. the so-called "ideal" painting, entitled *Suspiro decreciente en función del logaritmo de pi* (Breath diminishing in function of the logarithm of pi);
7. an unfinished canvas painted with a few strokes of red with which the story closes.

How the story proceeds, and Daniel's and the reader's ability to solve the crime, depend upon the interpretation of each of these pieces of art, as well as the catena of meanings that manifests between them. But while the clues that the reader needs to resolve the case are buried in the composition of these works of art, and although what amounts to Walsh's treatise on aesthetics is framed by them, the author and the murderer both use art as a diversion to distract the reader and detective from staying the proper course. This danger can be resolved in a single dictum that should serve, at least in retrospect, as an important key to the crime: do not trust art. Or, understood as an aesthetics reframed within a future political context: art will reveal, if we only learn to look otherwise, crimes that remain obscured before us.

Walsh works out this slippery aesthetic field by setting up the works of art in a complex network of referral and deferral, so that one work is incapable of portraying its full or ideal meaning independent of its relationship with another work of art in the story. This creates an unstable hermeneutics that doesn't allow the reader—here, also the viewer—to trust her heretofore reliable methods of interpretation. While Walsh hints at this challenge from the beginning of the story, it becomes manifestly clear about halfway through; at this point, the reader realizes that any further reference to art might either, or perhaps simultaneously, obscure the truth or hide the key to the crime. In either case, art acts here to cover something up, and thus confirms the pitfalls of a mimetic ideal. The story finally reveals to its reader evidence hidden in an unfinished work of art introduced as the "ideal painting." The truth, Walsh intimates, can indeed be accessed if only we learn how to properly *perceive*—from Latin: obtain, grasp, collect, all important gestures when dealing with art—and read the ideal, which may show up where we least expect it.

Walsh's "Variaciones en rojo" recalls Foucault's well-known analysis of Velázquez's *Las Meninas* (figure 1.1) at the beginning of *The Order of Things*. In his description of the painting, Foucault brings into relief a network of sightlines and system of representation that manifests a space that far exceeds the scene that the painting frames. Velázquez's masterpiece succeeds in opening up "an essential void: the necessary disappearance of that which is its foundation."[22] In Velázquez's painting, and in Foucault's analysis, what gets elided is the subject itself: "the person it resembles and the person in whose eyes it is only a resemblance."[23] Both the subject of the painting—the king and queen of Spain viewed doubly by the artist himself who figures in the work—and the spectator of the scene who sees the pair reflected in the mirror behind the painting are elided. The viewer, victim of so many eyes

Figure 1.1 Diego Velázquez, *Las Meninas*, 1656. Museo del Prado, Madrid.

staring out at her, finds her likeness in the form of the sovereign reflected at the back of the painting; she is displaced and both her subjecthood and subjectivity, per Foucault, disappear in the spatial abyss of the painting opened up by a repetition of crossed gazes. The arrangement of viewing and interpretation that Walsh sets up in his short story functions in a similar manner. The author builds a network of art in various stages of completion that multiple spectators view, at the center of which is caught the reader herself. Because each piece of art can only be fully interpreted by way of its relation to the other pieces of art in the story, and because, ultimately, this network of representation includes Walsh's story itself, the reader is caught dead center in an entanglement of deferred vision whose instability disappears the object of art, here Walsh's subject, and calls into question the interpretive practices of the reader-viewer. This system of hermeneutics grounds and innervates a dynamic aesthetics of disappearance that proves fundamental to Walsh's larger narrative project.

In each of the stories that makes up Walsh's trilogy, the possibility of deduction hinges upon how well the reader is able to decipher the significance of a disappearing object or subject whose presence or occasion is dissimulated by the guilty party. But in "Variaciones en rojo," the reader herself gets trapped in the act of reading, which in this case is also the multivalent act of viewing. Walsh is concerned, then, with how a reader locates and interprets disappearance despite its dissimulation and, more importantly, with how she manages to enact some sort of agency despite the epistemological instabilities that disappearance manifests. He asks us to consider how a reader might assert her own subjectivity, here bound up with interpretive practices, in the face of an art that threatens to defer her gaze and the world she knows ad infinitum. The challenge here is one of aesthetics, but it serves as practice for what will later become both a political task and one of survival. And Walsh embeds within his story an answer, at least in theory, and a way out of the entanglement of art, disappearance, and crime: logic.

Privileged Sight

In "Variaciones en rojo," the police arrive not long after Carmen Sandoval faints upon entering her employer's studio; they find Carla de Velde still laid out upon the floor, and Peruzzi with her. Peruzzi greets the police "con un gesto de gran señor" (with a high-minded gesture), lamenting the horror of the crime loudly and peppering his speech with convoluted bastardizations of French and Latin to accentuate his exaggerated gesticulations and terror. The police are about to take him down to the station when Daniel, who has accompanied Jiménez to the crime scene, points out that they have not found the weapon or resolved the problem of the room being locked from the outside. The police chief does not care; in his estimation, Peruzzi will either be the murderer or an accomplice. For how else, he asks, could he come to have been locked alone in the room with the victim? But Peruzzi has the improbable answer for him in the form of a handkerchief doused in chloroform that he is holding in his hand: the murderer overtook him, chloroformed him, and then killed Carla. When he came to, he explains, Carla was dead, the murderer gone, and he was left behind locked inside his studio.

Jiménez begins to look for the weapon, which the police find shortly thereafter outside the studio: a small dagger lying at the bottom of the stairs behind the door that leads to the street. Peruzzi is overjoyed that they should have found the dagger outside of the studio itself locked from the outside and begs the police chief not to apologize for his misplaced conclusions. Meanwhile, Daniel examines a miniature cityscape that he has found in the corner of the studio:

> ¡Qué tabladillo tan curioso! ¿Será una ilusión óptica?—agregó dirigiéndose a Peruzzi—. Pero aún falta algo. Yo no entiendo de escenografía ni de pintura, y en realidad no sé qué es lo que falta aquí, pero algo falta.
>
> ¡Ah, *mon ami*!—se exaltó Peruzzi—. ¡Esa perspicacia me entusiasma! ¡Usted tiene la visión intuitiva a la que rara vez accede el burgués estragado por el *affiche* y las revistas! ¡Usted merece empedernirse en el encumbrado ejercicio de la crítica! Es justamente lo que yo me dije anoche cuando entré y vi el escenario de Hans. ¡Este animal de Hans! Casi un año trabajando para mí, y aún no ha adquirido el sentido de la composición . . . ¡Ah, pero lo despido, esta misma noche lo despido! *Sale bête*![24]

"What a curious little scene! Is it an optical illusion?," he added, turning to Peruzzi. "But something is still missing. I don't know anything about stage design or painting, and really, I don't know what's missing here. But something's missing."

"Ah, *mon ami*!" enthused Peruzzi. "Your perceptiveness is thrilling! You have an intuitive vision rarely exhibited by the bourgeois, so ruined by *l'affiche* and magazines. You should dedicate yourself to the lofty enterprise of the critic. It's just exactly what I said to myself last night when I came in and saw Han's miniature. That animal! Almost a whole year working for me, and he still hasn't acquired a sense of composition . . . Oh, but I'll fire him, tonight I'll fire him! *Sale bête*!"

Peruzzi's studio is filled with paintings, sculptures, empty canvases, brushes; the police look through it all and find no clues. But Daniel is attracted by a miniature scene set up in a corner of the room wherein large bats fly over cardboard skyscrapers and a crane digs up earth decorated with little wooden crosses. What a strange little scene, comments the myopic and self-effacing amateur who perceives in its composition a certain lack. The reader learns later that Baldung constructs these miniature scenes so that Peruzzi will have something to paint; his assistant provides him with new landscapes and, according to the artist, new emotions, which Peruzzi then interprets on canvas. Jiménez asks the artist to point out to him what is missing from this one. But Peruzzi refuses, telling the chief that while something is indeed missing, it is not something in particular, but something in general: "Una figura, un árbol, cualquier cosa. Cada uno debe suplirlo a su manera" (A person, a tree, whatever. We can each fill it in however we please).[25] Here Walsh hints at to the inherent deficiencies of art, but he also alerts the reader to a series of clues: 1) the miniature might be an optical illusion; 2) something is missing from the scene, a lack which is manifested, according to Peruzzi, in the totality of the composition; 3) Peruzzi saw the miniature for the first time last night; and 4) Peruzzi does not esteem Baldung, whose work he copies. These facts all point to the resolution of the crime while also instructing the reader as to how to proceed. Where Walsh equates the detective with the critic, a dual role that the reader already implicitly fills, she should know to look for clues in the works of art in the studio in the same way that a critic investigates art or literature. This will guide her reading as Daniel begins to wander around the rest of the studio until he finds himself in the adjacent gallery, or *sala de cuadros*, a blueprint of which appears here as figure 1.2.[26]

In the gallery, Daniel is intrigued by a painting that is, per Walsh's description, some avant-garde combination of Goya and Bosch. In the painting, a man stands backward on the edge of a high ravine; his head hangs back, arms outstretched, his eyes pierce the heavens directly above. His bruised and devastated body hangs just above an abyss, and from his chest a little door gives way to threads of blood that run across the rocks below. These small rivers of blood are populated by tiny, disproportionate people, dreamlike figures; a little man with jars on his hands looks down a well of blood bordered by stars. The painting is dark, and Daniel sees in it the heights of loneliness, "la muerte absoluta" (absolute death).[27] As he looks at the canvas that he recognizes as the work of a serious and studied

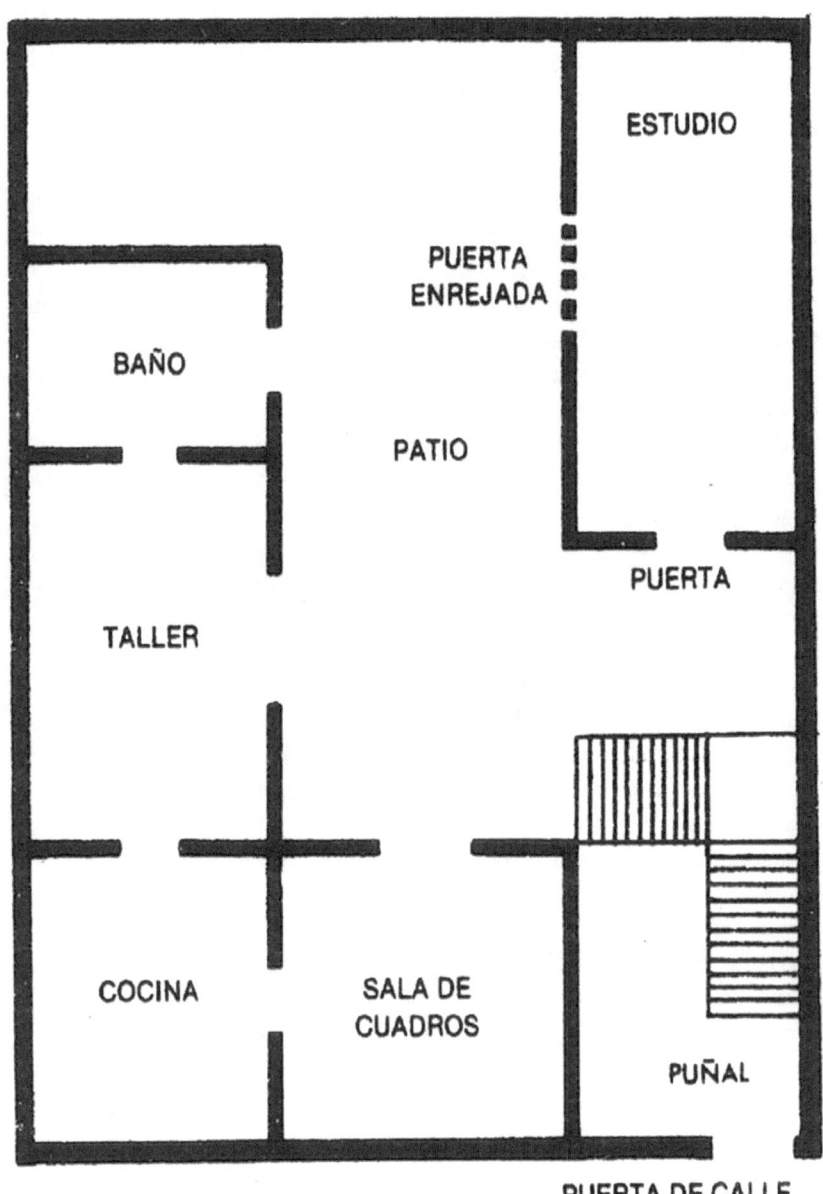

Figure 1.2 Blueprint of Peruzzi's studio. Rodolfo Walsh, *Variaciones en rojo*, 2002. Originally published in 1953 by Editorial Hachette.

painter, Daniel realizes that Peruzzi cannot be the pompous buffoon he is pretending to be. Somebody that ridiculous, thinks Daniel, could not have painted such a refined and poetic work. Peruzzi comes in and finds the amateur detective considering his painting.

The artist interrupts Daniel—complimenting him on his "visión privilegiada" (privileged sight)—by declaring that he will join the ranks of history's most important painters because he has just founded a new school of art: "Usted es el primero en saberlo. ¡Ja, ja, ja! ¡Qué broma colosal! ¡Quiero ver la cara de los críticos cuando lean mis primeros cuadros!" (You are the first to know. Ha, ha, ha! What a colossal joke! I can't wait to see the critics' faces when they read my first paintings!) Daniel responds, confused, "¿Cuando *lean* sus cuadros?" (When they *read* your paintings?)[28] And here Peruzzi launches into a description of his new school of art, a movement dedicated to creating paintings that defy the material necessity of frame, canvas, paint, and brush. What is, definitively, a painting, Peruzzi asks Daniel, aside from the complex of emotions and ideas that it offers up to the spectator? Peruzzi proposes a school of painting that abolishes the need for the material existence of art, renders superfluous the painting as we know it, and relies solely on the mathematical expression of light, color, and form. He aims to represent a painting via its mathematical transcription that will communicate—to those few who can conceptually perceive or "read" art—its texture, surface, content, and material dimensions. He imagines a painting that a viewer might *visualize* without needing *to see*. To do this, the artist discards material art and leaves in its stead symbolic transcription that functions as or points to a single whole. In short, Peruzzi proposes the construction and expression of the ideal painting. He assures Daniel that any artist who knows how to interpret the list of symbols that makes up the painting will be able to copy it exactly. This process corresponds, he claims, to the one that musicians follow when they read a score; they don't need to hear the music to know what it sounds like. This art will be, for Peruzzi, the embodiment of the Platonic ideal; its consequences for the art world, he insists, are vast.

The artist explains:

> ¿Prevé usted la trascendencia de esta teoría? ¿Puede seguirla hasta sus últimas consecuencias? ¿La imagina proyectada a las demás artes? ¿Imagina, por ejemplo, un drama o una novela que consista en un solo, vasto número, que para el iniciado represente inconfundiblemente todas las descripciones de caracteres, todos

los incidentes, todos los diálogos, todas las honduras psicológicas de la obra?[29]

Can you foresee the transcendence of this theory? Can you follow it to its necessary end? Can you imagine it projected onto the other arts? Imagine, for example, a play or a novel that consists of a single, vast number that for the initiated represents unmistakably all the character descriptions, all the incidents, all the dialogues, all the psychological depths of the work?

Peruzzi aims to create a mimetic ideal. But this is an aesthetic and philosophical trap, for if the copy is ideal, then there is no inaccessible original, no parable of the cave, nothing to represent beyond what the imagination might conjure up. The artist asks Daniel if he can imagine the consequences of this project: all literature would be reduced to a single, illimitable number that would represent every possible combination of human event, speech, and emotion; the passage of time and its lived experience would be rendered superfluous; and space would be condensed in a cipher. Peruzzi ultimately calls for the dissolution of art. Daniel is taken aback, but not as much as when the artist pulls out a sheet of paper from his pocket and shows the detective his first painting: a long list of symbols collected under the title *Suspiro decreciente en función del logaritmo de pi* (Breath diminishing in function of the logarithm of pi).

Peruzzi's first ideal painting is the representation of a prolonged and eternal death, a picture that Walsh juxtaposes with the painting in the gallery that Daniel has been admiring. But the Goyaesque allegory of humanity perched precariously on the edge of the abyss does not quite approximate death, and neither does *Suspiro decreciente*. However one might imagine Peruzzi's ideal painting, his protagonist does not ever die, as determined by the infinite and irreducible extension of the digits that make up pi (π). For pi is both an "irrational number," in that the digits to the right of its decimal never repeat in any formal pattern, and a "transcendental number," because it cannot be constructed via a finite sequence of algebraic operations. Peruzzi's painting, an attempt to represent symbolically a slow death, is both irrational and transcendental; it cannot be *seen*, but only visualized. And this, the artist tells us, only by a privileged few. *Suspiro decreciente*, while a well-placed philosophical distraction for both Daniel and the reader, defers and dissimulates death where death does not ever quite come. Instead of simulating an ideal work of art, the "painting" dissimulates a false mimetic corollary. The death withheld in this potential work of art serves to cover up for the real death of Carla de Velde.

Walsh presents Peruzzi's description of his new school of art in great detail and affords it a prominent place near the center of the narrative. The artist's proposition is intellectually complex, if in its simplicity, and appears to be an important clue in solving Carla de Velde's murder. But of course Peruzzi's painting is a red herring. The artist introduces it to Daniel in order to distract him from the scene that is right before him, and Walsh introduces it to the reader in order to test where her attention lies. But the reader must remember this one basic rule of detective fiction, as put forth by Umberto Eco in his analysis of Bustos Domecq's *Seis problemas para Don Isidro Parodi*, "Abduction in Uqbar": "In detective novels the author (who acts in the place of God) guarantees the correspondence between the Possible World imagined by the detective and the Real World."[30] Eco's "mechanism of conjecture in a sick Spinozist universe"[31] requires that whatever hypothesis a story's detective comes up with must find its correspondence in a real and empirical world; the author guarantees this. If he doesn't, the work ceases to be a work of detection and crosses over into the realm of the fantastic, the supernatural, or horror. Walsh has to be able to guarantee that whatever conclusions Daniel draws regarding Peruzzi's mathematical painting are possible in corresponding real worlds both internal and external to the text; Daniel, and the reader alongside him, cannot conclude anything that cannot be proven. So if *Suspiro decreciente* is a ruse, where lie the clues that correspond to the real world populated with material, and not symbolic, art? The mimetic ideal covers up for death, but in so doing reveals a possible connection between art and death that the careful reader will want to pursue further by looking for possible similarities between the crime scene and the other artworks that Walsh describes in the story. For Walsh hides—or perhaps better, frames—an important key to the crime in the abyss of mimesis that he sets up in the narrative.

The Framing and Unframing of Art

Both the frame and framing—variously a border, limitation, tool to clarify a spatial field, the obfuscation of vision, and a set up—feature throughout Walsh's short story to disable and enable the interpretation of art and the solving of the crime at hand. Carla de Velde's death scene is represented in the painting by Peruzzi that Daniel comes across in the artist's gallery. This explains why Peruzzi turns to such histrionics to distract the detective. In the painting, a man stands on an abyss with a thin river of blood emerging from his chest; Carla died from a single stab wound to her chest and we see, at the scene of the crime, a comparable thread of blood trailing onto the floor. Peruzzi represented Carla's death long before her murder occurred. But this fact alone is not what convinces Daniel that Peruzzi murdered his lover. Walsh's myopic amateur is persuaded instead by the very material impossibility of Peruzzi's ideal painting. This is to say, Walsh's red herring functions as a frame to the real clue, which is Peruzzi's goal to construct a painting that transcends material necessity and is visible only to a select few. Here Walsh reaffirms the significance of the false clue in the detective genre, which plays a crucial role in aiding detection and interpretation. He achieves in writing about painting what Foucault aptly spies in Velázquez: "The image should stand out from the frame."[32] Here the image exceeds the boundaries of the frame in its interpolation of the viewer; the image cannot be framed—neither limited nor set up—and the frame works to obscure our vision. But Walsh does not free this image from the physical and interpretive constraints that frame it until the end of the story, when Daniel offers up a seventeen-page description of how he solved the crime:

> . . . inmediatamente se lanzó a una desesperada tentativa por convencerme de que, efectivamente, era un polichinela. Durante diez minutos esgrimió una ardua teoría que era la estricta negación de todo credo artístico. Y sin embargo, esa teoría también me sugirió algo. Peruzzi se refería, si no me equivoco, a un cuadro ideal, que existiría sin ser pintado, pero que no todos podrían ver. El asesinato de Carla de Velde es como ese cuadro, y pocos pueden imaginarlo.[33]

> . . . he immediately began a desperate attempt to convince me that he really was a buffoon. For ten minutes he defended an arduous theory that was the strict negation of all artistic creed. But this theory also made me think of something. Peruzzi referred, if I am not mistaken, to an ideal painting that would exist without being painted, but that not everyone could see. Carla de Velde's murder is like this painting, and few can imagine it.

Daniel sees here the mise en abyme that Peruzzi has constructed in order to simultaneously distract the police and boast of the ingenuity of his crime. Carla's murder was both his crime and an ideal work of art that defied material necessity, and as promised, that only a select few might see. His studio—both an open and closed space—was his canvas, Carla's death his subject, the wild red lighting his immaterial paint. Peruzzi was too impressed with his "art" not to leave clues, also by way of art, around the studio. The seven pieces of art listed earlier function as a network of clues that refer to one another, reflect or frame one another, or hide within them yet another clue. They work together as a series of mirrors that repeat what they reflect, which is the crime that lies outside of them but that is comprised precisely of these replications. Walsh folds the keys to the crime into the crime scene and into the thematic structure of the story. Peruzzi calls for the construction of the ideal via the negation of art—and here Walsh anticipates, if in slightly different terms, Blanchot's disappearance of literature—all of which is put into practice by a death that is staged to look like art. There is no way out of Walsh's crime scene; art is his trap. He emphasizes this on the very last page of the story when Peruzzi tells Daniel he is missing a fingerprint, and Daniel tells him he knows well where his fingerprints are hidden: on the bloody cloth that he used to wipe the murder weapon clean and that he then painted over with the first red strokes of the "cuadro inconcluso" (unfinished, but also unresolved, painting) that hangs in the corner of his studio.

Walsh buries another clue to the crime, however, in Peruzzi's promotion of a painting founded on material impossibility: namely, the material impossibilities of the crime that the artist claims secure his innocence. First, the fact that the crime was committed in a closed room locked from the outside, and second, that the murder weapon was found downstairs, far outside of the room where Peruzzi sat imprisoned. These two material realities, says Peruzzi, safeguard his innocence since he was locked inside his studio with the victim. Yet Daniel does not agree, and this is where Walsh turns to logic to ground what appears to be a quickly disappearing playing field. Daniel explains that, depending on the sequence of events that the crime followed, there might have been just one material impossibility: locking the door on the outside, for Peruzzi could have taken the murder weapon outside before locking the door. But the artist, from the beginning, has explained that *two* material impossibilities ensure that he did not commit the crime. For Daniel, this is where Peruzzi missteps. That he keeps referring to two apparent material obstacles confirms for Daniel, even if he does not yet know how, that the artist indeed manages to lock the door on the outside *and* remove the murder weapon from the room.

Daniel suffers, to Jiménez's annoyance, the habit of wandering around the crime scene, examining parts of the scene, the building, the landscape that the police overlook. This is how he comes to consider Peruzzi's art, Baldung's miniature city, and the impenetrable metal bars on the door that leads to the patio. Unlike Chief Jiménez, Daniel depends first on his powers of observation in studying the parameters of the crime scene and then opts for the simplest possible hypothesis. Early on in the story, Daniel spends some time analyzing Baldung's miniature and concludes that something is missing from it, although he cannot say exactly what that might be. Indeed, he locates what he believes is missing in the sketch that Peruzzi drew of the cityscape that Baldung built for him to copy. In Peruzzi's drawing of this miniature, a ferocious truck drives through the center of the city, devouring in its lights little men that it excretes in the form of little white crosses. The truck in this sketch—as does its artist—produces death, a key move in the aesthetics of disappearance that Walsh is here constructing. Walsh provides this description of Peruzzi's drawing to the reader but does not at the same time give us Daniel's interpretation of it. The reader does not hear about the truck again until Daniel presents his hypothesis of how the crime was committed.

The amateur detective also spends some time examining the metal bars on the patio door. Jiménez laughs at him and imagines he is trying to see if a man could fit through the bars, which are ten centimeters apart. But Daniel explains that he was instead "practicando una modesta versión de lo que después de Euler se llamó *Anaylsis situs*, es decir, un examen del terreno, referido no a las dimensiones, sino a la configuración" (practicing a modest version of what, since Euler, has been called *Analysis situs*; that is to say, a field test, referring not to dimensions but rather to configuration).[34] Here composition—how objects are related in space and the spaces they take up—is paramount for Daniel, as is Leonhard Euler's—the eighteenth-century Swiss mathematician—work on calculus, curves, and logic. Euler's *analysis situs*, or "geometry of position" will become the study of topology that interprets form from spatial arrangement.[35] Here the composition that organizes Peruzzi's paintings finds it parallel expression in the physical world; but it becomes, insomuch as it pertains to the solid and logical world instead of an aesthetic one, evidence Daniel can use instead of a false lead. We learn that Daniel is attempting to solve the problem of how the dagger left the room and arrived at the bottom of the stairs. He does not think it was deposited there by Baldung as he left the crime scene, as imagined by Jiménez, but rather that Peruzzi managed to leave it there from inside the locked room. He turns to graph theory to test his proof:

Yo me tracé mentalmente tres puntos: uno situado en la reja, otro en el extremo superior de la escalera—por donde evidentemente tenía que bajar el estilete, ya fuera llevado por manos humanas o no—, y el tercero en el sitio exacto donde se había encontrado el puñal. Uní imaginariamente esos puntos con una línea que, por supuesto, no debía atravesar ningún insuperable obstáculo material. Esto es lo que se llama trazar una gráfica, la más elemental de las gráficas, compuesta de tres vértices y dos arcos. Después me pregunté si de algún modo el estilete podía haber recorrido esa gráfica. En otras palabras, me pregunté si el puñal podía haber recorrido una doble línea curva, con una caída en el extremo representado por los escalones.[36]

I traced three points in my mind: one situated at the metal bars, another at the highest end of the stairs—where the dagger clearly would have gone down, carried by human hand or not—, and the third at the exact point where the dagger was found. In my mind's eye, I joined these points with a line that did not have to cross, of course, any unsurpassable material object. This is what is called plotting a graph, the most elementary of graphs, comprised of three points and two arcs. Then, I asked myself if the dagger could have in some way traveled in a double curved line, with a drop at the furthest point represented by the stairs.

In configuring his hypothesis as to who committed the crime, Daniel is concerned first with determining how the murder weapon left the room. This process is the inverse of the steps followed by Jiménez, who decides that if he knows who murdered Carla, he will know how the dagger got to the bottom of the stairs. But Daniel draws his conclusions from the physical world around him and the possibilities that its spatial configuration allows for to construct a plausible hypothesis as to how the artist might have removed the dagger from the crime scene while locked inside his studio. He identifies the three vertices upon which this removal must depend and mentally draws the two arcs that connect them to see if they comprise a plausible description of how the dagger traveled. When the sketch conforms to the physical laws of the real world, he must only determine how the dagger was transported. Daniel works backward from the physical conditions of the crime scene and deduces what opportunities the space of the setting affords for crime. Two things are significant: first, he does not move beyond the spatial boundaries of the scene of the crime, which is to say that his field

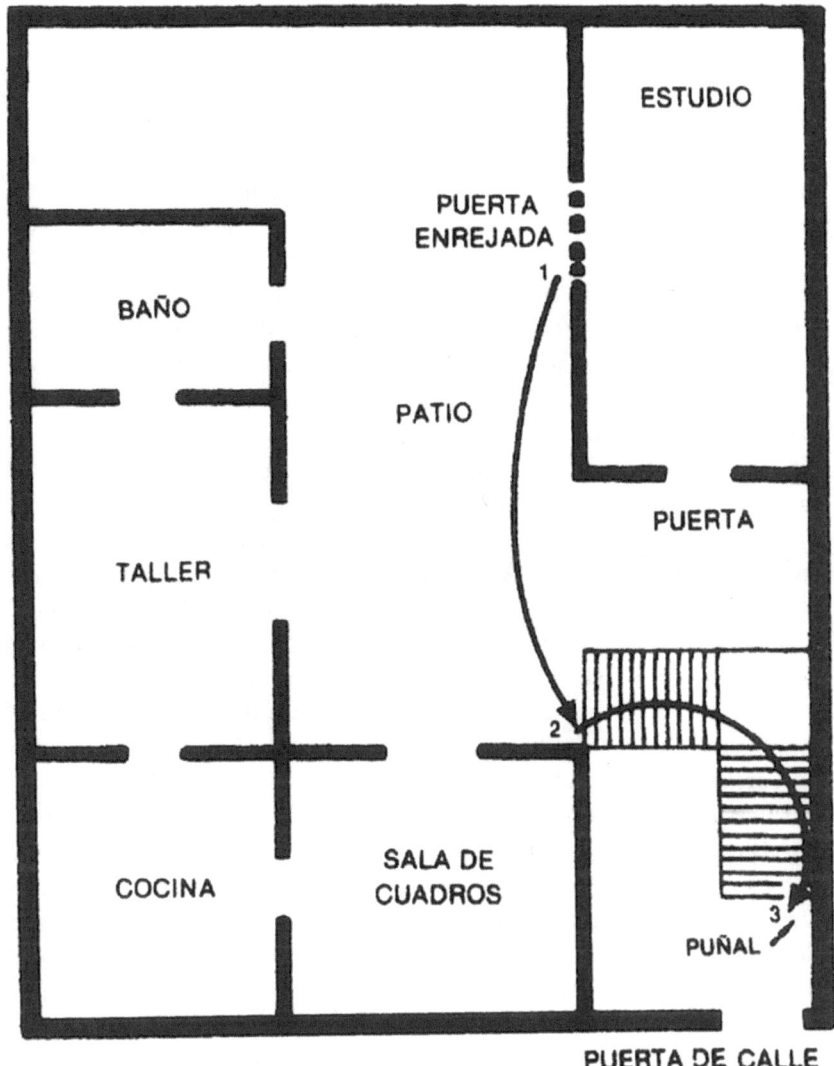

Figure 1.3 Daniel's hypothesis. Rodolfo Walsh, *Variaciones en rojo*, 2002. Originally published in 1953 by Editorial Hachette.

of investigation provides him with all the answers he needs; second, it is, literally, by connecting the dots—here logic worked out on the ground—that Daniel might perceive and read the organization that facilitates the central act of disappearance that motivates the story's narrative arc. Ultimately, the parsing of space, and Daniel's ability to imagine its configuration and construction, vacates Peruzzi's attempts to render immaterial the material necessities of art and therein cover over the clues that his art reveals. The immanent, material world abides and offers up everything the proofreader needs to solve the crime. Walsh uses Daniel's skill of spatial interpretation to make manifest that which has been disappeared and concealed, but also to build the logical mise en abyme that ensnares Peruzzi, the reader, and art itself.

Peruzzi covers up his murder of Carla de Velde by offering up two apparent material impossibilities: the fact that he is shut up in a locked room with the victim, and that the murder weapon is found some distance from the crime scene. But each impossibility can be dismantled. Peruzzi kills his lover, but only after he summons Baldung to work. The artist feigns one of his infamous violent outbursts and Baldung, fearing for his life, runs out of the studio. As he leaves, hypothesizes Daniel, it occurs to Baldung in a flash that the only way to set up an obstacle between himself and Peruzzi is to lock the door. He turns the key in the lock and flees; this is why witnesses place Baldung leaving the scene of the crime at a quarter to midnight, which is the principal evidence that the police chief uses to indict Baldung. Peruzzi banked on the immaterial—psychology—to construct a material obstacle in the form of a locked door. He takes the chance that Baldung will react exactly as he does; if he hadn't, Peruzzi would have just gone ahead with his portrait of Carla and postponed her murder for another night.

Peruzzi, now locked inside with his lover, kills her with a small knife. He then has to dispose of the murder weapon, which is where he gives himself away. For he attempts to make disappear the tool he uses to remove the dagger, which creates a glaring absence that will allow Daniel to crack the crime. Peruzzi removes the little red truck, which is also a wind-up truck, from Baldung's miniature cityscape; he affixes the dagger to its top and a thread to its back, winds the toy up, and lets it go from between the metal bars of the patio door. The truck propels itself across the patio with the knife on top, hits the stairs, falls down them, and deposits the knife at the bottom of the stairway. Peruzzi then brings the truck back upstairs via the little thread he has attached to it. Daniel notes that the toy's front axle is bent, which he proposes is evidence of the second arc the truck traveled, when it would have hit the far wall of the staircase. The murderer recovers this tool, and as Daniel points out, "No podía hacer *desaparecer* el juguete, pero podía *disimularlo*" (He couldn't make the toy disappear, but he could *make it look like* he had).[37] Peruzzi could not make the wind-up truck disappear, but he could hide it in plain sight and rely on art to cover over its original absence. The murderer's dissimulation fails in the end. Walsh here confirms the impossibility of ever fully covering up for disappearance, for Peruzzi's attempts to produce the appearance of absence prove the key to the story's crime.

Dissimulation—per Baudrillard, "to pretend not to have what one has"[38]—signals the presence of something even as it aims to mask or conceal that possession. In this case, Peruzzi stakes his impunity on the possibility that all art reveals a constitutive lack, or at least that a viewer might think so, such that anything missing would go unnoticed. He removes the truck from Baldung's cityscape, whose composition, had Daniel not recovered Peruzzi's sketch of the work, never would have betrayed the fact of its original presence. The work of art would have covered over the truck's absence, a lack easily attributed to all art's insurmountable mimetic failure. Peruzzi dissembles this absence in order to cover up his attempted disappearance of the means by which he displaced the murder weapon. He resorts to hiding the resolution to his crime in plain sight, integrating it into the fabric of the ordinary, the "given-to-be-seen," where disappearance will not be noted, and where the murderer's theatrics of dissimulation might deter close analysis of the scene in the first place. Here Walsh reveals that disappearance and dissimulation are already, as mechanisms that intervene in knowledge production, inextricably connected. For disappearance works to dissimulate both what it possesses and its own part in constructing that absence. So even as Peruzzi feigns not to have what he has because he cannot make something entirely disappear, he performs here in a staged aesthetic intervention the machinations that will become the constitutive and moving parts of enforced political disappearance. In so doing, he exposes that 1) dissimulation as disappearance signals a crime; 2) disappearance hides itself in plain sight; 3) the act of disappearance aims to cover something up; and 4) per Baudrillard, "pretending or dissimulating leaves the principle of reality intact,"[39] which is to say that dissimulation may obfuscate the truth but does not negate it. So at the core of Walsh's detective fiction, we find already the logical deconstruction of the legal and political defense of disappearance as a tool of state repression. Walsh would not have realized the stakes of what he was working out, particularly so many years before he would begin to explicate it more carefully in his works of documentary narrative. But here laid out in a work of fiction, his treatise on aesthetics—on what art is capable of communicating and providing for—offers up a blueprint of the complicated ways that disappearance functions as a tool of authoritarianism and how it works on society at large. Art, much as in Walsh's story, is a cipher by which we might decode the framework, composition, and interpretation of mortal crime.

After recovering the wind-up truck, Peruzzi sculpts a plaster head inside of which he hides the tool that allowed him to displace the murder weapon and thus set the stage for a version of events that might distract from the true crime. The artist here reifies and gives a body to the dissemblance he has thus far enacted; his artifice of distraction culminates when he conceals the key to the crime inside a copy of a head, which we might also read as visage, likeness, guise. Here dissemblance becomes semblance, art proper, the copy that cannot help but communicate—at least in the version of aesthetics that Walsh constructs—that it belongs to a secondary order. Peruzzi fashions the face to imitate his own sardonic expression and puts it on display on a pedestal in the center of the room. As Daniel nears the end of his explication of the crime, he asks the artist if he values the head. Peruzzi tells him he does not; Daniel knocks it to the ground where it breaks, revealing the truck buried inside and confirming the proofreader's theory of the crime. Walsh's narrative here enacts the shattering of the cover-up in a veritable *rompecabezas*—a puzzle, in Spanish, literally, a "head-breaker." Daniel has to break open the mind of the criminal in order to prove his theory of the crime. Peruzzi has dissimulated his participation in Carla de Velde's murder by way of a dissembled and disassembled disappearance; the series of negations required to hide the crime multiply throughout the narrative. But in the end, Daniel extracts the key to the crime from the head of the criminal, and Peruzzi's cover-up lies in pieces on the floor. It is the final victim in the prolonged battle of wits between the two, and proof that disappearance—even its appearance—cannot be masked, dissembled, or hidden.

Bloody Dawn

At the end of Walsh's trilogy, Chief Jiménez and Daniel drive away into the distance and see that, "sobre el mar, en el esfumado horizonte, se dibujaban las primeras pinceladas rojas del sangriento amanecer" (above the sea, on the vanishing horizon, the first red brushstrokes of the bloody dawn were appearing).[40] Walsh closes his collection as his detective drives off into a new day, yet one that promises new violence all the same. The horizon disappears alongside him, giving way to a dislocated and future orientation marked only, if here in the vein of pulp fiction, by the bloody trace of morning light. The move is at once aesthetic and politically avant-garde.

In "Variaciones en rojo," Walsh offers up a work of fiction that serves, before its time, as meditation on the relationship between art, crime, and the production of knowledge. Its political potential is still latent when first published, but as the tactics and consequences of Argentina's military dictatorship come into focus, the story gains in its capacity to function as cipher for understanding how dissimulation and disappearance work in concert as symptoms of violence and as catalysts for the production of new logic-based knowledge. These possibilities, if in hindsight, confirm that disappearance can be dismantled by logic and the careful parsing of spatial composition, and the violence at its core revealed. Walsh's short story also lays bare the ways in which art might participate in this larger task. The successful resolution of both Peruzzi's crime and the narrative depends on the masking and unmasking of disappearance by way of art such that Walsh anticipates the ways in which aesthetics can intervene in and recalibrate the political in the context of state terror. He asks his reader to consider how the examination and interpretation of aesthetics, of what it promises as well as obscures, galvanizes new forms of knowledge that dismantle violence. In Walsh's work, closely reading the conception and composition of visual art, space, and received logic negates the hypervisibility of dissimulation that attempts to cover up for disappearance. Walsh trains his reader in oblique reading practices that reject art's mimetic aspirations for its indexical capacity; instead of copying a lived world, art points us back to it, if newly reconfigured or reframed. In Walsh's narrative universe art recontextualizes what we see before us, a possibility that takes on significant political valence as later authors, Cortázar and Martínez among them, begin to work with disappearance as narrative device and mode decades later.

Walsh proves that art already deals in disappearance on various fronts and can engage with the vanishing, the excised, and the absent as both medium and interpretive method. Art, for Walsh, is a useful and productive container for disappearance, and his contemporaries—those that survived the dictatorship in exile at home or abroad—will expand the limits of this possibility. But Walsh also cautions that disappearance might itself also serve as a cover-up for some larger criminal act, as it did for Peruzzi's murder of Carla de Velde. And this is where his short story issues a dire warning, if indeed a message legible only from a distance: he demands that his readers investigate the larger context in which disappearance is enacted, that they learn to read disappearance as part of a larger text. Cortázar and Martínez will remember and repeat this demand in their future works—which together provide for forms and spaces of disappearance—as they build on, expand, and revitalize Walsh's early efforts to propose and parse a narrative aesthetics of disappearance. Walsh would go on to make a career of applying the oblique reading practices he honed as an author of detective fiction to the documentation and analysis of extralegal state crimes. Two decades later, he would take on disappearance, not only as indicator of some larger crime but as a fully embodied tool of torture and systematic state repression. His "Carta abierta de un escritor a la junta militar" (Open letter from a writer to the military junta) of March 24, 1977, would cost him his life and compel his disappearance. Walsh died for the *violento oficio de escribir*, the violent task of writing, but not before leaving behind a legacy of work that asks us how to read more carefully the oblique and complicated ways that art and disappearance signal each other and cross over, by deferral and referral, to our lived world.

2

Double Exposure

The Hermeneutics of Catastrophe in Julio Cortázar's *Fantomas contra los vampiros multinacionales*

Enforced disappearance, because it depends on its own official denial to function, operated during Argentina's military dictatorships by way of a kind of double-speak that rejected the absence at its core. While not a cover-up for some original violence, as we see in Walsh's early detective fiction, disappearance as a fundamental tool of state repression performs and propagates its own cover-up in the interest of protecting a larger, more entrenched system of ongoing violence. This constitutive doubling made discussing disappearance, particularly in the early years of the dictatorship, complicated. As a tool of genocide, its very structure rendered speaking about disappearance a doubed gesture—as evidenced in the well-known leitmotif and call to action "¡Presente!"—as such acts attempted to signal the very real lives lost at the core of, in Diana Taylor's formulation, the "given-to-be-invisible."[1]

Writing about disappearance and representing it aesthetically are similarly burdened with taking on, laying bare, and dismantling the protective double-speak that defines and enables both its initial systematization and its insidious devastation across generations. This taking apart of the doubled nature of disappearance exposes its constituent parts as fictive apparatuses, themselves evidence of the fictions of power that authorize and buttress authoritarianism. Once dismantled, this political anatomy becomes newly legible—if in different ways, both at the time and years later—within historical contexts beset by crisis or catastrophe. Part of the task of late twentieth-century Argentine narrative is rendering these fictions decipherable so that they might be held accountable for the gross human rights abuses for which they are responsible. But this is only one part of a larger dynamic system in which the political informs an aesthetics that in turn makes possible new forms of the political and the historical. Here the work of aesthetics serves as an ethico-political response to the crimes of state terror as it renders absence materially present and a critical agent in the form, structure, and techniques of storytelling and world-building that populate Argentine fiction.

The violence of enforced disappearance materializes as a fundamental catalyst of Julio Cortázar's 1975 graphic novella *Fantomas contra los vampiros multinacionales: una utopía realizable* (*Fantomas versus the Multinational Vampires: An Attainable Utopia*). But this core catastrophe appears only upon navigating complex intersecting narrative worlds that work not in the service of fiction, but toward fomenting in the reader a self-reflective historical consciousness with the capacity to activate real change in the lived world. This chapter examines, in particular, Cortázar's techniques of doubling and displacement as part of a hermeneutics of catastrophe that exposes and dismantles the doubled nature of disappearance so that we might properly attend to its political fictions, including historical determination, and lived realities. These literary techniques—manifested in *Fantomas* as repetition, duplication, splicing, recursive and embedded ontologies, and narrative smokescreen—disclose the constitutive parts of disappearance and reveal how it works to both signal and cover up for a larger network of violence in Argentina, and across Latin America more generally, in the final year before the coup that installed the Videla dictatorship. Doubling and displacement as a literary mode of disappearance—in this case, as a way in which disappearance both functions as narrative catalyst and allows us to understand history otherwise—here invites the reader to enter multiple, embedded fictional worlds in order to instruct us in how catastrophe is constructed and how we might avoid it by paying closer attention to the social and political urgencies of the lived world. In this, Cortázar's novella is as relevant two decades into the new millennium as it was on the eve of the Videla dictatorship.

The textual instantiation of doubling and displacement in *Fantomas* as form, narrative technique, and device by which the production of historical consciousness might be apprehended finds an important counterpart also in the extratextual. Cortázar's early graphic novel—already a text whose words find their double in images—bears the traces of a work written from within a nascent political exile since returning to Argentina from France, where he had lived since 1951, had by 1975 become a risk to the author's safety. The double life of the exile, and what emerges as the Cortazarian philosophy of exile that I discuss later, becomes a critical frame for understanding the techniques of doubling that the author uses to construct *Fantomas* and for how the ludic functions as a hinge for political agency. The hybrid work—part first-order narrative, part embedded comic—also serves as important evidence of the division that Cortázar felt between his dedication to the literary and the political. He was never able to reconcile his commitment to the literary and what he felt were a writer's responsibilities, as a public intellectual, to informing a wider reading public about political realities and motivating these readers to political action. The weight of this doubled task, and the complexities of the relationship between art and politics, shows up throughout the various diegetic levels of the novella, and indeed helps forge pathways between these worlds. These doubled and displaced authorial positions provide a critical context for the narrative techniques that Cortázar employs to show how disappearance functions as both index and smokescreen for an entrenched and insidious system of neoliberal violence, here a product of the long-standing legacy of US economic intervention in Latin America. Doubling and displacement, at multiple extratextual and textual levels, expose the space of disappearance to be catastrophic. But the force of its form also instructs Cortázar's readers that seeing the historical present otherwise might allow the future past of this catastrophe to unfold differently. *Fantomas*'s literary investment is at once historical and in our future.

A Fellowship of Exile

Cortázar left Argentina in 1951 in order to settle in Paris, where he would live until his death in 1984. When he left Argentina, Perón was nearing the end of his first term as president and the country was in the grip of what Cortázar would come to identify as "the first great convulsion, the first great shock of the masses in the country." If the author reveals his own bourgeois upbringing when he imagines he emigrated to the metropole when the noise from the neighboring mass Peronist demonstrations prevented his enjoyment of an Alban Berg concert, he later admits that his anti-Peronist leanings prevented him from seeing past the figures of Perón and Evita to realize the historical significance of Peronism, to see that "a new Argentine history" had begun.[2] Furthermore, he points out, history is paradoxical,[3] because it took his leaving Argentina for him to come to understand what was going on in his own country and respond to its historical transformation.

Cortázar took a job as a translator for UNESCO in Paris, a position he held off and on until 1975. Although he could not have foretold it at the time, when he left Argentina in 1951, he would not again live in his native country. The author's decision to live abroad was not without precedent: he was born in Brussels and spent two years in Barcelona before his family returned to Argentina. His peripatetic life, he summarized with a wink, was the product of tourism and diplomacy. Cortázar was always careful to report, in his interviews and essays, that when he moved to Paris, he did so voluntarily. It was not until the mid-1970s that he would begin to identify himself as a political, and then cultural, exile rather than a writer simply living abroad. It became clear to him in 1974 that although he might be free to return to Argentina, Isabel Perón's government would not allow him to leave again. Not long afterward, Videla's censorship panels refused to allow him to publish the volume *Alguien que anda por ahí* (1977) unless he omitted from it the now-canonical short stories "Apocalipsis en Solentiname" ("Apocalypse at Solentiname") and "Segunda vez" ("Second Time Around"), both of which implicitly critique state violence and, in the case of the latter, the use of disappearance as a tool of state repression. Cortázar's new condition as political exile under the military dictatorship corresponded with a solidification of his political commitment on an international stage, and the growing extent to which he was willing to explicitly and self-consciously merge his literature with politics.

While careful to acknowledge the potential devastations of exile, Cortázar advocated, however, for a different approach to its experience. In his 1978 essay "América Latina: exilio y literatura" ("The Fellowship of Exile"), Cortázar expounds, with caution, upon the possibility of a positive view of exile. He warns that nostalgia is a sentimental trap, that silence has wasted more than a few great writers, and that the bitterness of exile works on behalf of the exiling regime. He claims that an effective way to combat the original purpose of exile is to remain positive and adopt humor as a weapon of resistance and creative productivity. He writes:

> ¿Y si los exilados optaran también por considerar como positivo ese exilio? No estoy haciendo una broma de mal gusto, porque sé que me muevo en un territorio de heridas abiertas y de irrestañables llantos. Pero sí apelo a una distanciación expresa, apoyada en esas fuerzas interiores que tantas veces han salvado al hombre del aniquilamiento total, y que se manifiestan entre otras formas a través del sentido del humor, ese humor que a lo

largo de la historia de la humanidad ha servido para vehicular ideas y praxis que sin él parecerían locura o delirio.⁴

But what if exiles were also to take a positive view of exile? This is not a joke in bad taste, since I know full well that I am touching upon an area of open wounds and unimaginable pain. What I am calling for is a deliberate act of distancing; and at the same time, I am making an appeal to those inner resources that have so often saved man from total annihilation, surfacing in various ways, one of them being a sense of humor, the same humor which throughout history has served as a vehicle for ideas and strategies that would otherwise have seemed like madness or delirium.

In language that reflects exile's concern with territory and distance—although distance here becomes *distancing*, a gerund that insists on action and an express agency—Cortázar proposes to undermine exile as a strategy of oppression by rendering it an ineffectual method of silencing. He locates in humor—and the proof of this for Cortázar is in his publication of the ludic *Fantomas* a few years prior—a resource that can represent and transport ideas and practices that might otherwise be reduced to mere evidence of insanity, and thus excluded from circulation. As both exile and writer, he feels there is work to be done, stories to be invented, and ideas to be communicated that operate outside the system of logic of the military regime.

He goes on to speak of his own experience of exile and the fact that he prefers to consider it "una beca de full-time" (a full-time fellowship) of which he must take ready advantage. He writes:

> . . . los verdaderos exilios son las regímenes fascistas de nuestro continente, exiliados de la auténtica realidad nacional, exiliados de la justicia social, exiliados de la alegría, exiliados de la paz. Nosotros somos más libres y estamos más en nuestra tierra que ellos. He hablado de demencia; también ella, como el humor, es una manera de romper los moldes y abrir un camino positivo que no encontraremos jamás si seguimos plegándonos a las frías y sensatas reglas del juego del enemigo.⁵

> . . . the real exiles are the fascist regimes of our continent who are exiled from the true realities of their countries, from social

> justice, happiness, and peace. We are freer, more at home than they. I have spoken of insanity. Like humor, it too is a way of breaking the mold and opening a positive path that we will never find if we continue to adhere to the enemy's cold and calculating rules of the game.

Cortázar here locates national belonging and its attendant freedom, justice, and potential for happiness outside the geographical boundaries of the nation-state. He reclaims what it means to be Argentine when he identifies the states of exception that Latin America's various fascist governments have enacted as the real state of exile, and he recalibrates what it means to be at home. This proposition—at once introspective and an outward gesture to a fellowship of exiles living abroad—could only have been arrived at by someone denied access to his country and seeking other modes of national identity. Where the doubled state of exile exerts this pressure, Cortázar responds with two means of resistance that have long been proven effective: madness and humor. Both operate outside the logic of dictatorship and work to undermine its structure and weaken its source of power. Where the single goal of an authoritarian regime, to the exclusion of all other political operation, is to maintain its power, madness and humor compromise its execution. By working at the margins, manifesting unexpected apertures, and in their refusal to account for themselves, insanity and humor reveal the constructedness, the artifice, and the tautological logic of dictatorship. They are able to intervene and make change where playing by the rules of the regime will not. So Cortázar asks his fellow exiles to not only not reject their outsider status but to cement it by going even further afield into the always uncharted terrains of madness and laughter. This is a "deliberate act of distancing"—a thoughtful and conscientious separation, walking away from, giving space to—that will at once interrupt the logic of the distance already imposed upon them and allow them to build new spaces of belonging.

That Cortázar offers up the carnivalesque as an agent of resistance and reform is not unrelated to his own craft of literary invention, itself often grounded in the ludic, the fantastic, and in efforts that trouble how we know what we know or how we perceive what we believe to be the world around us. If many of his short stories, such as the canonical "La noche boca arriba" ("The Night Face Up," 1956) or "Continuidad de los parques" ("Continuity of Parks," 1964), offer up parallel realities, techniques for transitioning between those realities, and then unexpected portals to ancillary worlds and a total estrangement of what we know to be our world and how, then these landscapes of literary invention also serve as a blueprint for how worlds might be doubled and as warning of an estrangement that we are already living, perhaps unwittingly. These works offer up significant, if latent, political instruction and function as early signs of Cortázar's later recognition that reality does not culminate in a book, but that the end game of the book is instead to parse the real world around us. This possibility will prove fundamental for the political action that Cortázar aims to catalyze in *Fantomas*.

In a letter that he wrote in May 1967 to his close friend Roberto Fernández Retamar, Cortázar outlines the evolution of this political consciousness, first awakened at the early age of twenty-two in response to the Spanish Civil War, strengthened throughout the fifties, and then finally cemented in the sixties in his firm commitment to the Cuban Revolution. He explains:

> De la Argentina se alejó un escritor para quien la realidad, como la imaginaba Mallarmé, debía culminar en un libro; en Paris nació un hombre para quien los libros deberán culminar en la realidad. . . . Incapaz de acción política, no renuncio a mi solitaria vocación de cultura, a mi empecinada búsqueda ontológica, a los juegos de la imaginación en sus planos más vertiginosos; pero todo eso no gira ya en sí mismo y por sí mismo. . . . En lo más gratuito que pueda yo escribir asomaré siempre una voluntad de contacto con el presente histórico del hombre, una participación en su larga marcha hacia lo mejor de sí mismo como colectividad y humanidad.[6]

> From Argentina left a writer for whom reality, as imagined by Mallarmé, should culminate in a book; in Paris was born a man for whom books should culminate in reality. . . . Incapable of political action, I will not give up my solitary vocation of culture, my determined ontological search, games of the imagination at their most dizzying heights; but all this doesn't revolve any longer around itself and for itself. . . . As freely as I can possibly write, I will always assume a willingness of contact with the historical present of man, a participation in his long march toward the best of himself as collective and humanity.

It takes Cortázar's moving to Paris for him to abandon the Mallarméan ideal that reality might be represented in a book. The inversion of book to world that he suffers—the idea that what literature might represent should lead to something worldly, some engagement with present circumstance—serves less as the basis of the author's political awakening than it does of a shift in opinion about the capacity of literature. Cortázar believes himself to be "incapable of political action" (*incapaz de acción política*), but at the same time confirms his commitment to participating in some human collective founded in "the historical present of man" (*el presente histórico del hombre*). He suffers a kind of authorial blind spot here. He has yet to realize that the very "games of the imagination" (*juegos de la imaginación*) that he has long been constructing are charged with political possibility, and he does not recognize that a preoccupation with man's historical present and participation in a plural humanity are a priori political gestures. Cortázar does not yet know himself to be a fully political animal; he knows that he is not willing to sacrifice culture to politics but also that his literature cannot exist in a vacuum. But he has not yet translated, and it will become a point of scholarly debate whether he is ever able to, this knowledge into a full and mature political agency.

Cortázar's latent political consciousness, here on the eve of the events of 1968 and still then after the rise of the Videla dictatorship, will continue to trouble him. He will not give himself or his literature over to a fully fledged political activism—in the style, for example, of his friend Walsh—but will continue to struggle with what he thinks his political commitment should be and how he might use literature to represent it.[7] *Fantomas* emerges as evidence of this continued internal struggle, as do his later reflections on exile and its possible forms of resistance. He reveals his literary and political preoccupations as parallel concerns but never manages to fully merge the two. Cortázar will remain doubled in his attention to literature and to world, even as he realizes himself to be living the double life of an exile, but he will attempt to close the distance between the two, in ways not unsimilar to his aforementioned efforts to reinterpret exile. In *Fantomas*, he will use the ludic, humor, and just a little bit of madness laid out in literature in an attempt to inform his fellow Latin Americans of the political and human rights abuses being committed by the governments in power across the continent. But the work's complex techniques of doubling and displacement; its double nature as part literature, part historical intervention; and his efforts to participate and intervene in the political life of his native country from a place of exile will betray his continued and self-conscious efforts to come to terms with what will ultimately remain separate variables in Cortázar's continued ontological search.

On Gaining Political Purchase

In 1967, Bertrand Russell and Jean-Paul Sartre convened the first sessions of the Russell Tribunal to investigate foreign policy and war crimes committed by the United States during its military occupation of Vietnam. In 1974, the Russell Tribunal II was formed to investigate the consequences of the United States' foreign policy in Latin America, including alleged human rights abuses perpetrated by the United States throughout various Latin American nations. Cortázar, along with Gabriel García Márquez, served on the tribunal, which found the United States guilty of unethical interventions across Latin America, as well as widespread human rights abuses. The tribunal noted and denounced the foreign backing of the Pinochet regime; sanctioned the Argentine government for its increasing use of detention, torture, and disappearance as methods of state repression; and deemed foreign ownership of multinational corporations based in Latin America, and their widespread appropriation of natural resources, unlawful and injurious to the prosperity of Latin American nations. Cortázar wrote *Fantomas* to record and make widely available these findings.

Fantomas is a slim volume printed on thick, glossy paper that looks and feels like a comic book. The work opens upon a narrator yet unnamed in the text, although the cover of the book already reveals the narrator of the story to be Julio Cortázar, traveling from Brussels back to Paris after serving on the tribunal. At the train station in Brussels, he buys a comic book titled *Inteligencia en llamas* (The mind on fire) to read on the trip home; the comic narrates the exploits of the superhero Fantomas—here the newest iteration of the turn-of-the-century villain who wreaked havoc on Paris and the later Robin Hood–like cult figure of 1960s Mexico[8]—who is called upon to put a stop to the nameless villain destroying books in public and private libraries around the world. Once back in Paris, the narrator finds that the world of the comic begins to merge with his own world—and here the recursive resonance with the author's earlier works—, confirmation of which is offered to the reader when Cortázar himself shows up as character in the comic book he is reading. Here a group of international writers and public intellectuals discover that the destruction wreaked upon the world's books by the anonymous villain is only a smokescreen for the more heinous and diffuse crimes committed by multinational corporations. The worlds of the parallel stories remain merged until the end of the book, when Cortázar bids farewell to Fantomas after participating in a collective phone conversation with representatives of a wider Latin American public. In an appendix to the work, the author includes a brief overview of the work of the second Russell Tribunal, and a complete copy of its findings.

Cortázar first had the idea for the work after reading episode 201 of the popular Mexican comic book *Fantomas, La amenaza elegante* (Fantomas: the elegant menace), written by Gonzalo Martré, illustrated by Víctor Cruz Mota, and sent to him by Luis Guillermo Piazza, his friend and founder of Novaro, the press that brought out the Mexican *Fantomas*.[9] In this episode, published in February 1975 and titled "Inteligencia en llamas," Fantomas battles against the same worldwide bibliocide that we see in the work that Cortázar brought out with the Mexican press Excelsior just a few months later in June 1975. Cortázar also appears here—alongside Octavio Paz, Alberto Moravia, and Susan Sontag—as a character in the comic. In conceiving of a work that might aid in making public the work of the Russell Tribunal, Cortázar drafts "Inteligencia en llamas," its characters (himself included), and its disappearing books as narrative foil for the larger story of economic and political catastrophe that he wants to tell.

The colorful and shiny cover of Cortázar's work introduces Fantomas as a chiseled caped crusader dressed in a blue evening suit complete with tie, cufflinks, and white gloves, but he also dons a full white face mask and a red and yellow belt bearing a capital red F at the waist beneath his cummerbund (figure 2.1). This combination of high-brow, elegant villain and low-brow masked superhero comes directly from Fantomas's Mexican counterpart, who recalls his own Parisian progenitor in his dress but then is also masked in the style of El Santo, the widely popular midcentury Mexican *lucha libre* wrestler turned folk icon and then comic book protagonist in the Novaro series. Where Santo was hailed as defender of the common man, a deliverer of justice in the ring, on the screen and page, and in a larger Mexican cultural imaginary, Cortázar's Fantomas would follow in his footsteps but with an equally popular air of literary menace inherited from his French counterpart. Equal parts Lord of Terror and El Santo, Fantomas is possessed of enough villain to meet the criminals he will battle on their own ground, but then also of enough superhero to right their wrongs and restore balance to a world beset by injustice and, in this case, crimes against humanity. Fantomas is a self divided—an ontological struggle common to the best of superheroes—between a villainous European progenitor and a Latin American champion of the people. Cortázar calls upon both figures in order to put a stop to the disappearance of the world's stores of knowledge,

Figure 2.1 Cover of Julio Cortázar's *Fantomas contra los vampiros multinacionales*. Cover by Oswaldo for Excélsior Cia. Editorial, June 1975, México D.F.

but in their configuration, Europe lends the bad and Latin America offers up the good, an arrangement that identifies the crimes being committed against the Latin American people by their own governments as the product of centuries of colonial devastation and the resources to battle them proper to the people of Latin America.

On the cover of the book, Fantomas stands amid a pile of burning books while holding in one arm a sampling of the books he has managed to rescue and in the other a kitschy laser gun pointed off the page at an unknown enemy. The illustration is reminiscent of pulp fiction and would have been attractive to consumers. But it also announces itself as a literary artifact in its own subtitle: *Una utopia realizable narrada por Julio Cortázar* (*An Attainable Utopia Narrated by Julio Cortázar*); Cortázar had already been heralded as one of the most important writers of his time, so that a publication that bore his name would have been a literary event. This was emphasized in the two-inch paper band that encircled the book and announced in black block letters "El último libro de Cortázar" (Cortázar's latest book). The announcement also featured a pair of scissors cutting through the author's name just after the first syllable, a visual interruption that serves as the first instance of the narrative cutting and splicing that the reader will find inside. The cover of the book, then, already reveals the author's desire that the work do double duty to both politics and literature.

Cortázar's hope was that, if packaged and presented as a comic, the work would be more easily and widely consumed. In conversation with González Bermejo, he reflects on the success of the marketing of the book:

> Conseguí que el libro se vendiera en edición popular, en los quioscos de diarios, y en él incluí la sentencia del Tribunal Russel [*sic*] concerniente a las dictaduras del Cono Sur. Salió muy bien, pues miles de personas se enteraron de cosas de las que no tenían la menor idea; el libro, por supuesto, apenas entró en mi país o en Chile, pero muchos ejemplares pasaron de bolsillo a bolsillo, y tuve la plena confirmación de su eficacia. Me parece, además, que fue una buena prueba de lo que puede hacer un escritor responsable cuando se trata de transmitir un mensaje ideológico a su pueblo.[10]

> I managed to get the book sold in a popular edition, in newspaper stands, and in it I included the sentence pronounced by

the Russell Tribunal on the dictatorships of the Southern Cone. It worked out really well, in that thousands of people found out about things about which they didn't have the slightest idea. The book hardly entered my country or Chile, of course, but many copies got passed around from hand to hand, and I had full confirmation of its efficacy. It seems to me, also, that it was a good test as to what a responsible writer can do when trying to transmit an ideological message to the people of his country.

The first print run of *Fantomas* produced twenty thousand copies of the work, which Cortázar arranged to sell in both bookstores and newspaper stands.[11] He here sounds pleased with how his experiment in public reading has turned out. But more interesting is that Cortázar views the whole project as a kind of test that proves that literature is capable of containing and circulating some larger ideological message. The latter was indeed his intention in writing the work, as he notes in his correspondence to friends just after finishing the project.[12] In a letter of August 28, 1975, he writes to Lelio Basso, the Italian organizer and president of the second Russell Tribunal:

> Hace años que me preocupaba la falta de difusión y de información en América Latina en todo lo que se refiere a la labor del Tribunal Bertrand Russell. Los silencios culpables, la deformación de las noticias por obra de las agencias de prensa imperialistas, y tantas otras cosas que conoces mejor que yo, son culpables de que los pueblos latinoamericanos no sepan con detalle la labor que realiza el Tribunal, los nombres de quienes lo forman, y el texto de sus sentencias.
> Tal vez este modesto *comic*, al llegar por la vía popular, sirva para mostrarle a mucha gente lo que no le llegaría nunca a través de diarios y revistas.
> Me alegra pensar, además, que la venta de *Fantomas* pueda dar algún dinero al Tribunal, puesto que conozco sus dificultades.[13]

I've been worried for years about the lack of circulation and of information in Latin America as to all the work undertaken by the Bertrand Russell Tribunal. The guilty silences, the deformation of the news at the hand of imperialist news agencies, and so many other things that you know better than I, are responsible for the fact that the Latin American people don't in any detail know the work carried out by the Tribunal, the names of its members, and the text of its sentences.

Perhaps this modest *comic*, arriving by more popular means, will be able to show to a lot of people what they'll never get from newspapers and magazines.

It makes me happy to think, too, that the sale of *Fantomas* might provide the Tribunal with some money, as I'm familiar with its difficulties.

This letter reveals a more socially engaged Cortázar concerned with facilitating the dissemination of accurate information about the work of the tribunal to a larger Latin American public. He emphasizes his hope that the work of a "modest comic" will succeed where mainstream print media fails to fully inform its readers, as well as help fund the tribunal. Cortázar here notes a gap in knowledge and knowledge production that he thinks *Fantomas* can help close. He privileges the social or political import of the work—perhaps to some extent magnified by the fact that he is writing to the founder of the tribunal—but puts the aesthetic in its service.

In a letter to Eduardo Jonquières of September 2, 1975, he writes:

> Aquí te va *Fantomas*, como verás *no es literatura sino el deseo de llevar una cierta información a niveles de público que carecen de ella por razones bien conocidas*. Vos me repetiste en el hospital que no creés en el poder de este tipo de cosas, pero yo sigo empecinando en creerlo y además en hacerlo. Confío en que por lo menos te diviertas con esta mezcla de realidad y ficción que me entretuvo mucho mientras lo escribía.[14]

> Here's *Fantomas*. As you'll see, *it is not literature, but rather the desire to get certain information to a portion of the public that lacks it, for reasons that are well known*. You told me in the hospital that you don't believe in this type of thing. But I'm still trying to believe it and also do it. I trust at least that you'll enjoy this mix of reality and fiction that kept me so entertained while I wrote it.

Cortázar is clear here—and so emphasizes in his letter—that *Fantomas* is not a work of literature but a project undertaken to facilitate information to a wider reading public. He might have here settled any debate about the purpose of the novella, except he goes on to encourage his friend to enjoy "this mix of reality and fiction," therein broaching again the possibility that the work marries political and literary efforts. In another letter written to Fernández Retamar on October 6, 1975, Cortázar refers to *Fantomas* as "un 'divertimento' que escribí para ayudar al Tribunal Russell" (an "amusement" that I wrote to help the Russell Tribunal).[15] Here, too, Cortázar reveals in the same tenor the dual purpose of the book as political intervention and aesthetic undertaking, or at least a project whose aesthetics—here an amusement and a distraction—are put in the service of the serious political work of the tribunal. In each of these letters, Cortázar lays bare the fact that he thinks art can serve politics, work to produce new knowledge, and effect some sort of real change in the world. Yet while his purpose might be political, his means are literary. So *Fantomas* is a hybrid work both in content and in conception, and we can fairly use one to help us understand the other. For, as will become evident shortly, this doubled extratextual context appears in the novella as portal and pathway between the intersecting narrative ontologies that Cortázar constructs in order to reveal the structure and function of disappearance.

While *Fantomas* has been to date largely overlooked in scholarship on Cortázar,[16] several scholars have noted the dynamic contradictions of the literary and the political at work in the book. Ellen McCracken in particular, in one of the earliest and most prescient scholarly responses to *Fantomas*, concludes that Cortázar fails at reconciling his dual desire to produce literature with a meaningful ideological message for a wide audience and to write for an elite readership. She writes:

> While Cortázar's politics urge him to write in a form which is widely disseminated, he finds it impossible to not be a high culture novelist. This helps to explain his insistence that his job is to be a revolutionary of literature. For Cortázar, this does not mean the writing of literature for a wider sector of the population and consequently, he is locked within the contradiction of producing elite literature while desiring to widely disseminate an important message.
>
> In both *Libro de Manuel* and *Fantomas* the use of mass culture represents Cortázar's failed attempt to resolve the dichotomy he saw between aesthetic innovations and political ones. His desire to remedy some of the media's negative effects on human consciousness and to join art, politics, and mass culture, led to

politically contradictory works of fiction. Cortázar, as self-proclaimed "revolutionary of literature," succeeded in aestheticizing two mass cultural forms but failed to achieve his political goals.[17]

McCracken identifies in Cortázar's work—and here particularly in works that foreground mixed media, collage, intercalation, or otherwise attempt to participate explicitly in the techniques of mass culture—an unresolved dichotomy between political and aesthetic interventions. Where Cortázar might have wanted to see himself as participating in some larger revolution of political consciousness, his first commitment was to work as a "revolutionary of literature." Any innovation and renovation he conceived was in the service, in the first instance, of art. Even, then, in composing and arranging for the wide circulation of *Fantomas*, McCracken proposes, Cortázar was not able to overcome his status as a writer of high literary culture.

David Kurnick, in the afterword to his recent translation into English of *Fantomas*, offers up an interpretation of Cortázar's contradictions acted out instead in the character of Fantomas. He recognizes Cortázar's version of Fantomas as a failed, solitary superhero, noting that indeed "the originality of Cortázar's book is the way it lets the superhero do his superhero thing only to have him admit in the end that his wizardry is inadequate to the task at hand."[18] In the end, Fantomas alone is not enough to save the world from the insidious influence of the multinational corporation, here a synecdoche for US intervention in Latin America, and Cortázar lays the responsibility for stemming large-scale human rights abuses in the hands of the people. Kurnick recognizes in this ultimate failure on the part of Fantomas a narrative that corresponds to the difficult position that Cortázar occupied as both author of high literary culture and cultural hero to the masses. He writes:

> Fantomas, who can do anything except figure out whom to fight and how to translate his talents to the proper sphere of action, was a dense and perfectly ambivalent fantasy object for the high-culture idol Cortázar had become: for the difficult writer, Fantomas serves as an emblem of a truly mass audience; for the culture hero, he is a compact illustration of the limitations of individual heroism in making political change.[19]

Fantomas's own ambivalence, in Kurnick's estimation, becomes the embodiment of and perfect foil for the pull the author feels between his creative commitment to revolutionizing literature and putting literature in the service of political action. Where Fantomas might be capable of stopping the world's books from disappearing, he is not up to the task of putting an end to the crimes against humanity documented by the Russell Tribunal that this bibliocide covers up for. And where *Fantomas* does its part to disseminate information about the tribunal to a wider reading public, the work does not ever rise to the level of a revolutionary political intervention. Both the text and its protagonist instead serve as evidence of the limitations that Cortázar felt as a political agent in a larger cultural sphere, of what he felt was the limited capacity of literature to house a political message, and of just how far he was willing to sacrifice the literary in order to privilege the political. *Fantomas* is proof and product of the author's divided loyalties to art and the political sphere, but more importantly of the struggle he suffered to unite them.

The dualities revealed in the enduring narrative of a failed Cortazarian reconciliation of aesthetics and politics serve as a critical frame for the textual techniques of doubling that emerge as fundamental to the construction of the novella and to Cortázar's larger philosophy of fiction. They also allow the work to succeed, if not properly as either literature or political intervention, then on a historiographical front. For the tension that emerges in Cortázar's struggle to satisfy both aesthetic and political revolution leaves us with a work in *Fantomas* that functions not only as a significant historical artifact but, by way of its narrative techniques of doubling, also as a primer for understanding the production of a dynamic, fluid, and abiding historical consciousness. Where Cortázar fails to work wholly in the service of either literature or politics, their interaction with each other—however marred, incomplete, asymmetrical—produces an important historiographical intervention by enacting on the page the processes at work in historical consciousness in general and in the recognition of historical crisis more particularly. Doubling and displacement as a mode of disappearance—a way to narrate and parse the disappearance that appears as context and core of *Fantomas*—works not only to render the looming catastrophe to which the novella responds visible, legible, and the site of new forms of knowledge, but it reveals history and our consciousness of it as the product of a doubled stance, perspective, and a critical stereoscopic vision. What remains of this chapter attends to the ways in which Cortázar uses the narrative techniques of doubling and displacement to expose this catastrophe of disappearance at the core of *Fantomas* so that we might better understand its structure, what it obscures from our view, and how catastrophe worked out on the page provides for an abiding and self-reflective historical consciousness.

Smokescreen

Cortázar leads his readers through the plot, which is also the political message, of *Fantomas* by way of a series of plunging, ascending, and intersecting diegetic transitions. The disappearing of the world's books that the work's superhero is engaged to halt turns out to be a cover-up for the far more heinous economic crimes that fund systematic enforced disappearance. Here the threat to free and accessible knowledge is a foil for the larger threat to the human life that produces that knowledge, but it takes navigating the complicated recursive worlds that Cortázar builds, as well as the persistent textual traces of his struggle to fully commit literature to politics, to get at what disappearance covers up for, and then the catastrophe that it points us toward, in *Fantomas*.

Fantomas opens upon an unnamed narrator returning home to Paris from the last meeting of the Russell Tribunal in Brussels. Before boarding his train, he stops in the station to buy something to read on the way home and is surprised to find that all the newspapers and magazines for sale are Mexican, a phenomenon for which the saleslady has no explanation. He selects a thin comic entitled "*FANTOMAS, La amenaza elegante*, presenta: LA INTELIGENCIA EN LLAMAS" ("FANTOMAS, the *Elegant Menace* presents THE MIND ON FIRE"),[20] and boards the train, where he shares a compartment with a woman who looks disdainfully at his choice of reading material:

> . . . la rubia platinada desprendía una ojeada cibernética hacia la revista, seguida de una expresión general entre parece-mentira-a-su-edad y cada-día-se-nos-meten-más-extranjeros-en-el-país, doble deducción que desde luego dificultaría toda intentona colonizadora del narrador cuando empezara a reinar la atmósfera solidaria que nace en los compartimentos de los trenes después del kilómetro noventa. Pero las revistas de tiras cómicas tienen eso, uno las desprecia y demás pero al mismo tiempo empieza a mirarlas y en una de esas, fotonovelas o Charlie Brown o Mafalda se te van ganando y entonces *FANTOMAS, La amenaza elegante*, presenta . . .[21]

[It was moreover impossible to miss] the cybernetic glance the blonde bestowed on the magazine, followed by a bland expression that conveyed something between can-you-believe-it-at-his-age and every-day-there-are-more-foreigners-pouring-into-the-country: a double conclusion which would of course render that much more difficult any seduction the narrator might attempt to undertake around ninety kilometers into their journey, when an atmosphere of solidarity tends to take over in train compartments. But there's something about comic books, one scoffs at them but one starts to leaf through them all the same, until one of them, a *fotonovela* or Charlie Brown or Mafalda, pulls you in . . . and in this case, FANTOMAS, *the Elegant Menace*, presents . . .

After identifying the narrator as a foreigner out of place in the country—a not insignificant reminder of Cortázar's outsider status—the passage introduces us to "La Inteligencia en llamas" by asking us to imagine ourselves as readers of a comic, torn between wanting to read it and recognizing that we really should not be reading such material at this age. Here Cortázar asks us, his readers, to reflect on our own reading choices while establishing the work we are holding in our hands as itself divided between high culture— the reading material of a member, for example, of an international human rights tribunal—and low culture—reading material looked down upon by a woman herself reading the French tabloids. He also asserts, by aligning the comic with the *fotonovela* or other comics like *Peanuts* or *Mafalda*,[22] the mechanical reproducibility of the book we are holding and the global, capitalist network in which it unavoidably participates. For we cannot read *Fantomas* without also reading the embedded comic whose world will come to merge with the world of the narrator. Here Cortázar lays bare the conflicted nature of the work, but asks the reader to reflect on it alongside him, so that the reading process that follows is doubled as soon as the work begins.

He then slips from the world of the narrator into the world of the comic on the back of the reflexive verb form in the present continuous of *ganarse* (*a alguien*), a structure that also proves key to his previous works of fantastic literature, namely, "La boca noche arriba" and "Continuidad de los parques." In the latter, an unnamed protagonist "gozaba del placer casi perverso de *irse desgajando* línea a línea de lo que le rodeaba" (tasted the almost perverse pleasure of *disengaging himself* line by line from the things around him),[23] until so fully immersed in the book he is reading that he does not realize the world of the book has become the world he is living. "Irse desgajando" indicates a disengagement from the world around him, but also a splitting off or a splitting off from, therein foreshadowing the fatal split that the protagonist-reader will suffer when his world merges with that of the book. Cortázar uses the same technique to move us into the embedded world of "Inteligencia" that will also later merge with the world of the narrator and also, in an even more complicated recursive move that is not more than inferred in "Continuidad," with the world of the reader. Those readers familiar with Cortázar's earlier works will recognize the move so that the previous world-splitting that the author has constructed—and the resulting caution that our failure to read actively is a fatal decision—accompanies us here as we let ourselves be pulled into the world of *Fantomas*, in turn itself another politically charged portal to our own world.

In "Inteligencia," here replicating its counterpart in Martré and Cruz Mota's version published earlier the same year, an unidentified enemy has begun to destroy the world's books. Libraries in London, Paris, Rome, Tokyo, and Moscow find their collections vanished, as individual writers and public intellectuals will theirs later in the text, including one Julio Cortázar, identified with a wink by the same caption given the author by Martré in the original comic, as the "Gran escritor argentino, contemporáneo" (Great Argentine writer, contemporary).[24] The author maintains his identity as a character in the world of the comic—although here displaced from Paris to Barcelona—creating a recursivity that will later double back on itself to connect the worlds of the book with the soon conjoined worlds of author and reader (figure 2.2). The international revelation of the disappearance of the world's books—of this bibliocide, as the narrator calls it, wherein books replace the human disappeared of state terror—progresses alongside the primary diegetic world of the story in which the narrator comments on the story he is reading, interacts with his fellow travelers in the train compartment, and reflects on the difficult human rights work performed by the Russell Tribunal over the last few days. The train reaches Paris, the passengers disembark, and the narrator heads to his apartment. Shortly after arriving home, he receives a phone call from his good friend Susan Sontag, who wants to know if he has heard about what is going on. When he tells her that he has not, Sontag wonders how this can be if Fantomas called Cortázar before he called her and tells him to hang up the phone and keep reading in order to find out more. Here the primary world of the narrator starts to merge with the embedded world of "Inteligencia" and Cortázar returns to the comic to find out what has happened. He finds Fantomas telling his assistant to get his entourage of writers and public intellectuals on the line so they can help him try to figure out who is causing the destruction of the world's books. But the situation is more dire: not only are books going missing, writers around the world are receiving death threats that will be carried out if they try to write or publish any future books.

Figure 2.2 Cortázar on the phone with Fantomas in "Inteligencia en llamas." Julio Cortázar, *Fantomas*, 1975. Drawing from no. 201 of the comic book series *Fantomas, La amenaza elegante*, February 1975, Ediciones Novaro, México D.F. Written by Gonzalo Martré with drawings by Víctor Cruz Mota.

The work will remain at the hypodiegetic level of "Inteligencia" until the end. But Cortázar points the reader back to the primary narrative level of the narrator, and from there to the extratextual world of the reader, on several occasions. When Fantomas, for example, thinks he has identified one George Steiner (not the literary critic) and his gang as the men perpetrating the bibliocide, Sontag tells the narrator—here named Julio for the first time—that it has all been a smokescreen, that the real culprit are those who have just been condemned by the Russell Tribunal:

—Julio, Julio, ¿quién es verdaderamente Steiner? ¿Cómo se llama los que el Tribunal Rusell [*sic*] acaba de condenar en Bruselas?
—Se llaman de mil, de diez mil, de cien mil maneras—dijo el narrador . . . —, pero se llaman sobre todo ITT, sobre todo Nixon y Ford, sobre todo Henry Kissinger o CIA o DIA, se llama sobre todo Pinochet o Banzer o López Rega, sobre todo General o Coronel o Tecnócrata o Fleury o Stroessner, se llaman de una manera tan especial que cada nombre significa miles de nombres, como la palabra *hormiga* significa siempre una multitud de hormigas aunque el diccionario la defina en singular.[25]

"Julio, Julio, who's the real Steiner? Whom did the Russell Tribunal just condemn in Brussels?"
"They have a thousand, ten thousand, a hundred thousand names," said the narrator . . . , "but above all they're called ITT, they're called Nixon and Ford, Henry Kissinger or CIA or DIA, they're called Pinochet or Banzer or López Rega, they're called General or Colonel or Technocrat or Fleury or Stroessner, they have those special names where every name means thousands of names, the way the word *ant* means a multitude of ants even though the dictionary defines it in the singular."

Sontag tells the narrator that Fantomas has fallen for the "Gran Engaño," the Big Lie. The destruction of the world's books is just a prologue to what will come, and besides, she asks, "Qué son los libros al lado de quienes los leen, Julio? ¿De qué nos sirven las bibliotecas enteritas si sólo les están dadas a unas pocos? También es una trampa para intelectuales. La pérdida de un solo libro nos agita más que el hambre en Etiopía, es lógico y comprensible y monstruoso al mismo tiempo" (What are books compared to those who read them, Julio? What are whole libraries worth if they're only available to a few? This is a trap for us intellectuals, too. We get more upset about the loss of a single book than about hunger in Ethiopia—it's logical and understandable and monstrous at the same time).[26] Here Sontag reveals that the worldwide destruction of knowledge and its production is a cover-up for a far more heinous crime that the world, including intellectuals, ignore.

The real crime, as the narrator reveals as he reports on the findings of the tribunal, is multitudinous in its singularity, insidious and diffuse and impossible to fully identify. Here ITT becomes Nixon then Kissinger, who is interchangeable with any number of Latin American dictators as the abuses they all provide for, sponsor, and implement become themselves as diffuse as their source and as difficult to curb. The risk to the production of human knowledge is signaled only asymmetrically by the destruction of the world's libraries. For the real risk is to the human life that produces this knowledge in the first place. But the network of destruction is too vast, interdependent, and self-replicating—not to mention well funded—to contain. This is why Sontag tells the narrator, in their first phone conversation, that the sentence pronounced by the Russell Tribunal "no servirá para nada, monono, si ustedes y nosotros no encontramos el camino, y cuando digo nosotros no hablo de los esbeltos intelectuales tan admirados por las élites, sino de nosotros y de millones de mujeres y de hombres del planeta" (doesn't mean squat, sweetheart, if all of us don't find a way forward, and when I say *us* I'm not talking about the slick intellectuals the elites admire so much, I'm talking about you and me and millions of men and women all over the planet).[27] The tribunal, Sontag asserts, is itself—in both composition and effectiveness—a placeholder for the grassroots work that needs to be taken up across the globe. It will not be the tribunal, comprised precisely of intellectuals and elites, but rather the networked masses who will take down the international network that feeds on the systematic production of inequalities in technology, labor, wage, food, and knowledge, and takes our lives in the balance.

The questions about the efficacy of the tribunal's work and Cortázar's plea to the people will return at the end of the book, and Sontag will continue to divide throughout the political work done by intellectuals from the work undertaken by the masses. She will also remind Cortázar, on several occasions that serve as pathways between the narrative levels of the book as well as reminders of the author's conflicted loyalties, of his responsibility as a writer to work on behalf of the people. This is clear evidence the author cannot shake the sense that he should be lending his talents to some larger political cause and an embedded defense—this another public version of the author's defensive position of his literary work's political engagement that Ricardo Piglia notes in conversation with Juan José Saer[28]—of the work he hopes *Fantomas* will perform on the ground. The political message that Cortázar aims to espouse in *Fantomas*—namely, that change is the responsibility of the people—survives the various narrative and ideological divisions throughout the book. But his view that the tribunal might contribute to this effort—a possibility underscored by the fact that the author cedes the work's rights to the Russell Tribunal on the copyright page, before the book even begins—emerges as unstable, contradicted on various fronts, and eventually displaced entirely by what appears to be the *real* work of the people. Cortázar wants to disseminate the findings of the tribunal and includes the full transcript of its findings in an appendix to which he directs interested readers in a footnote on the first page of the work. But once that information is made public, once the people are in possession of that knowledge, he intimates, then the work of change is in their hands.

What emerges intact from the handover of political responsibility that *Fantomas* facilitates is Cortázar's proposal that what we value in knowledge covers up for what we value in human life and can indeed impede our access to its protection. Cortázar instructs us in how to identify and read what he sees as a bourgeois cover-up that doubles as a genuine concern for the fate of humankind. Both the widespread bibliocide and the mortal risk to the production of new knowledge cover over the real danger in our midst; they are a smokescreen that distracts us and prevents us from seeing what we most need to witness. Our fevered reaction to these possible losses, both immediate and future, is a form of displacement that permits us not to attend to what really threatens the replenishing of the repositories of human knowledge: the very real disappearance of human life that is being effected by the governments in power across Latin American that receive the financial sponsorship, as well as the clandestine intelligence training, of the United States. Our valorization of this knowledge, Cortázar tells us, is suspect and functions as both foil and, more dangerously, absolution for not reading properly—here again his admonishment that we be active, engaged, responsible readers—what is going on around us. The consequences of this misreading in Argentina in particular, in the final year of Isabel Perón's defunct presidency and on the cusp of the Videla dictatorship, are fatal.

Catastrophe and Consciousness

To counter this misreading, Cortázar offers up in his narrative techniques of doubling and displacement new forms of knowledge and knowledge production proper to recognizing and to living historical catastrophe. Catastrophe enacts a reversal of what is expected as it signals the fatal turning point in a drama. Made up of the Greek *kata*, "down," and *streiphen*, "turn," catastrophe is a downturn, but in its linguistic history also an overturn, an overturning, a sudden end. *Streiphen*, related to strophe, indicates a physical turning by the chorus in the singing of an ode and marks a turn that is itself linguistic product of the Indo-European *strebh*, "to wind or turn," from which we also get whirl, whirlwind, that which is twisted. The overturning at work in catastrophe is then "an act of rotating," later "a place of bending," *turn* from the Greek *tornos*, "lathe, a tool for drawing circles," from the Indo-European root *tere*, "to rub, turn," that also gives us a violent overthrowing, ruin, and destruction. There is, in the very making of catastrophe, a circling, a going round and round, but also a turning back on, a violent change in direction that threatens ruin.

The end that catastrophe signals might be sudden, but it does not depend on a rupture from its context; instead it marks a new direction, a spiraling, and a going back over again. When we talk of a historical catastrophe, we are not pointing to an event that is separate from the social or political context in which it occurs. Catastrophe signals rather a twisting round, a turning around, a sudden turning back upon that marks a reversal in direction completely embedded in and dependent upon the conditions that provide for it in the first place. As a catalyst for new knowledge, then, catastrophe requires a going back over again with a difference, a turning over the same ground with an eye to something else, a revolution that does not shake its roots no matter how far out it spirals. Seeing catastrophe, recognizing historical event as catastrophe, necessitates a double vision that allows for a focus on the past and the future at the same time. The perception of catastrophe—the historical consciousness that something has turned away, turned back on itself, that we might be headed in a new direction or right toward ruin—depends on this split, on a stereoscopic sight that allows us to see ourselves and our historical context in two places at the same time. The techniques of doubling that Cortázar deploys provide for this stereoscopy, the production of a historical consciousness that allows us, in the moment and still from the distance of more than forty years later, to see a catastrophe in the making.

As a mode of narration, instantiations of doubling proliferate throughout the novel. *Fantomas* already announces, on the work's cover, that it straddles both low-brow and elite reading cultures. Cortázar then cedes the rights of the work to the Russell Tribunal at the bottom of the copyright page, where a footnote directs "el lector interesado" (the interested reader) to the appendix at the end of the book with "un consejo amistoso: lea el apéndice al final, para qué apurarse si aquí todo va de lo más bonito" (a friendly piece of advice: read the appendix last, why rush things when we've gotten off to such a good start).[29] Cortázar here makes the reader a promise only aesthetics can make: why hurry to the end when everything here is going so well, when everything right now is just beautiful. He separates here the fiction to follow from its historical double—the text's historicity emphasized when sent to heads of state around the world—which functions already as a warning that something in the story to follow is going to go downhill. He waves the reader away from the political intervention that motivates the book at the same time as he announces, before the first sentence of the story has even come to a close, that the work shares some intimate relationship with the tribunal. The message is mixed, but it should alert a cautious reader that whatever aesthetic reading pleasure she is about to derive from the text will be soon undone by some historical reality. The move appears to separate history from fiction—even as it links them inextricably between the shared covers of a book—and seems to protect the content of the story from any historical incursions so that the reader might choose one and leave the other. Cortázar offers up here a false aesthetic security that lulls the reader into thinking her fictional world is somehow protected when what awaits is a political intervention that will leave the responsibility for effecting social change in her very hands. But for now the reader's attention is displaced.

It will not take long for Cortázar to return to the matter of the tribunal, however, and to expand on its purpose. Just a few pages after the beginning of "Inteligencia," the narrator leans back to rests his eyes, preferring to "pasar por alto la ligera laguna cultural, máxime cuando lo que sucedía en la revista rebosaba de cultura, las bibliotecas europeas descubrían la desaparición de las obras de Víctor Hugo, Gautier, Proust, Dante, Petrarca y Petronio, sin hablar de los manuscritos de Chaucer, Chesterton y H. G. Wells . . ." (pass over this small cultural lacuna in silence, especially when the story in his comic book had culture to spare: the libraries of Europe were discovering the disappearance of the work of Victor Hugo, Gautier, Proust, Dante, Petrarch, and Petronius, not to mention the manuscripts of Chaucer, Chesterton, and H. G. Wells . . .).[30] Europe, the narrator esteems, is overflowing with culture, has culture to burn. So his attention turns from Europe's disappearing stores of knowledge back to the events of the tribunal. But the shift is interrupted by frames from Martré's and Cruz Mota's original comic in which Fantomas, disguised as a concert-goer, explains Brecht's vision in *The Threepenny Opera* to the young lady who accompanies him: "Brecht quiso parodiar las costumbres de la burguesía con las de los estafadores. . . . entreveía que la diferencia entre un hombre sin escrúpulos financieros, y un gángster, es mínima" (Brecht was satirizing the bourgeoisie by comparing them to crooks. . . . He saw there was little difference between an unscrupulous banker and a gangster).[31] This critical transition from Europe's disappearing books to the work of the tribunal—the transition back to the primary diegetic level of the book—connects the two events early on in the book, but splits in order to identify early on the real criminals responsible for both: the bourgeoisie are crooks, gangsters, responsible in their irresponsibility for the global inequalities that galvanize human rights abuses across Latin America. Cortázar's animated, intercalated meditation here is placeholder, anchor, and foreshadowing of the work's final thesis.

But for now the transition serves as a portal back to the world of the narrator, still en route to Paris. He closes his eyes and the comic in his hands and lets himself

> . . . resbalar despacito en el tobogán de la fatiga. Ocho días de trabajo en el Tribunal Russell, con una última reunión hasta la madrugada, horas y horas escuchando a relatores y testigos que aportaban pruebas sobre la represión en tantos países de América Latina y el papel de las sociedades transnacionales en el pillaje de las economías y la dominación en el plano político* y paralelamente, porque la dominación económica exigía otras dominaciones, otros cómplices y otras víctimas, la repetición hasta la náusea de testimonios sobre el asesinato, la tortura, la persecución, las cárceles en Chile, Brasil, Bolivia, Uruguay y no pare de contar. Como un símbolo que ya nadie nombraba, la sombra ensangrentada del Estadio Nacional de Santiago, el narrador creía escuchar otra vez las voces que se sumaban a lo largo del tiempo y los países. . . . Cada tanto, como una obstinada recurrencia, alguien subía para dar testimonio de muertes y torturas, un chileno que mostraba las técnicas empleadas por los militares, un argentino, un uruguayo, la repetición de infiernos sucesivos, la presencia infinita del mismo estupro, del mismo balde de excrementos donde se hunde la cara de un prisionero, de la misma corriente eléctrica en la piel, de la misma tenaza en las uñas. Y al salir de todo eso (de la representación mental de todo eso, podía corregir el narrador) se entraba de nuevo en lo personal (pero entonces lo personal también debía ser una representación mental de la vida, una cortina de humo, un cómodo tren Bruselas-Paris, un número de *Fantomas*, un cigarrillo negro, una nena platinada cuyo tobillo acababa de rozar el suyo y era

promisor y tibio aunque Onassis y Romy Schneider), una mera representación mental de la vida si todo lo otro se borraba con un simple parpadeo y un cambiar de tema.[32]

. . . glide slowly into fatigue. Eight days of work at the Russell Tribunal, with a final meeting until dawn, hours and hours listening to rapporteurs and witnesses bearing stories of repression in so many Latin American countries and of the role of multinational companies in economic plunder and political domination and also—because economic domination required other kinds of domination, other accomplices and other victims—the repetition ad nauseum of testimony about murder, torture, persecution, prisons in Chile, Brazil, Bolivia, Uruguay, endlessly. Like that symbol that already no one wanted to mention, the blood-stained shadow of Santiago's National Stadium, the narrator thought he could hear again the litany of countries and of voices. . . . From time to time, like an obstinate refrain, someone would stand up to give testimony of death and torture, a Chilean who demonstrated the techniques employed by the military, an Argentinian, a Uruguayan, the repetition of successive hells, the infinite presence of the same rape, the same bucket of excrement into which a prisoner's face was forced, the same electric cables attached to the skin, the same pliers applied to the fingernails. And on leaving all this behind (on leaving the mental representation of all this behind, the narrator corrected himself) he came back once again to the personal (but then the personal also must be only a mental representation of life, a smokescreen, a comfortable Brussels-Paris train, a *Fantomas* comic book, a cigarette filled with dark tobacco, a platinum blonde whose promisingly warm ankle had just grazed his, Onassis and Romy Schneider notwithstanding), a mere mental representation of life if all the rest could simply be erased with the blink of an eye and a change of topic.

Cortázar's narrator leaves behind the world of "Inteligencia" to sink back into his own world, where his fatigue is punctuated by memories of his work at the tribunal over the past few days. He hears testimony after testimony of the fundaments of disappearance—detention, torture, and murder—from people across Latin America. The singular acts of torture, rape, and pillage are repeated so often that they merge with one another, the same event narrated by one voice made up of hundreds. From the narrator's memory emerges a collective voice of witnessing and suffering that presages the same "single and uncontainable multitude"[33] that will interrupt his final phone conversation with Sontag at the end of the book and that together stands in juxtaposition to, or stands in for, the human collective to which Cortázar will hand over responsibility for working toward the "attainable utopia" the author identifies on the cover. The narrator's memories are interrupted on the facing page (the split text marked by an asterisk in the preceding passage) by an image of a metropolitan skyline repeated in fifteen tiles down the length of the page, so that this global economic center functions as a multiplying, metonymic source of political domination just before the narrator offers up in parallel the crueler consequences of this domination (figure 2.3).

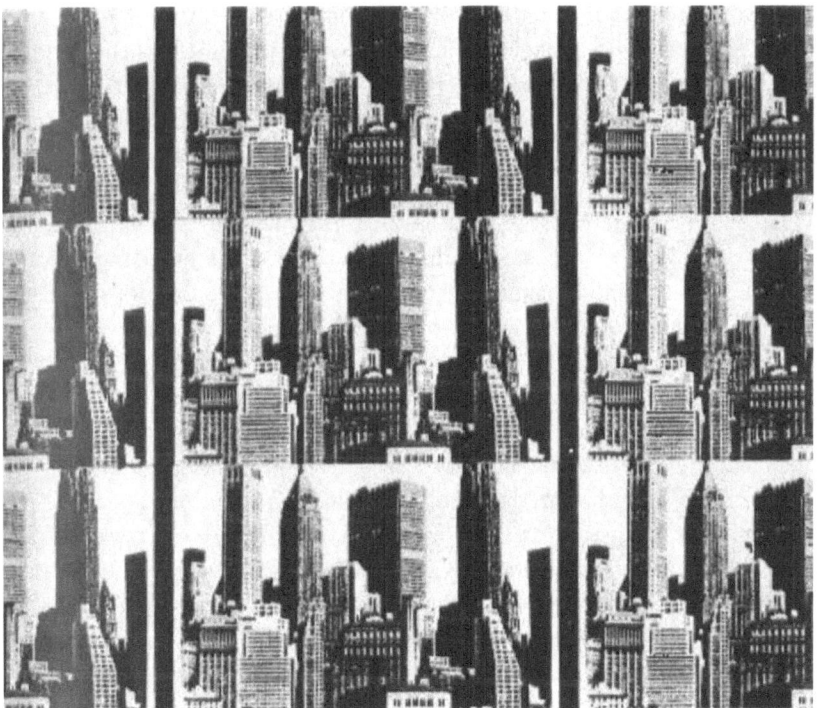

Figure 2.3 Metropolitan skyline. Julio Cortázar, *Fantomas*, 1975. Montage from no. 201 of the comic book series *Fantomas, La amenaza elegante*, February 1975, Ediciones Novaro, México D.F. Written by Gonzalo Martré with drawings by Víctor Cruz Mota.

Finally, the narrator gives up the public sphere of the tribunal that haunts his memories to return to his personal life, a reality that becomes more dubious, more unstable, more irresponsible—here a "mere mental representation of life"—if that other collective, and devastated, reality might be left behind with a simple "blink of an eye and a change of topic." The reality of collective human suffering renders his own life a mere invention of the mind, a copy, a smokescreen that stands in for some other world or world of experiences. This now unreachable world is covered over by the personal, here diminished to the status of placeholder by our human ability to ignore, reject, and leave behind the political even when presented with firsthand evidence of its capacity to devastate the personal. The narrator implicates *Fantomas*—the very work we hold in our hands—as bound up in this cover-up, and as also threatened by the political, so that reading or the very production of knowledge is complicit in obfuscating our access to the real or at least to what is really happening around us.

The preceding passage, the key moment in the book when Cortázar first details the work of the tribunal and confirms the disappearance at its core, offers up a series of divisions in which the personal finds its double, if troubled, in the political or vice versa. The narrative itself is split between the primary world of the narrator and the embedded world of "Inteligencia," where both the narrator and the author find themselves doubled—once and twice over—as a character in the comic accused by Sontag of the same difficulties in navigating the responsibilities that the literary might owe to the political. The narrator, here the author's own first double, is prevented from resting by the political realities to which he has just been made witness. The author's own act of witnessing, if we can identify both this narrative moment and Cortázar's *Fantomas* as such, is haunted by the doubled and redoubled voices of the people bearing witness to the crime of economic devastation that finds its own double in the metropolitan skyline itself repeated over and over again. The totality of the collective witnessing to the results of these crimes reveal the stark division between the political and the personal to be untenable and indeed the personal an impossible construction in the shadow of the political. If what is personal is not implicated in the political, then it is not a first-order personal, not proper to the immanent world, a world given-to-be-known, but instead a stand-in, a foil, and in its most nefarious instantiations, a cover-up for some diminished experience of the world.

This series of splitting, here perpetrated on the near shore of a text itself divided between competing ontologies and media, is not the fantastic division of worlds with which readers of Cortázar's more widely circulated "Axolotl" (1956) or "La Boca noche arriba," for example, are familiar. While these might offer up important, and unmistakable, political subtexts, the divisions that Cortázar perpetrates in *Fantomas* identify the political as the personal and any unpoliticized version of the personal as not an honest being-in-the-world. But where Cortázar's axolotl merges with the man who visits him in the Jardins de Paris every day and where his reader of novels find his own world implicated, and his life threatened in "Continuidad de los parques," so does *Fantomas*'s narrator find his personal world interrupted by and eventually taken over by its political double, not unlike the house taken over by a diffuse and unnamed Peronist threat in "Casa tomada" ("House Taken Over," 1946). This merging of worlds insists on a politicized reality, for if not, the train, the cigarette, even the book we hold in our hands are mere mental representations of life, not really life at all. The cost of living in a real world populated with the tangible, the mundane, and most especially the aesthetic, is that it be a political one. And from the textual, medial, and experiential divisions fundamental to *Fantomas* also emerges the groundwork for a historical consciousness that might recognize the larger import of this political moment. This recognition depends on a doubled vision, awareness, and being-in-the-world to function, which together force an important ontological displacement that allows for agency, change, and a return, if with a difference, to the very world it espies.

Cortázar wrote *Fantomas* just as Argentina came upon its own historical turning point. Videla's junta ousted Isabel de Perón's own disastrous presidency—one that ushered in skyrocketing inflation, the founding of the Triple A paramilitary death squad that practiced illegal detention and enforced disappearance well before the coup, and a state of siege declared in November 1974—but with the introduction of the so-called Process of National Reorganization, installed a yet unprecedented project of systematic national cleansing that would prove catastrophic in scope and consequence. The divisions that comprise *Fantomas* ask the work's readers to adopt a split vision that might take stock of these present historical circumstances and use them to imagine various future historical possibilities. This is not some exercise in historical divination but, as the late German historiographer Reinhart Koselleck sees it, an art of prognosis whose significance is espoused by thinkers such as Kant and Hamann and one of whose functions is to allow us to better identify a new or singular event against the backdrop of some larger historical structure or process that persists across "different velocities of change."[34] Kant's proposal that "we look about us from the standpoint of the present in order to determine something, or to be prepared for something,"[35] is coupled, in Koselleck's analysis, with Hamann's following meditation: "Can one recognize that which is past if one does not even understand that which is present? And who can conceptually appraise what the present is without knowing what is to come in the future? What is to come determines what is present, and this determines the past."[36] Both Kant and Hamann identify the future as the gauge for how we understand both the present and the past. Recognizing a present social or political event or condition as historical, and then again as a historical catastrophe, requires a vision that can read the present by way of what it might become. Reading catastrophe, then, is a project that requires a split historical vision whose doubled perspective allows an observer to inhabit multiple temporalities and espy a downturn, a place of bending, a change of direction in human events that promises ruin, destruction, an overthrowing of what has come before in order to allow for some future moment. This hermeneutics of catastrophe reveals what Koselleck recognizes elsewhere as the ambivalence of modern history, insomuch as we conceive of it as a totality, "but a totality that can never be complete, for, as we know, the future remains unknown."[37] Koselleck identifies here the open-endedness of modern history—an episteme, in his view, also accelerated and compressed by technological advances and a foreshortening of time[38]—whose striving is nonetheless bound by some imagined future moment that does not arrive but that promises to refract what we know of human experience so that the present, and the past, become legible at a moment of catastrophe. Cortázar works in *Fantomas* with history's structural ambivalence, and he puts his skill in splitting narrative worlds in its service so that his readers might simultaneously read catastrophe in the making and identify a revolutionary but "attainable utopia" as a possible, if yet unwritten, future outcome of this devastation.

If the promise of such a utopia, however, remains always in the indefinite future—and herein the political value of *Fantomas* never fully materializes—Cortázar's textual and graphic deconstruction of the mechanisms that facilitate systematic disappearance as a tool of state terror produces a split vision that allows for the possibility of resisting the historical groundswell toward catastrophe in the first place. Catastrophe is adjudicated always after the fact per a set of conditions that appear to congregate, from some outset, to provide for a crisis that answers always and only to its own logic. *Fantomas* breaks the moment of crisis down to its disparate parts—to the economic, the banal, the quotidian—so that we might see in the spaces that open between them the many missed opportunities, these

Benjamin's definition of tragedy, to interrupt their aggregation. Cortázar's literary techniques of doubling and displacement protract this moment so that what appears on the horizon, if ex post facto, as a state of exception might be understood as a series of smaller decisions that allow us, at any moment, to act otherwise. This reading of catastrophe aligns itself with Janet Roitman's assertion, per Koselleck, that "crisis is a historical 'super concept' (*Oberbegriffe*)," the very possibility of which signals a "certain philosophy of history"[39] that allows us to see some events while not seeing others. The "crisis narration" that Roitman analyzes in response to the financial crisis of 2008 serves as an important future corollary to the urgent disassembly of the logic of the multinational that Cortázar attempts decades earlier in *Fantomas*. But still more pressing is the possibility that narratives of crisis obscure the ground of their own knowledge because crisis, "like all observations or cognitions, does not account for the very conditions of its observation."[40] Crisis here becomes, in Roitman's *Anti-Crisis*, "a primary enabling blind spot for the production of knowledge":[41] a supra-category of knowledge that provides for itself while eclipsing other narratives that might make up some alternative history; a set of social and theoretical practices that brings into being our particular brand of contemporary history;[42] and an object of knowledge, founded on contingency and paradox, that raises more questions than offers answers. Roitman's reading of crisis, while *crisis* etymologically distinct from the *catastrophe* I see taken apart in *Fantomas*, reminds us that narrative and the form it takes makes up the very crises it chronicles. But Cortázar attempts—in his ludic, meticulous use of doubled and splitting characters and ontologies, recursive pathways between hypo- and hyperdiegetic planes, and by splicing the personal and political—to subvert the coming catastrophe rather than to provide for it. Instead of narrating the grounds of its proleptic arrival, his hermeneutics of catastrophe shows us rather that we cannot account for it and gives us multiple ways out of buying in to the crisis narrative.[43]

These spaces—apertures or potential exits—appear, among other places, in the divided reading strategies enacted in the primary diegetic plane of *Fantomas*, but also over again in the world of "Inteligencia" that Cortázar drafts as foil for the lived worlds of the narrator and of the reader. Intercalating into *Fantomas* panels from Martré and Cruz Mota's comic, Cortázar asks the reader to switch back and forth between the linear, if not necessarily stable, reading required by straightforward prose on the page and the synesthetic reading of both space and sound that a comic compels. The grammar of the comic means that its reader reads already doubled while also working to fill in the blank spaces that simultaneously hold the text up and move it forward. Scott McCloud calls this grammar "closure," even as he shows how it serves as an opening before the reader. "Closure," McCloud explains, is the cognitive process by which a reader fills in meaning left unresolved in the work's frames in the blank space between its panels; "the audience is a willing and conscious collaborator and closure is the agent of change, time, and motion."[44] The reader of "Inteligencia," then, reads into the disjunction manifested in the time frames between panels and becomes an active producer of the work's meaning, even as she must also navigate the cognitive slippage that necessarily occurs between the space and time of the comic and the world of the novella's narrator. These disjunctions—each occupying different diegetic worlds—are productive and allow the reader to imagine and experience the work's fragmentation as a "continuous, unified reality."[45] The reader makes sense and assembles order from within the dynamic interstice of disjunction that allows, in its repetition and cognitive accretion, for world expansion on the page. Closure, here doubled diegetically, functions as a productive aperture.

This dynamic opening out of Cortázar's text toward some whole and ordered, if fictional, ontology mirrors the kind of reading that Koselleck's understanding of history provides for. It looks to an undetermined future condition to make sense of a still unfolding present that, read together, make up a legible and cohesive whole. But this structure is itself comprised of disparate and fragmented parts that require assembly to be read, which finds its counterpart in Benjamin's constellated hermeneutics of history. "History," writes Benjamin, "is the subject of a construction whose site is not homogenous, empty time, but time filled full by now-time [*Jetztzeit*]."[46] This "now-time" in Benjamin's reading of history finds a correlate in the blank space constitutive to "Inteligencia" and in the interstice that connects it to the rest of the text. The blank space between the time frames of the comic and the blank space that binds these to the larger narrative of *Fantomas* provide, in tandem with the other narrative and medial interstices that the work opens up, for a dynamic and revolutionary consciousness of how history might be constructed. This new kind of historical consciousness is here product of the blank space that allows us to identify disappearance at the core of the present catastrophe, but is a consciousness also spatialized on the page. Where recent scholarship has looked at how the Latin American comic offers up, if after the fact, a crucial spatialization of cultural memory that informs how we understand and read the continent's dictatorships and postdictatorships,[47] I propose that *Fantomas* provides for and lays out for its readers also a certain spatialized historical awareness that is galvanized by the dynamic system of gaps, absences, and interstices that materialize in the doubled text. This new kind of historical consciousness derives from any given present reading moment—and thus might be always innervated anew—but looks toward the future to make sense in these present instances. The contours of the coming catastrophe, then, might always be in flux, and Cortázar's work offers up, with every reading, the opportunity to reshape the lived present before it becomes the historical future.

Double Vision

Cortázar's hermeneutics of catastrophe also depends throughout *Fantomas*, as it did in his *Libro de Manuel* (*A Manual for Manuel*, 1973), on the intercalation of other media that lay bare the brute economic and political mechanisms that provide for enforced disappearance and whose integration into the text demands, as does reading the frames of the embedded comic, a doubled vision. These media include found images, a newspaper article that reports on the attempted sale of deadly weapons to US intelligence agencies for resale outside the country, a map marking the locations around the world of coup d'états funded by the CIA, a memo from the International Telephone and Telegraph Corporation morally justifying the intervention of armed forces for an indefinite period of time, and a note that documents German big pharma's vested interest in securing the fall of the Allende government in Chile. The images that supplement "Inteligencia" or, as in the case of the aforementioned metropolitan photomontage, visually interrupt the primary diegetic world, include repeated, merged shots of monuments, riot police, and the IBM logo, as well as a series of black-and-white drawings. These images accompany Cortázar's explanation to Fantomas—after Sontag tells the failed superhero that the key to solving the crime lies in the events of the Russell Tribunal—that the international bibliocide wreaking havoc around the world is only a smokescreen for the crimes against humanity detailed in the tribunal's transcripts.

When Fantomas asks Cortázar about the tribunal, the author refers him to the appendix and shows him "las páginas finales de este mismísimo volumen" (the final pages of this very volume),[48] so that Fantomas moves into the same narrative plane as the reader or so that the reader is invited to occupy the embedded world of the comic alongside Fantomas. They both, as well as Cortázar, who holds a copy of the very book the reader is reading in his hands, are reading the same book and might, in this instance, both turn to the appendix at the same moment. This proleptic move toward the imagined wholeness of the book—a book whose end remains yet unknown to the reader—replicates the structural ambivalence that Koselleck identifies as proper to our particular historical moment. The narrative that we conceive of as a whole is open-ended on one end, so that we define our current circumstances by way of a recursivity whose future source is yet empty, which gives us far more room to act than we might imagine. Where Cortázar moves himself, Fantomas, and the reader all onto the same diegetic plane, he folds the collaborative future of his narrative back onto itself so that what is yet not more than an imagined space is already exerting pressure on how we read the book and, consequently, how the book unfolds. Cortázar forces the reader, if gently, into the position of finding herself already, textually, bound up in the book. This textual interpellation makes the reader complicit in what follows, so that she is responsible, before the fact and as the book takes shape, for the knowledge that will be proffered. Cortázar both positions the reader as an active part of the historical moment he comments on and arms her with knowledge about it. The reader becomes entangled here in both world and text, in full possession of the knowledge and the split vision required to understand this moment as historically charged.

This hinge moment in the text in which Cortázar uses intersecting ontologies to implicate the reader in her own world remains uncommented by the narrator-author who goes on to offer up ITT as representative of a larger network of multinational corporations, as well as a summary of what was discussed at the tribunal. He asks Fantomas, "¿Querés que te muestre cómo las veo yo?" (Should I explain to you how I see things?), and then, "Así las veo" (Here's how I see things) is followed by a full-page photomontage of a hand stabbing an eye with a knife (figure 2.4), to which Fantomas responds, "Parece el comienzo de *Un perro andaluz*" (It's like the beginning of *Un chien andalou*)."[49]

At the bottom of these facing pages is a black-and-white photomontage that lays out a multiplied, stacked sequence of what appears to be Capitol Hill. From the far right-hand side of the page to the left, we see a cropped shot where the whites are overexposed and the background is too dark; then from another angle, an underexposed shot with children playing in front of the building; and then again, with just one frame on the left-hand side of

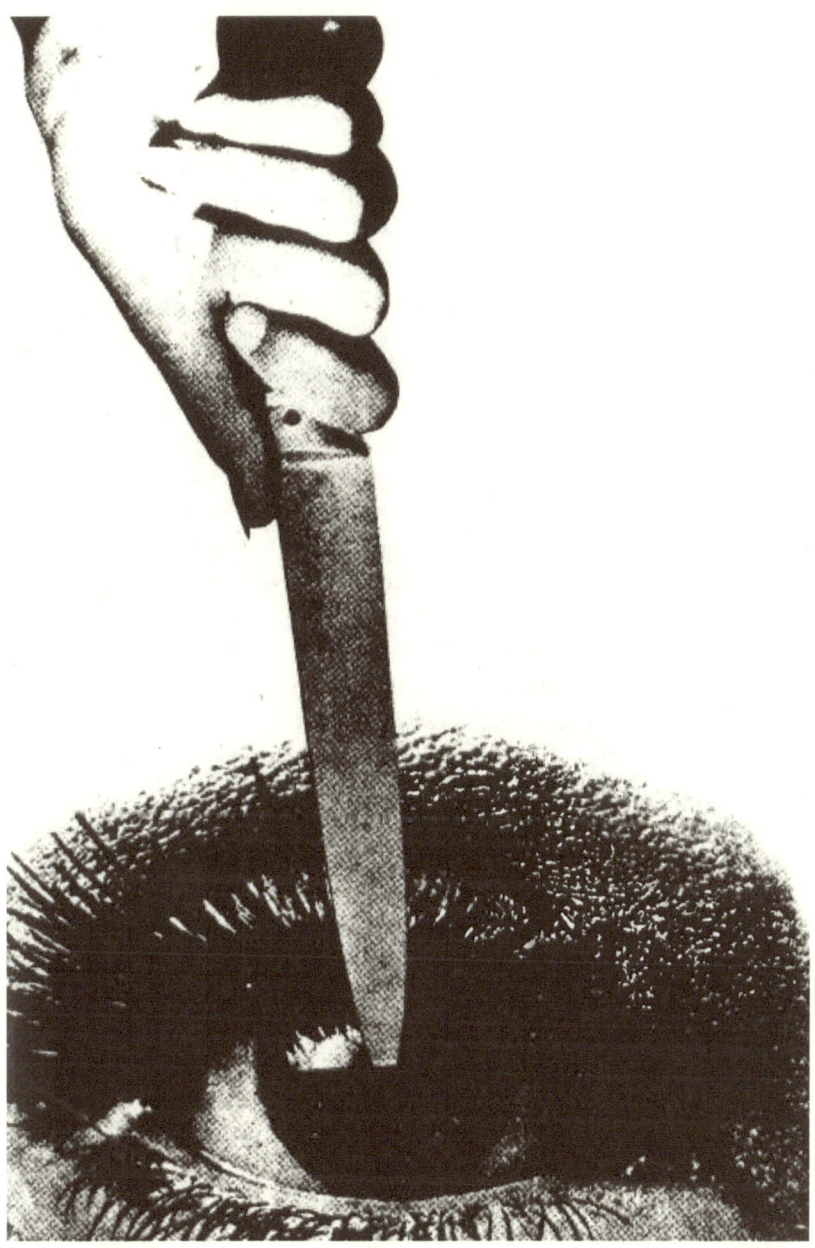

Figure 2.4 Buñuel reinterpreted. Julio Cortázar, *Fantomas*, 1975. Drawing from no. 201 of the comic book series *Fantomas, La amenaza elegante*, February 1975, Ediciones Novaro, México D.F. Written by Gonzalo Martré with drawings by Víctor Cruz Mota.

the page, the overexposure for the whole of the right-hand-side page (figure 2.5). The transition worked out here from overexposure that fades to normal and then back again corresponds visually to the narrator's response to Fantomas: "Todo en nuestra América es el comienzo de ese perro, viejo, pocas veces hemos llegado a mirar algo de frente sin que la navaja o el cuchillo vinieran a vaciarnos los ojos" (Everything in the Americas is like that, my friend, we've hardly ever gotten a look at anything head-on without that razor or that knife coming to cut our eyes out).[50] The narrator uses Buñuel's film—here present in the metonymy of the dog but then also vacated by the fact that the film features no such dog—in tandem with José Martí's revolutionary, anti-imperialist vision of "our America" to describe a Latin American vision routinely compromised by the colonial knife come to blind it, empty it out, "to cut our eyes out." This thwarted sight is worked out in the over- and underexposure of the grainy frames below so that we read the knife coming, the disabled sight, the play of darkness and too much empty light that repeats over and over again. Sight is again split, except here blindness is the reward for looking too directly at what is going on in Latin America. Cortázar cautions, and confirms this in his graphic sequence, that an oblique view also reveals critical information and can be a life-saving tactic when discerning catastrophe on the horizon. This obliquity of sight—modeled by Walsh and here drafted by Cortázar—will reappear in more mature form as a crucial narrative technique in works of fiction across the Southern Cone that respond to state terror during its various dictatorships and afterward. But before it becomes a signature narrative device that sees its way through the "given-to-be-invisible," obliquity shows up in *Fantomas* as an alternative to viewing catastrophe head on. The narrator's offer to show Fantomas how he sees things is accompanied by intercalated images until the final two pages of the book. *Fantomas*, which has already moved the reader into the graphic world of "Inteligencia," asks the reader to move now between concurrent, intersecting textual and visual narratives that work together as revolutionary clarifying agents to still the hand on the imperial knife and allow for multiple planes and angles of possible vision.

The nature of the visual texts that Cortázar integrates into his work—particularly the reproductions of the written texts—serve both as exemplification of the narrator's account of the work of the tribunal and as polyvalent sites of meaning in their own right. Cortázar interrupts the reader's reading experience with the news article, map, memo, and letter that also each operate at multiple narrative levels and within their own particular historical contexts; here the reader must navigate a simultane-

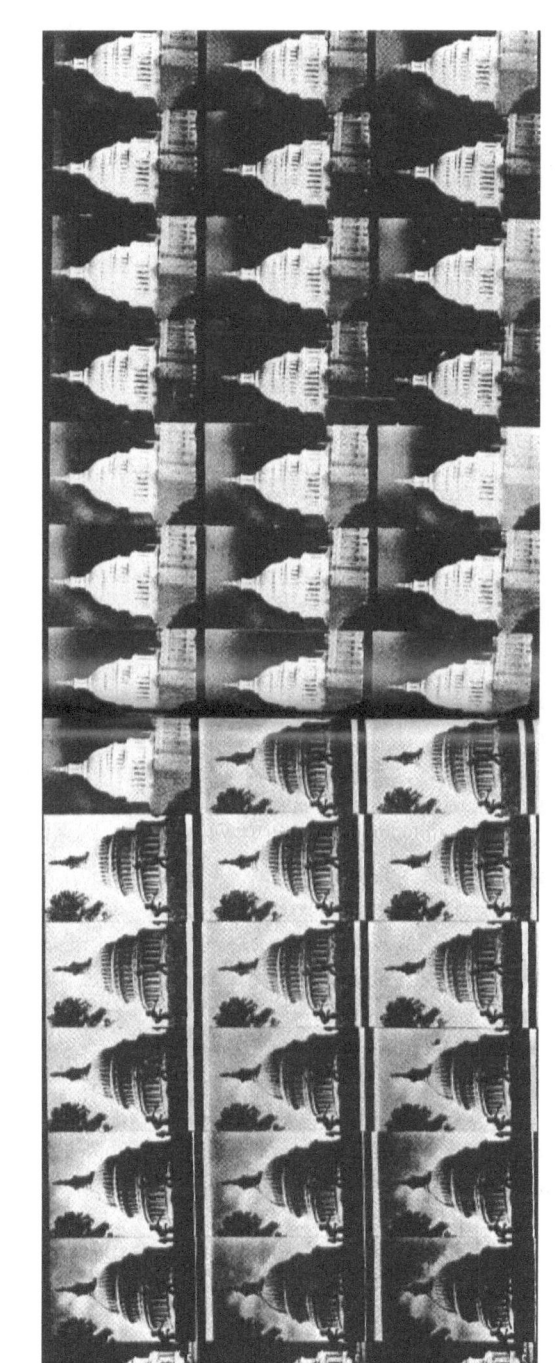

Figure 2.5 Exposures. Julio Cortázar, *Fantomas*, 1975. Montage from no. 201 of the comic book series *Fantomas, La amenaza elegante*, February 1975, Ediciones Novaro, México D.F. Written by Gonzalo Martré with drawings by Víctor Cruz Mota.

ously horizontal and vertical reading experience that juxtaposes, as if in a collage spread out over multiple pages, discrete moments in time that, read together, become evidence of history in the making. This history is the latest and perhaps most diffuse instantiation of a protracted colonial intervention whose insidiousness is only more pronounced when dissembled and put into conversation with its other constitutive parts here unearthed by the tribunal. Cortázar reenacts this protraction when he forces his reader to alternate between textual and visual fields, and study the ephemera that makes up the history of multinational intervention in the state affairs and lives of private citizens of Latin America. The careful reader will read through the written documents and connect the visual representations of Fantomas's varied attempts to infiltrate or undermine the workings of these global corporations to the larger narrative. She pieces together bit by bit the history that the narrator lays bare and in collecting it for herself comes to own this knowledge, which will in the end, Cortázar hopes, translate into some kind of political action in the lived world.

Whether or not this translation occurs, the found objects that Cortázar integrates into his narrative displace the reader's attention in order to allow her to engage with history in the making. This visual and cognitive displacement asks the reader to read simultaneously along two intersecting axes, for detail (vertical reading) and to take a broad view (horizontal reading) that allows the different parts of the text to fall into relation with one another so that the larger text make sense. All reading requires some version of this combined effort, to be sure, but in *Fantomas* the reader must be conscious of the process, and of the forestalling and thereby amplification of time that it manifests, so that Cortázar's larger narrative of social justice make sense. This consciousness is here the product of a hermeneutic displacement that reveals a catastrophe *in the making*, a crisis to come that although espied on the horizon or all around us, has yet to fully materialize; for the fullness of the moment that will become the present—its consequences and capacity for reform or revolution—belongs yet to some future state. The pressure that this axial collage-work exerts on the reader is to find herself immersed and implicated in a crisis-in-progress, the full effects of which are as yet unknown but in this open-endedness shape a current and, according to Hamann, a past historical knowledge. Cortázar writes from within the protraction of this coming catastrophe, manifesting a kind of Benjaminian fullness of time on the page in which the visual and textual interruptions that intercalate his already diegetically buried narrative function as nodes of a larger historical constellation.

Both the space they take up in the textual and political valences they document and the intersecting interstices that become legible between them in the form of Cortázar's narrative and in their shared efforts to communicate the many different entry points to the same protracted late capitalist event, these found objects occupy a split reading plane that catalyzes historical consciousness. Although *Fantomas* responds to a particular moment in time parsed and adjudicated in the mid-seventies by the Russell Tribunal, that moment has not yet wholly passed. The coming catastrophe is still a crisis-in-the-making, so that the possibility of a more acute historical consciousness that Cortázar's work provided for when *Fantomas* was first published abides today. The axial and radiating reading strategies that Cortázar provided for in constructing his text are still charged as we live out the consequences of the ongoing catastrophe of global neoliberal politics. From our vantage point on this side of the millennium, Argentina's military dictatorship—where it was for Cortázar to become the most immediate and pressing social and historical catastrophe—becomes for us a crucial articulation of a larger historical constellation that includes also all the other economic, ecological, and ideological devastation that the multinational corporation has effected across Latin America in the last half century. In this way, despite its references to particular historical events contemporary to its writing, *Fantomas* manages to not date itself but instead remain to us now as useful and dynamic a primer of how to read catastrophe in the making as it would have been in the seventies.

Force of Form

Form in Cortázar's work—in the embedding and recursivity of hypodiegetic worlds that split the text, the intercalation of panels and found images and texts from "Inteligencia," and the revelation of disappearance as both smoke-screen and core of the coming political catastrophe—becomes a force that directs the reader back to the world by first ensnaring her in the text. The reader is returned to the world with new, or at least renewed, knowledge about the historical forces at work around her; but, more importantly, her vision of historical process and her place in it has been split or doubled so that she might be both an agent and a spectator in a historical world. This force of form operates at the level of the visual until the last pages of the novella when Cortázar and Sontag are back on the phone, trying to figure out the effects of Fantomas's various interventions into multinational campaigns around the globe. They cannot locate him and imagine he has failed to make any real change, a failure that Sontag absolves him of because the real problem, she tells the narrator, is elsewhere than Fantomas originally imagined. A superhero will not fix this mess, she intimates, and we are done for "hasta que mucha gente comprenda esto, y haga también lo suyo a su manera" (until many other people understand this, and do their part in their way).[51] Sontag tells Cortázar that the mistake is waiting for a leader to come along and show us the way or gather us together:

> Por supuesto que necesitamos líderes, es natural que surja y se impongan; pero el error (¿era realmente Susan la que hablaba? Otras voces se mezclaban ahora en el teléfono, frases en idiomas y acentos diferentes, hombres y mujeres hablando de cerca y de lejos), el error está en presuponer al líder, Julio, en no mover ni un dedo si nos falta, en esperar sentados que aparezca y nos reúna y nos dé consignas y nos ponga en marcha. El error es tener ahí delante de las narices cosas como la realidad de todos los días, como la sentencia del Tribunal Russell, ya que anduviste en eso y me sirve de ejemplo, y seguir esperando a que sea siempre otro el que lance el primer llamado.[52]

> "Of course we need leaders, it's only natural that they rise up and assert themselves; but the mistake"—was it really Susan talking? Other voices were mixing with hers now on the telephone, phrases in different languages and accents, men and women speaking from close by and from far away—"the mistake is to think we need a leader, to refuse to lift a finger until we have one, to sit waiting for this leader to appear and unite us and give us our slogans and get us moving. The mistake is to be content to let realities stare us in the face, realities like the Russell Tribunal's verdict (you were there, you know what I mean) and still to keep waiting until somebody else—always somebody else—raises the first cry."

When Cortázar counterproposes that people are ill-informed and not aware of the horrors going on around them, Sontag goes on to explain that we know the dire straits of our reality by way of the events of our daily lives and the things around us that seem commonplace, in birdsong or making love or in the price of potatoes, that we know it all already deep down. We choose to ignore it because the material consequences of this reality are not immediately violent or pronounced. The coming catastrophe, Sontag tells us, can be read—if we choose to read them—in the very smallest components of the quotidian.

As Cortázar and Sontag go back and forth in this conversation that will close the book, strange things begin to happen on the line. We see it first when Cortázar hears other voices coming through on the telephone, men and women speaking in different languages and in accents from near and far. These voices interrupt Sontag's exhortations that we not wait for someone else to act, that our excuses for not acting first amount only to laziness or brainwashing. And then, "además de las palabras venían imágenes más bien borrosas pero reconocibles"—accompanied here by an image of a city skyline repeated from different angles—"y de cuando en cuando una voz de locutor repetía frases que el narrador conocía muy bien porque muy pocos días antes había participado en su redacción" (aside from words, images were coming through, blurry but recognizable and from time to time an announcer's voice repeated sentences that the narrator knew very well because just a few days before he had helped draft them).[53] Here different voices from around the Spanish-speaking world pronounce excerpts from the verdict of the Russell Tribunal, accompanied by multiplied photographic frames of riot police, IBM Systems, and an automatic assault rifle. The reader receives both aural and visual versions of the verdict that work on separate diegetic planes. For while the transcription of the phone conversation respects the narrative limits of the embedded world of "Inteligencia," the images that Cortázar includes here do not. Only the reader might view these images in the pages of the book she holds in her hands, so that she here becomes—with the visual evidence to back up the diegetic displacement—the person on the receiving end of the call.

As he does in the passage previously cited where he directs Fantomas to the appendix of the book, the author transgresses the narrative boundaries he has constructed to make the reader complicit in his call for social action. This tandem discursive move displaces the content of the narrative to a hyperdiegetic world outside of the text, as well as asks the reader to double for the already doubled author-as-character in the novella. The reader takes up the same position of witness to the strange collective phone call that Cortázar inhabits in the book. By this point, the reader, the author, the novella, and the work of the tribunal are so entangled that Cortázar has effectively used literature to ensnare the reader in her own present world. He builds a narrative structure that is not isomorphic to our primary world—what Thomas Pavel calls a "salient structure"[54]—that works here not in the service of fiction but instead to cement the reader more firmly in the historical and social surroundings of the world she inhabits. Where Cortázar's previous short fiction works to displace the reader by way of shifting ontological possibilities, the displacement that *Fantomas* effects works to shift the reader back to solid ground in a move that proves the ethical function of fiction. Where the rules of fiction dictate, again according to Pavel, that the reader first suspend her disbelief in order to enter into a fictional world, and then again suspend that suspension so that she might fully participate in that world with "minimal departure,"[55] Cortázar asks his reader to relinquish whatever suspension of disbelief might have allowed her to enter the world of Fantomas and to find herself back in her lived world. As she returns to this extratextual space, she is accompanied by images and voices in her ear that were not there when she started out and armed with knowledge that she did not previously possess. She has now the tools she needs to recognize before her the constitutive elements of a coming historical catastrophe.

Fantomas arrives at the narrator's apartment to interrupt the phone call. He complains of political inaction, that he has seen no change: "Me pregunto si no tenían razón, intelectuales de mierda—dijo Fantomas—días y días de acción internacional y no parece que las cosas cambien demasiado." His *compañeros* console him, tell him that soon he will begin to see things change:

> Lo bueno de las utopías—dijo claramente una voz afrocubana que resonaba como una cascabel—, es que son realizables. Hay que entrar a fajarse, compañero, del otro lado está el amanecer, y yo te planteo que . . .
>
> Fantomas había bajado la cabeza, pero la máscara blanca no impidió que el narrador viera una lenta, hermosa sonrisa que era como un inventario de dientes blanquísimos. Del hueco sonoro venían voces, acentos, gritos, llamadas, afirmaciones, noticias; se sentía como si muchedumbres lejanísimas se juntaran en el oído del narrador para fundirse en una sola, incontenible multitud. Frases sueltas saltaban con acentos brasileños, guatemaltecos, paraguayos, y los chilenos pulidos y los argentinos a grito pelado, un arcoiris de voces, una inatajable catarata de pechos y de voluntades.[56]

"I'm asking myself if you fucking intellectuals weren't right," said Fantomas. "Days and days of international action and it looks like things are hardly changing at all" . . . "The good thing about utopias," said a clear Afro-Cuban voice that rang like a bell, "is that they're attainable. You have to get ready to fight, comrade, the dawn is still ahead, I'm telling you . . ."

Fantomas had lowered his head, but the mask didn't prevent the narrator from seeing a slow, lovely smile, like an inventory of the whitest teeth. From the receiver there poured voices, accents, shouts, cries, affirmations, news; the narrator felt as if distant crowds were gathering in his ear, coalescing there into a single and uncontainable multitude. Stray phrases leapt out in Brazilian, Guatemalan, Paraguayan accents, he heard the refined voice of Chileans and he heard Argentinians shouting their heads off, a rainbow of voices, an unstoppable cataract of lungs and of wills.

The Latin American collective on the other end of the line promises change, understands the promise of a utopia. The first Afro-Cuban voice tells the deflated superhero that utopias are attainable, the sun will shine on a new day, he just has to enter the fray to make it happen. A torrent of voices follows with affirmations and news, an "uncontainable multitude" and "an unstoppable cataract of lungs and wills." The Latin American people offer up the verdict of the Russell Tribunal and then promise to work toward the "attainable utopia" announced in the book's title. This ending is optimistic, forward-looking, which is only confirmed by the last few passages of the novella in which Fantomas takes off, having done what he could in his estimation, while the narrator watches the sun fall on the head of a little blond boy playing in the street. Cortázar closes the work neatly, in an exaggerated nod to the pulp fiction it is indebted to. But he leaves an opening in the text here, just at the start of the end, when this Afro-Cuban voice confirms that a utopia is not out of reach. Because this voice, while clear as a bell, does not get the chance to offer up any details about how to make this happen. She tells us we have to fight, even that things might come to blows, but as she begins a new thought, Cortázar cuts to the description of Fantomas. He redirects our focus just as she says, "Y yo te planteo que . . ." (And I suggest that . . .[57]), which sounds very much like the beginning of a plan of action. So we are left without any instruction as to how we might come together to fight for political change. This is the principal gap in the text, an aporetic call to action, that the reader has to fill in for herself.

Fantomas is built out of techniques of doubling and displacement that work to ensnare the reader in the lived catastrophe of her own world; perhaps the most significant of these is this final displacement of a possible utopia with which Cortázar ends the novella. He does not represent this utopia—beyond the symbolic promise of a new day that closes out the narrative—nor does he tell us how it might be achieved. But in identifying it, both here at the end and on the cover of the book, as "attainable," he creates a kind of prolepsis whose open-endedness functions to redefine the present catastrophe. Where Koselleck argues that understanding our present is predicated on how our future plays out, Cortázar offers up a future as-yet-undefined utopia that allows the reader to reimagine her present moment. He does not offer a way out of the catastrophe but shows us instead that the consequences of its downturn, turning back, or overturning are not yet written. They remain, from our present vantage and in Cortázar's view, ever unwritten so that our present is as dynamic and transformable into some other historical version of itself as our future. The blank space that Cortázar's hybrid voice on the line manifests is the space of transformation; its urgency manifests precisely by moving us toward some unknown future state that requires immediate attention.

The "attainable utopia," then, that opens and closes *Fantomas* functions as a placeholder for an always present future, which is another way of saying, for the present. Cortázar does not here instruct his reader how to act, rather only tells her that she must. The utopia that Cortázar promises his reader is no place, but it is the promise of a place that can be enacted at any moment. This promise is a placeholder wherein place becomes a dynamic structure that can be activated any time and in many different ways. The revolution that Cortázar urges is a way to dismantle the catastrophe that he sees on the horizon; in Cortázar's estimation, it is never too late for that action. The utopia that he signals, both on the cover of the book and here at its end, contains—encloses, holds together, and in a not insignificant etymological turn, stretches or tenses—the possibility of political action that *Fantomas* strives to galvanize. We will see later in chapter 4 another container model activated exactly twenty years later in Tomás Eloy Martínez's novel *Santa Evita*, but where here Martínez endeavors to give shape to disappearance, Cortázar uses the catastrophe of disappearance to signal the place of revolution, which is a fluid, malleable, and always present node in a historical constellation that need only be activated to gain in force. Cortázar's utopia promises the force of form, of formulation, of forming. This no-place is the shared commons and becomes, by way of *Fantomas*, a narrative commons with the potential to change our present—an ever-present moment—by imagining for ourselves a different future. This is what the strange, intermedial, heteroglossic phone call at the end of the novella enacts. Cortázar's attainable utopia urges us to look beyond ourselves so that we might most properly recognize where we stand. This task, on the eve of the incoming Argentine dictatorship, is about to become increasingly urgent. But Cortázar has here shown us a year in advance that disappearance—in stark contrast to what the dictatorship will avow—can be taken apart, dismantled, unveiled. *Fantomas* serves as a placeholder for this knowledge and for the realization that we might, at any moment, put this knowledge to good use.

The mode of disappearance at work in *Fantomas* discloses how disappearance as a tool of state repression works, both as an event proper to a particular historical moment and as systemic to the vast economic inequalities across Latin America fomented by the United States and its networks of globalization. Cortázar deconstructs the disappearance of knowledge on the page to show how disappearance might cover over—in its facelessness, disavowal, absence, and carefully organized insidiousness—still other crimes. He gets at these crimes and their consequences through a complex structure of spliced, recursive, and moving ontologies that work to reposition and reorient the book's reader within the context of catastrophe. This moment of crisis, *Fantomas* instructs us, is as much a way out as a way in. The points of entry and departure that Cortázar establishes throughout the work by way of the embedded world of "Inteligencia," shared hypo- and hyperdiegetic ontologies, and graphic and visual axes facilitate a fluid and self-reflective historical consciousness that cements the reader in her own world and allows her to see into catastrophe so that she might then see her way out of it. The work of literature here becomes the work of historical and political action that takes place in the points of intersection between an invented and a lived world. The keen hermeneutics of disappearance that Cortázar enacts in his use of doubling and displacement throughout *Fantomas* is a self-reflective mode of revelation and commitment. It shows us what we are missing and calls upon us—on the historical precipice of 1975 but also today and at any moment that the quotidian threats of catastrophe might reappear—to construct something different from this knowledge, to know history otherwise, and to act avant la lettre.

3

In Abeyance

Strategies of Suspension in Tomás Eloy Martínez's *La novela de Perón*

> . . . si bien la historia nace de la realidad, hay ciertas realidades que sólo pueden nacer de la ficción.
>
> —Tomás Eloy Martínez, "Ficción e historia en *La Novela de Perón*"

Other Logics

In February 1970, Argentine journalist Tomás Eloy Martínez—then completing a master's degree in Latin American literature while working as a correspondent for Editorial Abril in Paris—phoned deposed Argentine president Juan Domingo Perón at his residence in Puerta de Hierro on the outskirts of Madrid and asked for an interview. Perón caught the journalist off guard when he asked him what kind of questions he had in mind. Martínez, out of instinct, answered, "Me gustaría que me cuente su vida, desde el principio. Tal vez ya es hora." . . . "Tiene razón," responded Perón, "Ya es hora" ("I'd like you to tell me the story of your life, from the beginning. Maybe it's time." . . . "You're right. It's time"). The following month, Martínez drove from Paris to Madrid where he interviewed the exiled Perón over a span of four days. Perón told the story of his life to Martínez, who then brought out a serialized version of the biography in the *porteño* magazine *Panorama*. The biography covered the first fifty years of Perón's life. "Lo que pasó después," the president told him, "no son memorias. Es historia" (What happened afterward are not memories. It's history).[1]

This encounter marks an important turn in Martínez's interest in Perón, Evita, and "esa especie de profunda cicatriz en la historia argentina que es el Peronismo" (that sort of deep scar in Argentine history that is Peronism).[2] Martínez was never happy with the complete transcription of his interview with Perón. When he had finally transcribed the interview's seven audiotapes and crafted the former president's biography, he found it insufficiently matched to the realities of the General's life and political exploits. These insufficiencies, according to the author, are what prompted him to begin work instead on a novel—what would become *La novela de Perón*—that might more properly house the complicated details of Perón's life. The freedom of fiction would allow him to uncover, he hoped, the human dimension of Perón, to linger longer over the intimate details of the man behind the public figure, and to deal simultaneously with the many contradictions that seemed to define both his personal and political lives. Martínez explains the endeavor in a 1993 interview with Marily Martínez-Richter, who asks him why he always seeks to write about historical figures of such enormous stature: "Yo vi varias veces a Perón como periodista, y me parecía que la marca, como dije, que Perón había dejado sobre nuestra historia, necesitaba de algún modo ser reflexionada, revisada, reescrita, y que la escritura de un personaje tan enorme era una tentación a la que no debía resistirme si la tentación existía" (As a journalist, I saw Perón on various occasions, and it seemed to me that the mark, as I said, that Perón had left on our history needed in some way to be reconsidered, revisited, rewritten, and that writing about such an enormous person was a temptation that I shouldn't resist if indeed the temptation was there).[3] Martínez here lays out the scaffolding of his project: he wanted to reflect on Perón's influence in Argentine history, revisit it, and *rewrite* it. The biographical material offered to him during his interview with Perón had not answered the author's questions about why this man in particular should have left such a tremendous mark on the historical life of his nation. To learn that, he would have to lose the journalist's objectivity, and get close to Perón in a way that only the flexibility of the form of the novel might allow.

In addition to supplementing biographical insufficiencies, Martínez also wanted to trouble the discourses of history and modes of historiography—already an intergeneric enterprise in the history of Argentine letters and an endangered episteme in the poststructuralist shift of a decade prior—in ways that ended up serving as a challenge to the systematic historical manipulations that had such devastating consequences during the recent military dictatorship. In his 1988 article "Ficción e historia en *La novela de Perón*" (Fiction and history in *The Perón Novel*) he reflects on these efforts:

> En *La novela de Perón* . . . se llega a la misma verdad a la que ha llegado la Historia, pero a través de otros caminos: el camino de lo que pudo ser, el camino de lo que tal vez fue y sin embargo no se puede probar. Hay personajes ficticios que dialogan con personajes reales, publicaciones ficticias que narran hechos reales y publicaciones reales que narran ficciones, así como también hay personajes reales que viven acontecimientos imaginarios, si bien cuando los viven están sujetos no a la lógica de la Historia sino a la lógica de la verosimilitud novelesca.
>
> In *The Perón Novel* . . . we arrive at the same truth History arrives at, but by way of other paths: the path of what could be, the path of what maybe was and yet cannot be proven. There are fictitious characters that dialogue with real characters, fictitious publications that narrate real events and real publications that narrate fictions, as well as real characters who live imaginary events, even if when they live them they are subject not to the logic of History but to the logic of novelistic verisimilitude.[4]

The end result of both fiction and history writ large, proposes Martínez, is the same; they only take different routes to get there and submit to distinct systems of logic along the way. If the fiction of the Latin American Boom substitutes aesthetics for politics, as Idelber Avelar proposes,[5] the postdictatorship fiction of the post-Boom puts aesthetics, politics, and history on a level playing field, in a fluid and dynamic dialogue that calls into question each of their discursive and epistemological limits. The slippage between historical and fictional enterprise enjoyed increased critical attention particularly in the 1980s and early '90s—New Historicism here just one theoretical branch of various that investigate the relationship between history and fiction—and quickly became the cornerstone of the late Martínez's larger authorial project.[6] Martínez frequently repeats—with a nod to Hayden White's defense of the autonomous discursive properties of fiction[7]—that he sees no reason why fiction, "the lie that dares to speak its name,"[8] should be any less qualified to represent history than the store of falsified documents that the Argentine government for years offered up as the official version of his nation's history. *La novela de Perón* does not just foreground these efforts; it offers up the dialogue between history and fiction as proxy protagonist of a work that withholds its own purported protagonist from the reader, as this chapter argues, in a prolonged and inaccessible state of suspension. This project is as political as it is aesthetic, and history is its raw material and mutable synergist.[9]

This prolonged effort to rewrite historical misinformation, foreground and supplement textual gaps, and make up for biographical insufficiencies is an important framework for the analysis of the modes of disappearance that emerge in Martínez's work. For disappearance—here manifested, this chapter argues, in recursive strategies of suspension, withholding, and cancellation that function as critical narrative mechanisms to structure the novel and define the reader's access to Perón—works in service of the kinds of fictional reconstruction that Martínez proposes as much as historiographical limitations evidence what is not seen, what cannot be accessed or recovered, and what is missing. Suspension appears as the defining formal feature of *La novela de Perón*. It serves as the central scaffolding of the work, itself a fully formed narrative ontology that then gives shape to and contains the novel's embedded diegetic levels; emerges as catalyst in the complex intersections of these worlds; and functions throughout as a narrative device that becomes, in its repeated and varied use, a philosophical remainder and sociopolitical index of a particular historical moment that compels a recalibration of how we understand the work of history and fiction and the capacity of things withheld, receding, or vanishing to shape this work. As form, technique, and thematic preoccupation, suspension provides for a counterhistory that validates, in the context of Argentina's transition to democracy, tandem claims to historical realities manifested by parallel strategies. In this, Martínez's work illustrates, if at different moments and in different ways, Ricardo Piglia's "postmodern strategy," Nelly Richard's "aesthetics of the discard," and Idelber Avelar's "task of mourning" in postdictatorial fiction. The novel also here functions, in necessarily oblique fashion, as a kind of anticipatory fiction. It serves as model for other histories constructed out of absence or disappearance, and also then as fundamental to, per the genre's particular capacity to buttress emerging forms and expressions of democracy, a collective narrative commons itself capable of housing, giving shape to, and transforming what is absent. The strategies of suspension that Martínez activates in *La novela de Perón*, and that this chapter parses as a catalyst of new knowledge production in the postdictatorship, gesture toward novel forms of historical representation wherein abeyance, withholding, and suspension communicate their own set of political terms and possibilities.

A Deliberate Gap

La novela de Perón recounts the General's return from Madrid, where he lived in exile from the early 1960s on as a guest of Franco. Ousted in 1955 by a violent military coup that installed in his place Eduardo Lonardi, the deposed president spent his first days of exile aboard a Paraguayan gunboat docked in the Río de la Plata, then went on to Paraguay, Venezuela, Cuba, and the Dominican Republic. He finally settled in Madrid, where he lived with his third wife, Isabel de Perón, until he returned to reassume the Argentine presidency on June 20, 1973. Perón maintained close ties with Argentina for the duration of his exile. He sent emissaries to Buenos Aires to represent him; retained control over the important unions; played Peronist factions off one another, favoring all sides in what historian David Rock identifies as his political "pendular technique";[10] and otherwise kept the hope alive, if from a distance, that he would return to power. As his years in exile waned on, however, advancing in tandem to the political and economic instability of Argentina that reigned from 1955 to 1973, the possibility of this return began to take on somewhat mythical proportions. But in November 1972, under the government of Alejandro Agustín Lanusse, Perón returned for the first time to Buenos Aires for a short visit. In March 1973, the Frente Justicialista de Liberación, or the Peronist alliance, won nearly 49 percent of the vote in national elections; although Perón was prevented by a law that required residency in the country to take office, the road to his return was being deftly prepared. In Perón's absence, his ally Dr. Héctor Cámpora became the new Peronist president-elect, holding office essentially as a placeholder for Perón. Cámpora served a rocky term as president for forty-nine days until June when Perón returned to the country. The violent massacre that ensued at the airport in Ezeiza marked Perón's controversial return to Buenos Aires as well as foregrounded Cámpora's inability to maintain control over the divisive Peronist factions. In July 1973, Perón withdrew his support for the government and Cámpora was replaced by Raúl Lastiri, who served as temporary president until the upcoming September elections. Perón then won the national presidential elections with a return of 60 percent of the vote and in October began his third term as Argentina's president, exactly twenty-eight years after he first took office. Isabel de Perón was installed as her husband's vice president, assuming a historical role that many supporters had wanted Eva Perón to fill twenty years prior. Perón's return as president, however, lasted only until July 1, 1974, when he died of heart failure. Isabelita then became Argentina's first woman president, a post she held until she was ousted by the coup d'état led by Videla on March 24, 1976, that marked the beginning of Argentina's seven-year military dictatorship.[11]

Martínez's novel, if followed chronologically, narrates the events of just a single day, the day Perón left Madrid and flew back to Buenos Aires: June 20, 1973. But condensed into the significance of this flight are the three decades of Peronism that precede it and the ten years of a failed Peronist government and subsequent violent state repression that follow it. Martínez is purposeful in leaving a huge temporal and historical gap unfilled on either side of the day of Perón's return out of exile. In a 2002 interview with Argentine journalist Juan Pablo Neyret, he explains: "Si te das cuenta de cómo está estructurada la novela, vas a ver que desde el 17 de octubre del '45 hasta la caída de Perón, todo eso está excluido, es un hueco deliberado" (If you realize how the novel is structured, you'll see that from the 17th of October of '45 to the fall of Perón, all of this is excluded, it's a deliberate gap).[12] Throughout the novel, Martínez uses the material garnered from his earlier interview with Perón to narrate his childhood, his days in the army as a young man, and his early rise through military and government ranks. He intercalates these biographical memories with the story of Perón's arrival at the Ezeiza airport and, in an epilogue, records Perón's death. But the author stops short right on the historical edge of Perón's rise, and return, to power.

In early October 1945—the beginning where Martínez leaves off—Perón is removed from office as head of the National Labor Department in Buenos Aires and imprisoned by the government of the largely defunct president General Edelmiro Farrell. But the government misjudged public opposition to Perón and on October 17, 1945, thousands of Perón's allies march on the Plaza de Mayo and call for the General's release. He rejoins the ailing government, which sets a date of February 24, 1946, for the upcoming national elections. Perón, with his new wife Eva Duarte de Perón at his side, wins the presidency that year.[13] Yet Martínez does not document this in *La novela de Perón*. He turns Perón's terms as president of Argentina into a narrative sinkhole bordered by muddy before-and-after versions of Perón. This narrative strategy allows Martínez to achieve his desired effect that the reader know a more intimate version of Perón—we know him as a young and an old man—but never the man in power. He presents a portrait of the man while preventing access to the president, which effectively erases the public version of Perón. This aporia is the central organizing device of the novel, a work premised on an absence whose gaping presence looms large throughout and largely governs its historical and literary value. The rest of the novel, then, is built upon the empty space left behind by Perón's presidency. This is no baseless structure, however; the narrative inaccessibility of Perón's terms in office make room for other histories and other truths that allow the reader to know the contradictions and complexities that confronted Martínez when he began to assemble Perón's biography. This historical gap at the core of the novel also proves just the first of the many other holes and forms of displacement that Martínez uses to structure his work. For these strategies of suspension, in withholding Perón from the action of the novel, make space throughout for embedded modes of emplacement that should, but do not, function to ground the work. Even efforts at emplacement of the material and physical world end up giving way to unstable narrative ground, which only underscores the novel's formal response to Argentina's legacy of disappearance in the early years of the transition.

The novel opens onto Perón suspended in mid-flight traveling from the longest to the shortest day of the year on the solstice. He has taken off from Madrid in the northern hemisphere, where it is summer, and is flying toward Buenos Aires in the southern hemisphere, where it is winter. Martínez sets the beginning of his story at a spatial and temporal crossroads whose logical instantaneity endures for the length of the novel, which is also the time that Perón is in the air. In his conversation with Neyret, Martínez discusses the significance of this hyperdiegetic frame:

> Me pareció que el día de Ezeiza era muy significativo como día, en el momento en que me di cuenta de que Perón estaba viajando desde el día más largo del año hacia el día más corto del año. Me pareció un elemento simbólico curioso. Y, además, Perón suspendido en el tiempo. Fue la primera imagen que tuve: la suspensión de Perón en el no-tiempo, lo que se enfatiza una o dos veces en la novela para marcar que está fuera del tiempo mientras está en el avión. Y viene hacia un tiempo real, que es el tiempo de su caída. . . . Entonces, Ezeiza, que es el punto crucial de su caída, de su derrumbe, me pareció que servía para dividir el antes y el después. Y es también una divisoria de aguas entre los Peronistas de una línea y los Peronistas de otra línea opuesta.
>
> Ezeiza seemed to me, at the moment when I realized that Perón was traveling from the longest day of the year toward

the shortest day of the year, to be a really important day. It seemed a curious symbolic element. And also, Perón suspended in time. It was the first image I had: the suspension of Perón in a nontime, which is emphasized one or two times in the novel to show that he's outside of time while on the plane. And he's coming toward a real time, which is the time of his fall. . . . So Ezeiza, which is the crucial moment of his fall, of his collapse, seemed to function to divide the before and after. And it's also a watershed moment between the Peronists on one side and Peronists on the opposite side.[14]

This image of Perón suspended in time is the axis around which Martínez builds his novel. While he is on the plane, flying from the summer solstice to the winter, he exists outside of time. Perón's dislocation from time and event serves as the narrative frame of the work within which Martínez reconstructs his intimate version of the president. This bipartite diegesis allows the novel to move forward on split temporal and narrative levels that are only reconciled at the end of the work. The massacre at Ezeiza—from which Perón remains wholly removed throughout the novel—defines Perón's return to Argentina and power, confirms his political demise, and also marks the moment at which the Peronist party is irreversibly divided.[15] Martínez narrates his fictional version of the events at Ezeiza and the violent fragmentation of Peronism while keeping Perón at a remove. This violence and suspension finally dovetail, in their irresolution, at the end of the novel.

The reader's first image of Perón is one in which the exiled general is suspended above the earth, outside of time and, as the novel will show, also outside of history:

Una vez más, el general Juan Perón soñó que caminaba hasta la entrada del Polo Sur y que una jauría de mujeres no lo dejaba pasar. Cuando despertó, tuvo la sensación de no estar en ningún tiempo. Sabía que era el 20 de junio de 1973, pero eso nada significaba. Volaba en un avión que había despegado de Madrid al amanecer del día más largo del año, e iba rumbo a la noche del día más corto, en Buenos Aires. El horóscopo le vaticinaba una adversidad desconocida. ¿De cuál podría tratarse, si la única que le faltaba vivir era la deseada adversidad de la muerte?[16]

Yet again, General Juan Perón dreamed that he was walking toward the entrance to the South Pole and that a pack of women wouldn't let him past. When he woke up, he had the sensation of not being in any time. He knew that it was June 20, 1973, but that meant nothing. He was flying on a plane that had taken off from Madrid at dawn on the longest day of the year, and was heading for the night of the shortest day, in Buenos Aires. His horoscope predicted an unknown adversity. What could it be, if the only thing he hadn't yet experienced in his life was the yearned-for adversity of death?

Perón has fallen asleep as he travels back to Argentina and wakes up caught in the protracted time lapse of cross-Atlantic travel. He dreams a recurring dream—we find out at the end of the book that he had the same dream the next-to-last night before he left—of trying to conquer the South Pole, but he is refused access. He awakens from his dream state suspended, with the feeling that he is flying steadily outside of time. He knows what day of the year it is, yet June 20, 1973, has not yet become the historical marker it will be when he lands at the Ezeiza airport. His horoscope has predicted an unknown adversity, which leaves the General uneasy and confused, as the only hardship he has still to live is death. Martínez here opens *La novela de Perón* with a series of states of suspension: a flight, a dream, a vague premonition, a longing for death. Perón is returning from exile, but nothing is settled, nothing is sure.

Martínez positions Perón's return—and Perón himself—outside, or above, the action of the novel. Perón functions as a kind of narrative superscript that forms a suspended and mobile framework for what will take place in the rest of the book. We see Perón on the plane at the beginning of the novel and at the end; the chronological superstructure of the book is concerned with getting the General in the air and then landing his flight amid the throngs that have gathered to welcome his return at the Ezeiza airport outside of Buenos Aires. This flight facilitates the rest of the novel, which provides an account of the life of the General, yet is the only space in which the reader sees Perón in narrative real time. In limiting Perón's participation in the advancing events of the novel to the work's narrative framework, Martínez effects a series of suspensions that keeps Perón in abeyance for the duration of this novel that purports to offer up a portrait of the man. Perón is kept at a remove, just out of reach; but the inaccessibility to the historical Perón that Martínez crafts opens up the narrative space for an intimate account of what history leaves out, offers a challenge to what counts as historically significant, and aligns itself with an alternative system of signs and meaning-making that, as Nelly Richard proposes, works to dismantle the strict discursive and ideological binaries fomented by dictatorship. Correspondences with Richard's "strategies of the refractory" and "aesthetics of the discard" appear here—if these reconfigured at times in the deadly serious ludic vein promoted before the dictatorship by Cortázar—in the narrative strategies of suspension that *defigure* the totalizing function of Perón and of dictatorship more generally so that they not only mean otherwise but provide for new forms of meaning and knowledge-production in which withholding and disappearance are active and critical agents.[17]

This bears out in Martínez's removal of Perón from both lived time and history for almost the entire duration of the novel. The only time we see him in chronological time is when he is flying headlong *contretemps*. As the plane takes off, Perón asks his wife what time it is: "—En Madrid son ya las nueve y cuarto—respondió la esposa—. Pero en Buenos Aires falta mucho todavía para que amanezca. Aquí arriba no puede saber uno en qué hora está viviendo. Ya ha oído a Daniel: este avión va en dirección contraria a la del tiempo ("It's now nine-thirty in Madrid," his wife replied. "But in Buenos Aires it's still long before dawn. Up here there's no way to tell what time it is for us. You heard what Daniel said: this plane is flying in the opposite direction from time").[18] It is morning in Madrid when they leave but not even close to sunrise in Buenos Aires, and while they are in the air, it is impossible, Isabel tells Perón, to know what time one is living. The flight operates outside of time; they are flying in a direction opposite to the lived time that they know, headlong into a new era that they cannot yet imagine. What the reader understands here is that Perón is out of time: both outside of time and flying directly toward the moment at which he will become residual to the lived future of Argentina. Perón's time is up.

Martínez's portrayal of Perón suspended in air while fighting against a retrograde move toward the future enacts Walter Benjamin's canonical description of Paul Klee's Angel of History, who struggles against being pushed into the future by the forces of Progress, the single catastrophe of History piled up in wreckage at his feet. It is an image that Martínez returns to in different places and in various ways throughout both *La novela de Perón* and *Santa Evita*, and will become a central leitmotif of his work. Here Martínez pushes Perón forward toward the future by constructing a personal narrative that carries him back toward the presidency, so that the General appears to the reader as suspended in time, as occupying some kind of Eliotesque still moment, another image to which Martínez also returns elsewhere. This image of a suspended Perón corresponds to that of Evita as butterfly in *Santa Evita*, half of whose wings move toward the future and the other half toward the past, so that she ends up going nowhere, here suspended between history and myth. Keeping Perón suspended physically outside of time allows Martínez to present an account of the General's life while never actually representing him in a contemporary moment. The temporal suspension is a productive withholding that makes space for the lived time of the rest of the novel and means that Perón's absence functions throughout as an abysmal narrative receptacle. Biography is buried within fiction that has emptied or cleared out its own referent. The work of fiction here at the beginning of Argentina's return to democracy is to make room for moments of time that are not historical within a structure crafted out of absence. This absence then becomes in its own right an important container model that manifests on the page the logic of an alternate historiography.

To foster this, Martínez places Perón in the framework of the novel, in a purely speculative space removed from history. The reader might expect that Perón recognize the importance of his return to Argentina, but Martínez does not afford him this consciousness. The General, after living eighteen years in exile, is tired and old and feels that history, in his words, has already paid its debt to him. His secretary, José López Rega, makes him stay in a first-class compartment so that he will be fresh when he lands. But Perón knows this is only so that when he greets the crowd, "lo viese como al otro: el Perón del pasado" ([it] would see him as the other Perón: the one of the past).[19] Martínez's fictional version of Perón realizes that he is used up, neither the leader that he once was nor the leader the people are waiting to welcome home. From the outset then, Perón has no use for history; he does not understand its logic and allows whatever historical role he is to play to be constructed by others. Martínez removes Perón from the history he is making, despite the fact that his return to Argentina—the most significant historical event of the past eighteen years—will provoke an irreparably fractured Peronism to turn violently in on itself and will incite the massacre at Ezeiza that will see at least thirteen dead and hundreds more injured. The betrayal welcomes a confused and exhausted Perón home and marks the beginning of his presidential demise. But in the novel, Perón witnesses the events at Ezeiza from the air and hears about them secondhand from his secretary. And he only responds to them, in the end, virtually. By opening the novel with Perón suspended in midair somewhere above the Atlantic and by leaving him there until the end of the work, Martínez dislocates Perón from the history that is taking place all around him so that fiction might narrate what history cannot.

The state of suspension with which Martínez opens his novel makes space for the rest of the work, asks readers to suspend what they think they know of Perón and his legacies, and gestures toward a conception of history that undermines the materialist and linear historical teleologies that the military junta used to justify itself and its violence in the first place. The architects of the Process of National Reorganization—a formal constitutional amendment that disbanded the country's congress and recognized the junta as the supreme organ of the nation with the power to appoint the country's president—relied on a series of suspensions to establish and maintain their dictatorship, systematize disappearance, and ensure impunity for crimes against humanity well beyond the duration of the regime. Conceptions of legal subjectivity were altered so that the disappeared were not considered citizens before the law and their exclusion from the state then not a crime;[20] habeas corpus and other civil liberties were suspended in courtrooms and across the country; Argentine citizens were inculcated into a certain "percepticide" in which they were unwittingly trained to see, per Diana Taylor, the "given-to-be-seen" and not the "not-given-to-be-seen" by the regime and its entrenched networks of power; and families and friends of the disappeared were made to live in a state of suspended knowledge in which they did not know if their loved ones were dead or, if so, how they died and where their bodies were located.[21] The dictatorship itself was a seven-year hiatus from the social and political affordances of democracy. The strategies of suspension that Martínez adopts to construct his novel are not fictional correlatives to real-world events. But they do recall and stand in for the country's recent sociopolitical suspensions. Suspension in its many forms exerted pressures on how knowledge was produced, acquired, and disseminated and how this knowledge then helped shape both daily life and historical consciousness. Suspension became a mode of daily and historical existence in the 1970s and '80s, and becomes a critical narrative tool in the art that seeks to assimilate the events of these decades into a larger cultural and aesthetic consciousness.

While suspension appears in *La novela de Perón* as literary theme, it does its most important work as a dynamic instrument of form. Martínez drafts strategies of suspension as generic and structural narrative agents that allow him to tell the story about Perón he wants to tell. Suspension is constitutive to the craft of the novel, to the conflicted portrait of Perón that Martínez offers up, and to how we receive, interpret, and make sense of the work. The concerns worked out in the contemporary scholarly conversation about the relationship between literary form and human rights extend backward in time and ask for new inquiries into *how* the political and social preoccupations that shape the evolving discourse of human rights and their abuses show up in literature that responds to the many authoritarian regimes of the twentieth century. Literary form—as genre, but also as structural device and narrative technique—is itself the site of crucial epistemological inquiry in the wake of state terror. In the case of *La novela de Perón*, this inquiry asks how we know, engage with, and interpret the strategies of suspension that Martínez employs at the same time that we understand suspension as a larger sociopolitical agent in Argentine history. That is to say, the methods Martínez uses to craft his novel make visible, make legible, and allow for renewed interpretations of forms of human suffering under dictatorial regimes. This is an exercise not in cursory parallelism between the aesthetic and lived worlds but in reevaluating how knowledge is constituted and put to use. Martínez's strategies of suspension—overwriting and writing over generic expectations, withholding Perón from lived time and history, and in techniques of simulacra and simulation—allow for and become (a replication also proper to historico-political techniques of suspension)—the content of the novel. Where suspension is in this case a mode of disappearance, that mode materializes and takes shape in the evolving defiguration of Perón as a historical agent.

Dead Center

Betelgeuse prepares to land already at the end of the novel's first short chapter, "Farewell to Madrid." But the book has hardly begun and goes on for another 337 pages. The plane does not land until the last chapter, "The Shortest Day of the Year," nine pages from the end of the book. Martínez begins *La novela de Perón* with a location and ends with a reflection on time; everything that occurs in the novel takes place between these narrative parentheses that bracket the single, enduring instant of Perón's flight. The reader never witnesses Perón's flight landing, however; instead we learn of the scene by way of the Montonero Nun Antezana, who watches it on TV. The General's entourage deplanes, arms upraised, at the military base in Morón where they have been rerouted to avoid the violence at Ezeiza. At Ezeiza, the militant right-wing Peronists have already opened fire on the left after trapping them before the dais where they had gathered to meet Perón. But Perón never greets the crowd awaiting him, for he never actually arrives. Martínez takes advantage of this historically accurate detour to Morón, as well as new media technologies, to underpin Perón's historical and virtual absence even upon his long-awaited return to Argentina.

When he does narrate the plane's landing, Martínez describes a disoriented Perón who, looking through the plane's windows, sees "las amenazadoras hebras de humedad que se clavaban, como espectros, en el aire" (the threatening strands of dampness hanging suspended, like ghosts, in the air).[22] The politicians and journalists at the back of the plane applaud, shouting, "Viva la patria!" and López Rega tries to convince Perón that it was better to land at the isolated military base instead of among the throng of people waiting for him at Ezeiza. But the General is confused, which is only compounded by the fact that he and his wife have to wait onboard the plane until Cámpora is reinstated as president:

> Tuvieron que permanecer abordo hasta que el vicepresidente devolvió el mando a Cámpora. Luego en la oscuridad, bajaron. Unos pocos fotógrafos los iluminaban con flashes, desde lejos. Al General lo intranquilizó que la Betelgeuse hubiese caído tan bruscamente en los desconciertos de la noche. Llevaban dieciocho horas volando con luz de día, tantos como los años de su exilio, y de pronto, al asomarse a la ventanilla, encontró un horizonte sin crepúsculo: sólo había estrellas y una luna esquelética, en menguante.
>
> They had to remain aboard until the vice president had handed power back to Cámpora. Then, in the darkness, they came down the stairs. A few photographers lighted their way with flashes, from a distance. The General was upset that Betelgeuse had fallen so abruptly into the confusions of nighttime. They had been flying in daylight for eighteen hours, the number of years of his exile, and all of a sudden, on peering out the passenger window, he found a horizon with no twilight: there were only stars and a skeletal waning moon.[23]

Perón's first view of Argentina is foggy, dark, and steeped in the threatening suspension of the past. He is surrounded by political ghosts. He cannot set foot on Argentine soil until the government is returned to Peronist hands, and is made to wait aboard. When he finally does deplane, it is under the cover of night, with no fanfare and no reception. This is not the return to Argentina that he had envisioned for himself. Perón is disturbed that Betelgeuse—the dying star that carried him home—should have descended so suddenly into night after flying for so many hours in stark daylight. All the night offers him is the illumination of a few distant flashbulbs, even more distant stars and a hapless moon disappearing on the horizon. The reception he should have received, miles away, has turned bloody in his own name. He receives reports on the plane as to the number of dead, the hundreds of injured, the hangings, the roadblocks, the whirlwind of violence that waits to welcome him home. All eyes are on the General, as the new Peronist government awaits his orders as to how to proceed. But Perón is, again, asleep. And when he awakes, he is confused and dejected. He craves routine and feels, "en el cuerpo la urgente necesidad de alguna casa" (bodily, the urgent need of a house),[24] a request that is denied him even as he is finally returned to his home country.

This is the last image that the reader has of Perón in the flesh in real-time. Several pages later, we see him again, but on television. He addresses the Republic, apologizes for not being able to receive his supporters, and explains that although they flew steadily, they arrived "fuera del tiempo" (outside of time).[25] For the first time in eighteen years, Perón's voice comes across the airwaves; people around Buenos Aires recognize it but do not believe what they hear. The General has dressed up, looks the part, and delivers an impromptu speech to the nation, the words of which inexplicably appear on López Rega's lips before Perón's. The families gathered before the television screens realize this, that Perón's secretary is feeding him the speech:

> El desencanto cayó sobre la gente como una enfermedad instantánea. Una de las mujeres se apartó llorando del televisor y fue a recostarse junto a los braseros. Otras empezaron a calentar la comida de los chicos. La casa entera quedó suspendida en ese abismo que hay entre la indiferencia y el estallido, hasta que uno de los campesinos se alzó por fin y dijo, sereno, irrefutable.
> —Ese hombre no puede ser Perón.
> —No puede ser—aprobaron las mujeres.
> —Cuando Perón se entere de lo que está pasando, volverá . . .
> . . . —Aunque vuelva, es demasiado tarde. Ya nunca más seremos como éramos.[26]

Disappointment came over the crowd like an instantaneous illness. One of the women walked away from the television set in tears and went to lie down along the braziers. Others began to warm the children's food. The entire house remained suspended in that abyss that exists between indifference and a violent outburst, until one of the peasants finally rose to his feet and said, calmly, irrefutably:

"That man can't be Perón."

"It can't be," the women agreed.

"When Perón finds out what's happening, he'll come back" . . .

. . . "Even if he returns, it's too late. We shall never be again as we were."

Perón's *descamisados*, after having traveled for days to greet him at Ezeiza, are devastated when they realize that Perón is no longer his own man, that the Perón who has returned to them is not the General whose return they have been anticipating all these years. As compensation, Martínez performs a narrative slippage that nods to the fine line between fiction and myth when Perón's supporters decide that the man they see on the screen is not Perón and begin again to wait for his return. Martínez here fictionalizes Argentina's recent history of myth construction by proposing that Perón is more useful, more valuable to Argentina, as myth than man. The novel closes upon the workers, and the journalist Zamora who has joined them, who listen together to the first broadcast of Perón's voice into their homes in years. They turn to look at the television, but something is wrong with the image that is "fuera del orden natural, como si lloviese para arriba" (outside the natural order of things, as though it were raining upward).[27] Perón's first televised image is skewed, inverted, and turns nature—here a foil for historical teleologies—on its head even as the General awaits to be reinstalled as president.

Martínez's account of Perón's return never returns Perón to Argentina. Martínez keeps the General instead in a state of suspension that keeps alive the possibility—and here the author's fictional account of the Peronist myth machine—that Perón will someday return. We never see Perón in the flesh beyond the confines of Betelgeuse or outside of a snowy television screen. The image of Perón projected on the screen does not speak for itself and is not believed by viewers to be the General returned. Here the projection of Perón, and of a revived Peronism headed by its original founder, fails. Martínez's novel narrates not the General's return out of exile but the propagation of Perón's mythic status fed best by his prolonged absence. *La novela de Perón* regenerates the myth—here of a tongue-in-cheek messianic potential—of Juan Domingo Perón, and in so doing sacrifices Perón as a documentable historical agent. The turn is as much cultural commentary as fictional necessity as Martínez hands over the reader's last, if misplaced, hope for a historical Perón to myth.

Jean Baudrillard works out the political and social rationale of Martínez's maneuver four years before the latter pens Perón's failed return. In his 1981 *Simulacra and Simulation*, he reflects on the propagation of power in the modern political imaginary:

> Everything happens as if Mao or Franco had already died several times and had been replaced by his double. From a political point of view, that a head of state remains the same or is someone else doesn't strictly change anything, so long as they resemble each other. For a long time now a head of state—*no matter which one*—is nothing but the simulacrum of himself, and *only that gives him the power and the quality to govern*. No one would grant the least consent, the least devotion, to a real person. It is to his double, he being always already *dead*, to which allegiance is given.[28]

Within a larger discussion on the political simulacrum of power in the realm of the hyperreal, Baudrillard lays out how heads of state maintain their singular power. Given the polemic as to the democratic or dictatorial role of Juan Domingo Perón, the examples of Mao and Franco are particularly relevant here. If we switch them out for Perón: *Everything happens as if Perón had already died several times and had been replaced by his double*. In history, but especially in Martínez's novel, Perón has suffered several figurative deaths before his bloody return to Argentina. He suffered a certain political end when he was ousted by General Lonardi in 1955, and in Martínez's version of the man, he was a defunct leader before he reassumed the presidency. But this is not Baudrillard's point. Baudrillard offers up a series of counterfactual cases—the past unreal conditional (as if the dictator had already died, had been replaced) and the future anterior (he being always already dead)—to propose that from a political perspective, a dictator governs avant la lettre from a position of proxy. Perón, per Baudrillard's example, is already a simulacrum of himself even before he appears muted and copied by television broadcast at the end of Martínez's novel.

Baudrillard works from a dual premise here, the first a philosophical one also taken up by Michel Foucault, René Girard, and Giorgio Agamben.[29] The well-known premise posits that the sovereignty of a head of state depends not on who is in power (e.g., the person of the king) but rather on the embodiment of the figure of the sovereign. The symbolic power of the body is paramount here and recalls, for example, the ancient sacred rite in which a part of the body of the king was consumed by his successor to ensure the uninterrupted transition of power. The resulting disjunction between the body of the sovereign and he who embodies the sovereign leaves a lot of room for play, especially in the contemporary landscape of the hyperreal. For, as Baudrillard and Martínez both demonstrate, the embodiment of power and its propagation is susceptible to all sorts of treacherous sleights-of-hand when performed in front of a lens and projected onto a screen. Baudrillard's second premise states that because of the strictures of the hyperreal—the duplicitous, flat dimension of the television, the projected historical image, advertising, the screen—the sovereign leader has already been replaced by his projected Other.

It does not matter, writes Baudrillard, that one head of state replace another so long as the two resemble each other by occupying the same function. By this logic, then, it should not matter to Perón's *descamisados* that El Viejo returns to them once-removed, on the television screen, rather than on the balcony of the Casa Rosada, where they are used to seeing him. Perón, according to Baudrillard, is already a simulacrum of himself—the copy with no locatable original—by virtue of the fact that he is head of state and replaces previous heads of state and will be himself replaced. Argentina does not give its loyalty to Perón the man but to his double because the real Perón has already succumbed to the power of the dictator's simulation. And this simulation, in Baudrillard's estimation, "is nothing but the object of a social *demand*, and thus as the object of the law of supply and demand, is no longer subject to violence and death. Completely purged of a political dimension, it, like any other commodity, is dependent on mass production and consumption. Its spark has disappeared, only the fiction of a *political* universe remains."[30] The mythical Perón, at the close of Martínez's novel, circulates protected from the vicissitudes of life and death within a system of supply and demand instead of that of political power. He is here a mass-produced commodity that answers to and circulates according to the social needs of a particular historical moment. The novel itself also bears out, from cover to cover, Baudrillard's logic that all that remains is "the fiction of a political universe."

But as much as the author enters into the social cycles of production and consumption with a work that revives the smoldering legacy of Perón, he also steps in and challenges Baudrillard, as well as those who presume to understand Perón and the complicated social legacies of Peronism via traditional historiographic discourse and systems of logic. For in Martínez's versions of events, the people *do* reject a simulated Perón. They recognize him as a copy and cling to the hope that the real Perón will return. They are sure that he will come back as soon as he finds out that somebody is impersonating him. *La novela de Perón* leaves off with this hope, ending with the promise of the event that provides for the narrative in the first place, the return of Perón. The novel is a closed system, a feedback loop in the style of Adolfo Bioy Casares's *La invención de Morel* (*The Invention of Morel*, 1940) that feeds itself over and over, the possible return of Perón operating as an endless and recorded cycle that will repeat ad nauseam into the future. Martínez has crafted here a gaping hole stuck on repeat into which disappears Perón's marriage to Eva Duarte, his first two presidential terms, his long exile from and return to Argentina. He also achieves his goal of constructing a more intimate, humane version of Perón after *Las memorias del general* left him so dissatisfied. He offers as model of its reception the characters at the end of the novel who reject the presidential Perón, confirming that his version of the man is more believable, reliable, or verisimilar than the mediated, historical version made out of propaganda, image, and falsification.

Perón's televised appearance the night of the Ezeiza massacre is the last time we see him in the body of the novel alive. Martínez ends his story with the passage cited earlier, which itself ends with the borrowed last line of Henry James's 1902 novel of nostalgia, illness, and betrayal on foreign soil, *The Wings of the Dove*: "We shall never be again as we were." Even if Perón were to *really* return, says the journalist Zamora, who has been interviewing the General's childhood friends and distant family members so he can put together a retrospective on the early days of the *real* Perón for the popular magazine *Horizonte*, it would never be the same. Argentina, he suggests, would never be the same. Here again, Martínez seems to reject Baudrillard's theories of sovereign simulation to offer up Perón as a singular man and Peronism as an irretrievable historical entity. But he delivers this final line via Zamora, the journalist/biographer who most resembles Martínez in the novel, so that his reflections are delivered with a metaleptic wink. Martínez confirms here the singularity not of the historical Perón but of the mythic proportions he has taken on in the passage of time. The turn rearticulates the value of his authorial project: to offer up an alternative model for the production of history that includes the fragment and the trace, but more importantly the productive empty spaces, the interstices, and the voids that these give way to.

These gaps are fundamental to the functioning of the novel but also prove an originary void into which the whole book fades in the work's epilogue. Here outside the confines of the novel proper, Martínez depicts the details of the General's death and the national mourning that ensues. A group of women who have stood in line for over fifteen hours to pay their respects to Perón, who is lying in state, give up their wait and return home to hold their own private funeral ceremony for him. They have the impression that Perón is already too far gone, out of their reach, receded into the reflective glare of history: "A la madrugada del miércoles 3 de julio de 1974, los informativos descerrajaron una telaraña de datos y opiniones para la historia, que pusieron al General aun más lejos del alcance de las comadres, como si se lo llevara un espejismo" (At daybreak on Wednesday, July 3, 1974, the news broadcasts fired off a jumble of facts and opinions for the benefit of history, thereby placing the General even further out of the reach of the women, as if a mirage had carried him off).[31] In the wake of Perón's death, Martínez seeks to foreground the deceptive properties of history. The *comadres* want to pay their respects to the Perón they know, not to the General who becomes less and less theirs the more historical he becomes. So the women appropriate what they have left of Perón—his image—and hold their own ceremony protected from the vicissitudes of history.

The mourners return home to Bajo Belgrano and build an altar out of apple crates upon which they place a television set. They light candles, arrange fake flowers, and cover the living room in black. They then tune in to the national broadcast of Perón's wake so that the image of his face looks out from the television. They file past their makeshift altar, touch the screen, clean the image of the General with a handkerchief. The women hold vigil over Perón until "el muerto fue hundiéndose lentamente en la espesura del blanco hasta que no quedaron en la pantalla sino ventisqueros y volcanes de hielo, como los del Polo" (the dead man slowly sank into the white depths until nothing was left on the screen but snowdrifts and ice volcanos, like those at the Pole).[32] Perón vanishes, remote and inaccessible, into the whitewash of the television screen, whose static stands in for the South Pole that in his dreams he could never access. He recedes here into death, and history, from within the intimate space of a private home where he is lovingly attended to. Martínez, beyond the limits of the novel, returns Perón to the people even as he becomes a void, a dead center. The people, he intimates, know how to tend to simulacrum and simulation, care for an originary absence, and what to make of it. Perón is in their hands now, no historical intervention required.

Martínez narrates Perón's return by exposing him as simulacrum and simulation and then returns him—much as he became in exile—to a state of myth. This series of suspended ontological conditions does more than ensure that the General never materializes; it signals an originary absence and the concerted masking of that absence. Martínez's reconstruction of the life of Perón works to reveal Perón's tenure as president as a kind of void and the discursive strategies that historiography has used to fill in that gap. History, Martínez tells us, as does Perón, feigns to have what it cannot ever have[33]—direct access to an irretrievable past—and makes up for that abiding lack via a series of discursive and narratological approximations that attempt to cover it over by giving "to real events the form of a story."[34] A historical narrative that orders and makes sense of human event, Hayden White proposes a few years before the publication of Martínez's novel, is not a product of the "chaotic form of 'historical records'" but an exercise in wish fulfillment that reveals a basic human desire for narrativity.[35] Fiction achieves—in recognizing, accounting for, and assimilating into its discursive structure its generic parameters and limitations—what history cannot. The central mode of disappearance at work in *La novela de Perón* converges upon an empty space at the novel's center that belies the very possibility of documentation. Where the historical archive houses at its core a gap that it works to supplement, cover over, or supplant, Martínez's novel works to disclose that original void and offer up alternate historiographical options that not only take that empty space into account but make something of it. What has not been recorded, cannot be remembered, the denied, discarded, stumbled upon, and the contingent become viable and valuable materials for the construction of a story whose validity resides in its capacity to represent itself and "speak its own name."

Perón's flight from the longest to the shortest day of the year forms the narrative backbone of the novel, while the epilogue then provides the author with the opportunity to lay bare his biographical and historical pretensions that prove so consequential to how we understand the book's reception. The journey from Madrid to Buenos Aires functions as a parenthesis, simultaneously withholding and providing for the interior action of the novel. Martínez has placed Perón in a state of suspension, never allowing him to operate on the ground; he suggests here that Perón has to be held back in order that his story, and the story of the complications of his own splintered political party, be told. A historical Perón is largely absented from the novel by an oblique view that allows Martínez to see Perón from multiple competing and complementary angles. Martínez compensates for what history obscures by constructing a composite view of Perón, but in so doing he also discloses the original void that historiography strives to cover over in the first place. This exposure, and subsequent crafting, of a gap in our knowledge is both complemented and magnified throughout the novel by the many entries into the life and consequence of Perón that Martínez offers up. These recede throughout the novel into complex structures of recursivity, hiding behind or within one another so that the most stable narrative foundation of the work is the superstructure suspended in midair that withholds Perón from the reader in the first place. If Martínez never gives us Perón, he does enact, in offering up recursivity as a salve to obliquity, the historiographic complexities innervated by the early postdictatorship. That is to say, if we cannot see what is directly before us, at least we can see how things disappear into each other, which becomes in Martínez's position on the far side of the dictatorship, a crucial mode of sight and legibility and an important new historical vantage.

What World Is This?

Martínez challenges what we know by constructing an elaborate network of possible worlds in the novel by embedding spatiotemporal box-worlds within a primary diegetic world itself split into the two central ontologies of the novel: Perón's flight back to Argentina and the events that lead up to and follow the Ezeiza massacre. Both the narrative container of the novel (Perón's flight) and the interior of the novel (what is happening on the ground as Betelgeuse nears Buenos Aires) give way to or are intersected by multiple worlds nested one within the other. These worlds unfold throughout the novel on an x-y axis that asks the reader to read vertically along plunging and climbing diegetic levels and, horizontally, between narratives unfolding into the past, future, and displaced presents. Martínez's work requires flexible reading strategies: that the reader of the novel be comfortable inhabiting multiple spaces simultaneously, finding narrative resolution on parallel or perpendicular planes, or reading on in a state of narrative suspension itself likely to be interrupted by another intersecting narrative that might move the reader again up or down or backward or forward.

This metaleptic organization aligns *La novela de Perón* with other works of post-Boom fiction that also ask the kind of ontological questions that emerge from such an embedded construction: What world is this? What makes this world possible? Where am I, the reader, headed? But if postmodern literature reveals itself to be inherently refractory in nature, then these questions also turn back toward or give way to epistemological concerns that ask: How can I be sure? How can I know where I am and what am I in this world?[36] These questions turn out to be an important ethical endpoint in Cortázar's *Fantomas*, but in Martínez's novel they give way to one another prismatically throughout, so that just as one possibility presents itself, it refracts in another direction into many more possibilities that make up the narrative unfolding of the work. Knowledge is here both product and precursor of ontological preoccupation, so that *La novela de Perón* requires the reader question what possible world she currently inhabits; that inquiry, however, leads to many more questions about how she can be sure of where she stands in relation to the text, what forms of knowledge production she might trust, and who she can share this knowledge with and how. The discursive limits of history and fiction are complicated in this inquiry, and so is the reader's participation in these limits and their ideological uses. We learn, in this refractory state of history and fiction, how to see differently what vanishes, recedes, is absented, and then how to make something different of disappearance. This endeavor today is different than it would have been in 1985 when the novel first came out, but the proposition remains. Martínez, like Cortázar, shows us that disappearance is something constructed, built, not at all organic, and that it can be taken apart, dismantled, and its working parts investigated. On the shore of the return to democracy—and indeed forty years later—this possibility is ethical, judicial, and political, and requires collective investigation as much as it innervates individual reflection.

Martínez constructs a series of embedded and recursive worlds, on an order with the techniques that Brian McHale describes in *Postmodernist Fiction* (1987), such as "Chinese box-worlds" or Russian matryoshka dolls, infinite regress, trompe-l'oeil, Douglas Hofstadter's "strange loops," and other forms of mise en abyme.[37] He embeds different temporalities and spatial constructs; buries historical and biographical information; and intercalates mixed media of real or apocryphal origin, including text from interviews, newspapers, different incarnations of Perón's memoirs, song lyrics, maps, letters, and ephemera. The recursive box-worlds that he constructs give way to shifting hypo- and hyperdiegetic planes, undermine a continuous and disinterested authorial presence, and ultimately deconstruct and foreclose the possibility of knowing the historical figure Juan Domingo Perón. They operate via a narrative mode of disappearance in which multiple hermeneutic horizons cross and diminish in their varied intersection, leaving the reader with access to many possible worlds but also on unstable footing before the text.

The central scaffolding of the novel, Perón's flight from Madrid to Buenos Aires, is the narrative container within which the rest of the action of the novel occurs. One level down from this superstructure are 1) Perón's recollections of his farewell to Madrid, in which are embedded: a) Perón's memories of his second wife, Evita, which will end up intersecting in important ways with *Santa Evita* ten years later; b) the beginning of the memoirs that he recounts to López Rega; and c) the story of Don José Cresto, Perón's third wife's godfather whom Isabelita invites to stay with the couple in Madrid. Also one level down from the story of Perón's flight is 2) the narrative level that focuses on the preparation in Buenos Aires for the General's landing at Ezeiza. Embedded within this world are three main hypo-ontologies: a) the story of the journalist Zamora, who is organizing a reunion for the family members and friends of Perón who contributed to his intimate retrospective of the General in *Horizonte*; embedded within this narrative thread is the reunion, and the biographies of its members, that takes place in the lobby of the international hotel at Ezeiza; b) the biography of the young Arcángelo Gobbi, who becomes López Rega's disciple and righthand man on the ground at Ezeiza; and c) the world of the Montoneros, headed up by Nun Antezana and his lover Diana Bronstein, who are planning a march to meet Perón at the airport.

Within this third world (2c), already two narrative levels down, Martínez embeds the General's "Countermemoirs," which is the story of his life as told to the magazine *Horizonte* by the people who claim to have really known him. The reader has access to this narrative because Nun is reading the retrospective, but the people who contributed to the piece are gathered in a contiguous world on the same diegetic level. Buried within the pseudo-biographical world of the retrospective are a series of narratives that tell the story of i) Juan Domingo Perón's ancestors; ii) Perón's childhood; iii) Perón's schooling and early years in the military; and iv) Perón's relationship with his first wife, Potota. These countermemories stand in contrast to the official memoirs collected and rewritten by López Rega, as well as, if extradiegetically, to the real-life interview of the General conducted by Martínez. Also buried within this third world is the story of López Rega's early years and the world of the Montoneros, embedded within which is the story of how Nun aided in the kidnapping and execution of President Aramburu, the rationale for which is dictated by Comrade Rodolfo Walsh.

Many of these ontologies collide at the end of the novel while the crowd is gathered to meet Perón's plane. Present at Ezeiza are Zamora and his group of witnesses to Perón's early life, Arca Gobbi who protects the dais where Perón is supposed to appear on behalf of López Rega, and Nun, Diana, and their group of Montoneros who travel to greet their General. Perón, aboard his plane that never lands at Ezeiza, remains diegetically removed from these three principal worlds that make up the main action of the novel. These worlds also intersect in still lower ones, buried deep within Martínez's narrative. For example, the reader learns about the fate of Eva Perón's corpse via a remembered conversation between Zamora and Nun that took place two years earlier; the violence of the massacre at the airport overflows into the hotel where Zamora is holding his reunion when Perón's press secretary speaks from the lobby on behalf of the General; and Arca Gobbi becomes obsessed with and murders Nun's lover, Diana Bronstein, at the end of the book.

In addition to allowing these interior narrative worlds to intersect and cross-pollinate each other, Martínez also inserts himself into the novel three diegetic levels down in order to both clear history out and make a space for new histories that have not yet been told. He extracts this embedded fragment of autofiction and lets it stand alone on a purported first-order plane in chapter 14, entitled "Primera persona" ("First Person"). Here he relates the story of his interview with Perón to Zamora—journalist to journalist, even if across the divide of four narrative ontologies—in a move that both historicizes and fictionalizes Martínez's real-life conversations with Perón and Martínez himself. The author reflects here, in the first person, on why he has separated himself from the narrative he has long been constructing. He begins:

> He contado muchas veces esta historia, pero nunca en primera persona, Zamora. No sé qué oscuro instinto defensivo me ha hecho tomar distancia de mí, hablar de mí como si fuera otro. Ya es tiempo de mostrarme tal como soy, de sacar mis flaquezas a la intemperie. . . . Por una vez voy a a ser el personaje principal de mi vida. No sé cómo. Quiero contar lo no escrito, limpiarme de lo no contado, desarmarme de la historia para poder armarme al fin con la verdad. Y ya lo ve, Zamora: ni siquiera sé por dónde empezar.[38]

> I have told this story many times, Zamora, but never in the first person. I don't know what obscure defensive instinct has caused me to take my distance from myself, to speak of myself as though I were another. The time has now come to show myself as I

am, to expose my weaknesses to the elements. . . . For once I'm going to be the main character in my life. I don't know how. I want to recount what hasn't been written, cleanse myself of what hasn't been told, disarm myself of history so as to be able at last to arm myself with the truth. And as I can already see, Zamora, I don't even know where to begin.

Martínez reveals *La novela de Perón* to be just one version among many of the same story. He hearkens back here to *Las memorias del general*, but also to other pieces he has written on Perón and other interviews with the former president. He also invokes, in having "told this story many times," perhaps more communitarian incarnations of the same story, such as versions told to friends or colleagues or students that more closely abut myth than either history or journalism.

He is explicit about moving himself, if within a work of fiction, to the realm of the first person and questions why it has taken him so long to recognize that he has been there all along, if as a secret other, in the texts he has written on Perón. Martínez, from within a complicated and ironic authorial metalepsis that does more to endanger the limits of fiction and history than to clarify a definitive subject position,[39] speaks in defense of the attempt to construct history from the first person and the emptying out that this requires. In a kind of authorial catharsis, Martínez wants to cleanse himself of the written word, here historiography, to clear a space for new truths that he will speak as the protagonist of his own life. The proof of his attempt as historical, and fictional, agent is the novel that the reader holds in her hands; here fiction supplants historical discourse in its proximity to possible truths, even as the author here foregrounds its unstable foundations and his own compromised authority.

After this halting introduction, Martínez recounts some of the details of his interview with the General and his impressions during their conversations. But he does so as a novelist, complete with the descriptive benefit of interior monologue, narrative displacement from real life to screen, remembered memories, and traces of a magical realism here updated to underscore his own role in the construction of a mythic Perón. He purports to come out of hiding—from under cover of the written word—but never shakes his command over invention. As a character in his own book, he is creating from the inside out; he lays bare here the construction of the novel as much as he confirms that, in his words, the author is by definition not more than a literary convention and "a partial, subjective, limited mediator, who is rarely able to transcend the frame of his own experience, or to rise above his personal deficiencies."[40] The author takes his place alongside the other characters in *La novela de Perón*, suffers limitations in knowledge and perspective, and cannot escape his own life, which is now embedded within the novel. The lived world stakes a claim at the core of the novel when Martínez positions himself in the interior of the work; the world that tells becomes the worlds of which Martínez tells and vice versa. This embedded metafictionality gives way to a network of discursive contingencies that reveal a productive reciprocity between the lived, the historical, and the invented; these reciprocities contribute to the larger mode of disappearance that governs the novel by effectively erasing the epistemological expectations that divide how we access or garner knowledge and that buttressed, in its moment and per Martínez, the empty logic of the dictatorship.

Where in the World?

The embedded box-worlds that Martínez builds within the space that Perón's suspended flight opens up in *La novela de Perón* perform their own kind of disappearance as they variously vanish into contiguous worlds. Buried within these worlds are a series of narrative techniques and preoccupations that work to reveal or cover over absence, gaps, something gone missing, or something irretrievable. This contrapuntal movement creates a text cut through with holes, the threat of absence, and the uncanny feeling that something is already missing beneath the surface of the story before us. It is facilitated, throughout the novel, by Martínez's descriptions of platial and temporal structures whose verifiability should help to ground this work that works, on so many levels, to escape us. Textual evidence or mechanisms of absence are juxtaposed with descriptions of place, place markers, landmarks, maps, and geographical and spatiotemporal awareness, but these do not end up proving the anchoring mechanism they might; they tend to blur, obscure, fall apart, or vanish so that the spatial solidity of the world of the novel gives way to a narrative ground cut through with disappearance. The space of disappearance becomes here proper to the material world and how we see it. Absence is revealed as constitutive of the world we inhabit, know, and move through and capable in its own right of serving as marker, map, and common ground. Martínez uses, among other techniques, missing memories of historical events, transposed and impenetrable landscapes, and competing lapses of time to work out how absence shapes the material world and the epistemological suspension it leaves in its stead.[41]

As Martínez says good-bye to Perón the last time they meet, according to his account of their interview, the General asks him what he remembers of the glory days of Peronism. Martínez responds:

> Lo único que recuerdo es lo que no he visto, respondí. Algo que jamás podré ver. Lo recuerdo a usted abriendo los brazos y saludando a las multitudes en la Plaza de Mayo. Veo los estandartes que flamean, los coros de obreros que no paran de cantar *Perón, Perón*, mientras usted sigue saludándolos, largo rato. Por fin, su mano contiene el vocerío. Nadie respira. Miles y miles de personas alzan los ojos en éxtasis hacia donde usted está, en los balcones de la Casa Rosada. En el hueco de aquel gigantesco silencio, se abre paso su voz: ¡Coompañeros! Le oigo esa sola palabra y luego vítores otra vez, clamores. Mi recuerdo es algo que conocí en los cines, que oí por la radio. Nada que haya pertenecido a mi realidad.[42]

> The only thing I remember is what I didn't see, I answered. Something I will never be able to see. I remember you spreading your arms wide and greeting the multitude in Plaza de Mayo. I see the banners fluttering, the workers chanting *Perón, Perón*, in unison, over and over, as you go on waving to them, for a long time. Finally your hand puts an end to the clamor. Nobody breathes. Thousands and thousands of people raise their eyes in ecstasy to where you are standing, on a balcony of the Casa Rosada. Your voice makes its way into the emptiness at the heart of that tremendous silence: Comraaades! I hear that one word from you and then cheers again, shouts. My memory is something that I saw in movie theaters, that I heard over the radio. Nothing that has been a part of my reality.

Martínez performs here a narrative sleight-of-hand to cover over a deftly laid absence: he reconstructs a historical scene in a politically charged location by way of what he does not remember. He will go on to repeat the technique in *Santa Evita*,[43] so that these twin novels are connected by their fictional efforts to feign memory where no memory has been had. This is a subtle undertaking that leaves the reader with the impression that something has taken place, and it becomes her task—the task of the active reader—to decide what to do with the gaps that the author exposes at the seams of fiction. She can proceed as if this fictional memory fills in for what might have taken place but was never witnessed; or she can read against the grain of the invented scene—which is to say, take the text at its word—and reject Martínez's portrayal of a historical Perón, aligning herself with the possibility that history is fundamentally irretrievable. In the latter scenario, absence becomes epistemological agent and narrative foundation for what follows in the novel. This aperture is critical for Martínez. It anchors his authorial project, but also reminds the reader that narrative, any narrative, is pure construction; in this case, most pointedly, it unmasks and puts on display techniques of fiction that also appear in the rhetoric used by the juntas in constructing their version of official history.[44] But the hermeneutic gap that Martínez opens up here also allows him to create a text that goes in two directions at the same time. His reconstruction works in the service of memory even as it confesses to the blank space of its source. The careful reader will halt on the precipice of this gap before reading on to find out what material the author is using to cover over this interstice. That is to say, to find out what invention—of memory, history, and fiction in this case—is made of without forgetting that it fills in for, covers over, makes up for, and builds upon what was not there to begin with. Martínez constructs a bifurcated text that asks the reader to reflect on the pressures that absence exerts upon the craft of reading as much as writing, and in so doing, holds her wholly complicit in the construction of this text.

The task corresponds to the Derridean tenets of difference and deferral in circulation in the mid-1980s and, in this way, functions as a marker of literary philosophy as much as historical intervention. The correspondence reveals a larger preoccupation with absence at work, with how it works, and with the latent violence—critical in postdictatorial Argentine fiction—signaled by what is not present. Martínez instructs us in how we—for the task is shared between author and reader—might build upon these gaps, holes, things missing. Bound up in this is the possibility that the play between memory/nonmemory is proper to a larger dynamic culture machine of cinema, radio, and fiction and that we the readers get to opt in or out of the various fabricated historical possibilities they offer up. Piglia, in conversation with Juan José Saer in the late eighties, identifies the incorporation into fiction of elements and techniques of other mass media as one of three principal tendencies of the late twentieth-century novel, and Avelar describes it as the "postmodern strategy" that "lays a wager on the possibility that the stylistic procedures of mass culture may be appropriated for goals not achievable through mass culture and that the role of literature would be precisely to explore further that possibility."[45] Where other forms of mass culture might fail, if in part because of the restrictions of their form, to adequately represent the complicated contemporary relationship between history and fiction in the aftermath of the dictatorship, the novel's expansiveness and flexibility allow Martínez to make use of popular technical and stylistic devices in order to lay bare and complicate the absences that recent history has itself wagered on. He uses the form of the novel, capable of subsuming and then also recalibrating the ideological capacity of other forms of mass-produced media, to refract and give shape to the ways in which absence and disappearance appear and intervene in more necessarily diffuse social iterations.

The image of Perón here on the balcony of the Casa Rosada—arms outstretched before a sea of supporters who chant his name, the anticipation, the charged expanse of silence before he speaks, all familiar to anyone who has watched newsreels of mass Peronist demonstrations—is a historical image that has been recorded many times over. But here Martínez empties out its content by framing it as a nonmemory garnered from historical record. He creates a hole in the narrative where his memory should be and fills it in with the proliferated and simulated image of the historical figure of Perón. His confessed efforts at reconstruction function as a screen memory for the proliferating historical empty space of Perón on the balcony of the Casa Rosada; Perón, at the very epicenter of his power, is absent. This disappearing act serves as a concentrated example of what Martínez wants to reveal in his larger project: that the historical center is void and covered over with narrative invention. *La novela de Perón* asks that we learn how to read these absences and what takes their place on the page and, by extension, in the lived world where these techniques of reading become more urgent.

Martínez asks us to apply these techniques of reading to a more personal version of Perón that comes, throughout the novel, to also stand in for what history does not recount. At the beginning of chapter 9, "La Hora de la espada" ("The Hour of the Sword") the reader is privy for the first time to Perón's voice in the first person at the novel's primary diegetic level. The chapter begins with the General recounting, in the present perfect and then the more remote past tense, the physical ailments that have troubled him in the days leading up to his return to Buenos Aires. He then switches to the present tense to lament the fact that he cannot take Madrid with him to Buenos Aires in the same way he can take with him his memories of his time there:

Y ya es junio 18. En pocas horas dejaré todo esto. Amanece. Al menos me consuela saber que lo vivido aquí, aquí se queda. Que a los recuerdos no los pudre el tiempo. Uno puede llevarlos de un lado a otro, bajo los pies, abrazados en los fondos del cuerpo. ¿Se podrá hacer lo mismo con los lugares? ¿Qué le parece, López? Mirar por la ventana en Buenos Aires y tener a Madrid del otro lado: el clima fresco y seco, los palomares, las perritas saltando bajo los álamos. ¡Ah, entonces otro sería el cantar! Imaginesé. Si yo pudiera bajar de la casa que tengo allá, en Vicente López, y salir a las sombras del Paseo del Prado por donde tanto me gusta caminar: si aquello fuera Madrid, ¡con qué distinto me yo iría!⁴⁶

And now it's June 18. In a few hours I'll be leaving all this. Dawn is breaking. At least I have the consolation of knowing that what I've experienced here is staying right here. That time is not rotting my memories away. One can take them from one place to another, underneath one's feet, held in a close embrace in the depths of one's body. Is it possible to do the same thing with places? What do you think, López? To look through the window in Buenos Aires and have Madrid out there—the cool, dry climate, the palm trees, the little dogs frisking about beneath the poplars. Ah, that would be another story then. Just imagine. If I could go out of the house I have there, on Vicente López, and step out into the shade of Paseo del Prado, there where I'm so fond of taking a stroll: if that were Madrid, in what a different frame of mind I'd be leaving here!

After this passage ends, the narration returns to the third person and the General becomes again remote. The rest of the chapter alternates between Perón's voice in the autobiographical *yo* (I) of the memoirs he is writing with López and an omniscient narrator that transcribes reported speech between the General and the secretary. Throughout this chapter, the reader has to keep track of the multiple narrative levels at which Perón appears as well as the strategies that Martínez employs to destabilize these appearances and to render inaccessible a single, localized version of the exiled president.

But in the preceding passage, for this brief parenthesis, Perón gets to speak for himself. It is two days before he is set to return to Argentina, he doesn't want to leave his home, and he consoles himself with the knowledge that he can take his memories of Madrid with him. What he really wants, though, is to take the whole city with him. Perón wants to live in his house in Buenos Aires but step out into Madrid, to transpose the city that has become home to him onto a Buenos Aires that will be largely foreign to him after two long decades. Martínez here foregrounds the trouble with exile: while the longing for an original home might never subside, another place might well become another home. This makes the return out of exile—Mario Benedetti's "dis-exile"[47]—a second loss that superimposes itself upon the first. Perón knows that Buenos Aires will be changed and wants to retain the familiarity he has with Madrid and his ease of routine. Madrid has for so long filled in for the absence of Buenos Aires that this vacated original space is no longer recoverable. Perón is more comfortable in the place of proxy—a lived place populated with habit and the quotidian—than in the empty space of origin. This passage proposes that Perón knows himself by way of place, but only where that place is the adopted space of exile that fills in for the gaping absence of home.

By nightfall of this same day, which in a protracted deferral Martínez does not arrive at until eight chapters later, the General is still preoccupied with the city. Perón wants to escape the villa and asks his gardener Lucas to take him for a drive through Madrid so he can be alone with his memories and the city. Chapter 17, "Si Evita viviera" ("If Evita Had Lived"), is comprised of Perón's observations of Madrid interrupted by his memories of Evita, which he narrates to his driver, and excerpts from his memoirs, which he carries with him in the car. Perón reflects on the tour that Evita made of Europe twenty-five years prior, when he sent her abroad as Argentina's cultural ambassador. She was received warmly by Franco in Spain and by the Pope at the Vatican, her tour made international headlines, and her presence in Europe ran the danger of eclipsing Perón's long shadow; Europe fell in love with Evita. He wants to drive by all the places she visited when she came to Madrid, and as he does, while holding his memoirs on his lap, he recounts how they met, how he won her over, her political desire, the fate of her corpse. Martínez buries Perón's memories of Eva—both oral and written—in the streets of Madrid. When Perón says earlier that he wants to take his memories of Madrid with him and replace Buenos Aires with Madrid at his doorstep, he is also looking for a way to return to Argentina with Evita and with her memory intact. Evita becomes here place, location, and orientation, if these are also vacated, mutable, and not fixed. Perón cannot separate his memories of Madrid from the memory of his second wife; Martínez renders her here an itinerant embodiment of place, a move that will later prove the narrative seed of *Santa Evita*.

The scene continues as their nocturnal tour of Madrid winds down, and Perón tells Lucas to head home:

> Afanoso por esquivar el tránsito de la plaza de España, el Mercedes se interna inadvertidamente en las tinieblas de la Rosaleda. Es medianoche y Madrid huele, como siempre, a fritangas. A lo lejos se mueve una procesión de antorchas. Unos caballeros de golilla y hábitos negros pasean entre los árboles, flanqueados por una guardia de alabarderos. La ciudad, una vez más, se ha dejado caer en el pasado, y si no fuera porque los chopos brillan con su verdor intacto, si no aparecieran en las ventanas tenues cabezas vivas, el General sentiría que Madrid, este refugio último de su vejez, está desapareciendo en el maelstrom de los tiempos; que Madrid retrocede hacia las oquedades de la historia, llevándoselo a cuestas. Esta ciudad soy yo, dice Perón. De repente lo atrapan unos buitres de frío. Aprieta las carpetas de Memorias contra el pecho, y, a duras penas, se abriga.[48]

> Anxious to avoid the traffic in Plaza de España, Lucas inadvertently heads the Mercedes into the pitch black darkness of the Rosaleda. It is midnight and Madrid smells, as usual, of fried food. In the distance a torchlight procession is moving slowly along. Gentlemen wearing ruffs and black garments are strolling amid the trees, flanked by a guard of halberdiers. Once again the city has allowed itself to fall into the past, and if it were not for the fact that the poplars are gleaming with all their greenness intact, if vague live heads did not appear at the windows, the General would feel that Madrid, this last refuge of his old age, was disappearing into the maelstrom of time; that Madrid was retreating to the hollows of history, carrying him on its back. I am this city, Perón says. Suddenly vultures of cold swoop down on him. He clasps the folders of Memoirs to his chest, and, with great difficulty, bundles himself up.

As Perón leaves the center of Madrid, he finds himself on a thin edge of time that separates the present from the past. Were it not for the subtle signs of life, he imagines the city vanishing entirely into the recesses of history. He recognizes himself in this retrograde move, in this city poised to become obsolete, historical, lost to the storms of time. If throughout the tour through Madrid, Perón has been guided by his memories of Eva—half of which are not his but rather the bothersome "flour-and-paste of someone else's memory"—he is now driven out of the city with the realization that its anachronism is his own. On the eve of returning to reassume the presidency, he knows himself to be a throwback in time; his memories are not enough to save him now. He wants to take the city with him to Buenos Aires because he recognizes himself in it; leaving Madrid will mean leaving himself behind when he returns home. Both Evita and Perón are embodied by place here, but this embodiment functions only to contain their absence. Madrid becomes a tropic container—Evita on the order of metonym and Perón of metaphor—for Evita in death and for Perón's swiftly approaching political obsolescence. The city contains, limits, organizes, and protects against the threat of disappearance, an indexical generosity that Martínez's Perón does not want to relinquish.

Spatial referents that slip, erode, recede, or otherwise fail to hold their ground continue to make an appearance after Perón boards the plane to Buenos Aires and still after he lands, which bears out the General's unstable footing as he returns to Argentina. After he bids farewell to Madrid, yet far in advance of the prolonged good-bye represented in the novel, Perón peruses maps of Argentina aboard Betelgeuse:

> En la butaca le habían dejado algunos mapas con los derroteros de Aerolíneas Argentinas marcados en líneas de puntos, las bases navales de la Antártida, las redes ferroviarias abandonadas desde 1955. Abrió el plano de Buenos Aires. Recorrió con el índice la autopista que se abría paso desde las fábricas de Villa Lugano hacia el aeropuerto de Ezeiza, a través de monobloques, piletas populares y plantaciones de eucaliptus. Trató de imaginar dónde estaría el puente al cual iban a llevarlo para que arengase a la multitud.[49]

> Several maps had been left on his seat, showing the courses of Aerolíneas Argentinas marked with dotted lines, the naval bases in the Antarctic, the railway lines abandoned since 1955. He unfolded the map of Buenos Aires. He ran his finger along the expressway that went from the factories in Villa Lugano to Ezeiza Airport, past high-rise housing projects, public swimming pools, and planted stands of eucalyptus. He tried to figure out

the exact location of the little dais he was going to be taken to in order to address the multitude.

From his suspended standpoint in the air, Perón unfolds old maps that track a geography abandoned since the year he left power. He opens a map of Buenos Aires and tries to trace the route he will follow from the airport at Ezeiza to the dais from which he will address his party. Martínez's readership knows that Perón will never follow this course, and in the novel, the route outlined here becomes the one the Montoneros will follow instead to the massacre. Martínez places the context of the historical tragedy in Perón's hands but performs by way of the map the slippage of a missed opportunity that will lead to bloodshed.[50] The map communicates what might have been and what might have been avoided so that place in the hands of Perón gives way to historical displacement that leaves both a gap and violence in the historical record.

Just beyond the midpoint of the novel, Perón looks out the window of his plane at his first glimpse of Argentina. His vision is no longer the telescopic one that earlier allowed him to make out the outdated details of the route he would never follow on the ground, but rather a frightening wide-lens view of the landscape of his native country into which vanishes his sense of personal and national belonging and place in the world:

> A las cuatro de la tarde el General divisa desde la ventanilla del avión los cráteres marrones de un campo despoblado. La vista del desierto lo sofoca. El calambre de un rió abre sobre la tierra vetas verdes. ¿Árboles, matorrales? Qué desamparo. ¿A este país vuelvo?, dirá después el General, esa noche. ¿A estas infinitas pampas saqueadas, exprimidas? No las reconozco. No son mías. Fue aquí donde siempre quise morir, y ahora ya no sé. ¿Algo me pertenece de todo esto? Y yo, ¿a qué pertenezco?[51]
>
> At four P.M. the General makes out from the window of the plane the dark brown craters of empty, open country. The sight of the desert suffocates him. Where a river has contracted, green streaks have opened out in the earth. Trees, scrub? What desolation. Is this the country I'm coming back to? the General will say later that night. To this endless pampas, plundered, squeezed dry? I don't recognize it. It's not mine. It was here that

> I always wanted to die, and now I don't know. Does any of all this belong to me? And what do I belong to?

The comforting minuteness and abstractness of the map has become the expansive detail of the pampas as seen from the air. Perón sees nothing from this great distance but a vast emptiness punctuated by feeble signs of life that suffocate him. There is too much openness here and the expanse contrasts vertiginously with the closed-in streets of Madrid; Argentina twenty years later is a wasteland. Perón, after all this time, does not recognize it and rejects it as his own. This country is foreign to him and he is not sure he belongs to it. His view is one-dimensional and empty.

Martínez affords Perón, and his readers, two contrasting views of Argentina. The first is the represented space of the map that Perón cannot and will never enter and the second an overview of the real world whose flat, limitless landscape prevents assimilation. Neither of these spaces are accessible to Perón and they both actively work against him. The scientific grid of the map of Buenos Aires proves the city is still there without providing access to it; it serves as both promise and rebuke and leads to violence in place of belonging. Similarly, the pampas—a space so crucial to the Argentine national imaginary—prohibit Perón from forging the affective bonds with his country that he will need to again be an effective leader and to feel at home. National belonging, except at a remove, is no longer an option for Perón. Martínez grafts Perón's view of the empty pampas, however, onto what will be the massacre at Ezeiza. For not until "later that night" does Perón ask himself if what he sees out the window is the country he is returning to. The natural space of the pampas opens up just long enough to house the historical event of Ezeiza; history, Martínez suggests, might be written into what seems the empty space of nature, but in this teleological relationship, neither of them communicate anything. The prolepsis of Perón's reflections closes and in so doing forecloses any possibility of belonging; place here shuts Perón out of both history and home. Argentina will remain for Perón an empty, inaccessible space—not more than a surface structure—even as it appears before him in various iterations. And it resists the possibility that he might, on any indexical order stand in, in any stable way, for the nation.

Anticipatory Fictions

Much of Martínez's novel works toward the scene on the ground at Ezeiza. But this historical moment ends up, like Perón's flight, premised on a gap, an interval, a final interstice of time that opens outward to contain all of the fatal events of the massacre. Trapped within the still moment of Perón's landing at Ezeiza—a moment that never materializes, which both cancels out and continues to fuel a certain problematic messianic potential in Perón's return—are the conflicting factions of a splintered Peronism, the people from Perón's past gathered together in a nearby hotel lobby, and the Montoneros Nun, Diana, and the rest of their cohort. Martínez narrates this static gap in time, in a somatic anticipation felt by the leader of the Montoneros, that divides the before and after of the massacre:

> Rara vez sucede algo en el intervalo entre dos pensamientos. Pero hay un intersticio ahora, piensa Nun, mientras el increíble Cabezón va trepando por los caños del puente con una Colt desenfundada, en que la realidad se siente: a la derecha, dentro del camión de víveres de Bienestar Social, vislumbra el latido de unas escopetas; en los terraplenes ha descubierto la telaraña de alambres y cables que se le viene encima; huele, atrás, el relámpago de las cachiporras que blanden los matones de brazalete verde. Quisiera darse cuenta si es él u otro quien está oyendo este silencio. Los bombos han cesado, los músicos se han esfumado en el aire, los altoparlantes cierran sus párpados, Favio ya no está más. El globo entre en una nube. Y justo en este desierto donde las cosas no pasan, el Cabezón Iriarte aprieta el gatillo.[52]

> It is rare for something to happen in the interval between two thoughts. But there's a gap now, Nun thinks, as the unbelievable Bighead climbs up the metal underpinning, holding a drawn Colt, and in that gap reality can be felt: to the right, inside the supply truck from Social Welfare, he senses guns at the ready; on the embankments he has spotted the web of wires and cables that is descending on him; he smells, behind him, the lightning flash of the truncheons that the thugs with green armbands are wielding. He would like to know for sure if it is he or someone else who is hearing this silence. The drums have stopped beating, the musicians have vanished into thin air, the loudspeakers are closing their eyelids. Favio is no longer there. The hot-air balloon enters a cloud. And precisely in this desert where things don't happen, Bighead Iriarte squeezes the trigger.

Martínez slows down the action of the story here, at perhaps its most crucial historical hinge, in a series of freeze-frames that take place in the nonspace between two thoughts. Thought is here suspended, giving way instead to a somatic knowledge that allows Nun to report on what is happening around him. Up until this moment, the narrative is a confused mass of movement. The different factions of Perón's party are all gathered in the clearing next to the eucalyptus grove outside the airport at Ezeiza. The police are present, López Rega's snipers are in place to shoot, and pilgrims and workers have lined the expressway from Villa Lugano. An orchestra is tuning up; the media is ready to record and report; supplies, vendors, and banners abound. In the middle of this frenzied scene, Martínez switches to a slow-motion narrative—a kind of cinematic panvision—in which Nun's sensorial awareness of the events around him is heightened in the blank space that emerges between his thoughts. This empty space is populated by time slowed down and interpreted bodily instead of cognitively, such that Nun's prescience functions as an alternate kind of knowledge proper perhaps only to a fatal moment—not unlike that of Bierce's Peyton Farquhar—but no less capacious in its capacity to catalog and perceive. Nun feels the government ready to shoot, sees the mass of media ready to descend, simultaneously smells and sees the police batons already striking their first blows. The interstice is populated with the gap of a weighted silence. His companion has left his side, the hot air balloon rumored to be carrying the General to the dais goes behind a cloud, and all motion stops. The standstill—with all the political weight this might connote—is ruptured when Bighead Iriarte fires the treacherous shot that provokes, in this fictional account, the historic and fatal violence at Ezeiza.[53]

Martínez renders this interstice a productive, full gap in time. He slows time down, allowing it to offer up a somatic consciousness that contrasts with the weight of the historical moment and to serve as both a political and fictional division that will usher in a more cohesive late-stage right-wing Peronism even as it spells the beginning of the end of Perón. But this interstice, insomuch as Nun perceives it to be an "interval between two thoughts" also signals a clearing out of or making up of space as much as it does time. "Interval," from the late Latin, points to the space cleared between two walls, posts, ramparts (*inter* + *vallum*); it indicates at the same time an opening up of space and a closing in or around a cleared space. This empty space is both defined by and provides for what contains it, which in the context of the novel lays bare the internal and conflictive innervation of Peronism on the ground in Perón's long historical absence. Martínez clears space here for this still time so that space and time work together to become a site of historical moment and action. The emplacement of this moment is possible only as interval; it makes what surrounds it legible even as it holds at bay that which defines it. Here Martínez materializes space out of time—from time, but also outside of time—that houses the historical trigger.

Absence here becomes its own full moment: prescient, felt, and dynamic. It stakes a claim to space in the narrative, shapes what precedes and what follows it, and allows us access to an embedded sensorial world that suggests that history cannot be known in the moment, but that historical consciousness functions as a form of embodied abeyance that perceives fragmented series of events in constellated arrangement from a certain and necessary remove. This arrangement is read only later and in any number of different ways. The interstice in thought that Martínez offers up here expands and fills with synesthetic cognition, revealing a grafting of senses and knowledge onto one another that, in turn, reveals new connections and possibilities in a historical playing field. The absent in this instance serves as a cipher for how we might read the historical and reminds us that what is gone, empty, or hollowed out is a rich proving ground for how we make sense, otherwise, of the world around us. Martínez cautions us that not only does the absent take up space and produce its own forms of logic and legibility, but that emplacement is itself a form of emptying, hollowing, or carving out space. So where we turn to the solidity of the emplaced world, we also turn to an opening up, out, or onto of a larger embedded expansiveness that contains other worlds in turn. In this final instance of embedded box-worlds that I read in this chapter, absence emerges as a still moment in time that makes use of new forms of embodied, present knowledge that in turn allow us to read what comes before and what comes after. The body and the knowledge it provides for become a fundamental part of the mode of disappearance that Martínez enacts here, and one that he will return to in full force in *Santa Evita*.

The descriptions of and gestures toward emplacement in the material world that Martínez makes use of in *La novela de Perón* function throughout as forms or markers of absence. More than just emptying out the solid narrative ground of the novel, however, the move indicates that suspension, withholding, and cancellation are—within the context of the postdictatorship most pointedly, but also as evidence of a more expansive postmodern condition—viable and valuable mechanisms by which to interpret the world. This is not a negative epistemology, nor an exercise in exhaustion. Instead these moments in the text that come apart or vanish suggest that we know the world, or might know the world, as much by what is receding, no longer manifest, or removed as by what remains before us. Where the emplaced world—platial structures, maps, landscape, embodied moments in time—recedes or is withheld, disappearance becomes a dynamic space by which to know and make room for the narrative world at hand, and an active agent in building new ones.

The embedded narrative structure of Martínez's novel bears this out by proffering intersecting ontologies that open onto or make space for what is no longer present and, inversely, by drafting what is absent as the catalyst for new spaces. From this box-world model, we learn to navigate the historical gaps, simulacra and simulations, and other strategies of suspension that together make up the mode of disappearance at work in the novel, and in many ways in Martínez's larger authorial project. This mode makes claims to disappearance as a manifold form of knowledge, a way to intervene in and make sense of the complex and productive relationship between history and fiction and, perhaps most importantly, as a constitutive component of world-building during Argentina's transition to democracy. Martínez shows us, in *La novela de Perón*, how this construction occurs—with all its complicated recursivity, intersection, and multiform division—upon shifting planes of discursive absence. The suspension this produces renders the work, at the beginning of the postdictatorship, a kind of anticipatory fiction whose purposeful and dynamic withholding signals a history still very much in the making and its readers necessary accomplices in that future.

4

Errant Metonymy

The Embodiment of Disappearance in Tomás Eloy Martínez's *Santa Evita*

> tú has de volver no importa tu fracaso
> nunca terminará es infinita esta riqueza
> abandonada
>
> —Edgar Bayley, "es infinita esta riqueza abandonada"

> Fluidity is the fundamental condition.
>
> —G. W. Leibniz, "Of the Simple Modes of Space"

Where the strategies of suspension in *La novela de Perón* give us an anticipatory fiction that opens Argentina's postdictatorship up to new and participatory historical possibilities, that anticipation reaches a material apotheosis in Tomás Eloy Martínez's next novel. *Santa Evita*, published ten years after its twin novel and twelve years after Argentina's return to democracy, is in a position to gauge—as much as a work of historical fiction might serve as barometer for a particular contemporary moment—which versions of the future have materialized in the early postdictatorship and how. Martínez's novel, this perhaps his most widely read across Latin America and beyond, reports back in the form of Eva Perón's copied, errant, and disappeared corpse whose multiplication, movement, many attempts at erasure, and hyperanonymity are met at every narrative turn, these part myth and part fact, with resistance. Martínez offers up a postmodern satire of the gothic novel—its correspondences with Faulkner's *As I Lay Dying* are many—to report on the busy afterlife of Eva Perón's dead body and the mythic proportions Evita's life and corpse took on in certain sectors of Argentine society and politics after her husband's fall from power in 1955. The work of satire, however, is here deadly serious. For it offers up an oblique view of one of the most visible female figures in Western history; and here her life and corpse begin to participate in new systems of meaning-making that recalibrate and recast their own place in history and in Argentina's recent past.

I argue throughout this chapter that Eva Perón's body functions in *Santa Evita* as metonym and metonymic structure that houses and gives form to historical absences and, not without complication, the place of the disappeared in literary history. Evita's corpse is the narrative mode of disappearance of the novel wherein the examples of disappearance as literary technique or form I have observed throughout this work here materialize in their most tangible, immediately discernible, and dynamic shape yet. The dead body is a force of form that exerts narrative pressure on every aspect of the novel: its structure, character development, central themes, as well as the work's capacity to communicate a critical ethics of resistance that informs how we construct history and remember and memorialize the disappeared dead. Most importantly, for the purposes of this chapter, the literary corpse of Eva Perón serves as a container to manifold forms of absence that simultaneously shapes the work's emplotment—its unfolding and intrigue in and across narrative spaces—and exceeds the capacity of literature and literary cartography to contain it. The corpse enacts the limits of fiction in its metonymic representation of the historically discarded or excised whose political, historical, and ethical significance shape Martínez's narrative from the inside out. These, including the disappeared, appear by way of Evita's body as the feminized superabundant; they are a structure of narrative and national excess that prove, if we follow Blanchot, both limit and fundament of the literary and Argentina's postdictatorship nation.

Liquid Sun

Eva Perón died in Buenos Aires at 8:25 p.m. on July 26, 1952, succumbing to a protracted battle with uterine cancer at age thirty-three. At 9 p.m. on the night she "passed into immortality," Perón handed his wife's body over to Dr. Pedro Ara, a Galician embalmer whom he brought to Argentina in anticipation of Evita's death. Dr. Ara began his work that night and concluded the project almost three years later, on July 10, 1955. On September 16, 1955, Perón's government was ousted, and Perón began his eighteen-year exile, at the invitation of Francisco Franco, on the outskirts of Madrid. Shortly after Perón left for Spain, Eva Perón's preserved body was taken by the new government from the powerful labor union group who had kept if for years under the care of Dr. Ara at the Confederación General de Trabajadores (CGT). Taking Evita's body into hiding proved a fundamental part of General Aramburu's vast efforts to deperonize the country that prohibited referring by name to the Peróns or their politics, displaying or circulating their images, and voting for the Peronist party.[1] In this context Eva Perón's body was a particularly charged political vestige with the power to serve as a lightning rod for future Peronist uprisings. That the corpse was embalmed, preserved, and remained still unburied left, and not at all metaphorically, a central component of Peronism intact, visible, and in circulation.

Aramburu quelled this threat to the stability of his new government by engaging members of the military—most notably the head of military intelligence, Colonel Carlos Eugenio Moori Koenig—to secretly bury the body in an unmarked plot in Chacarita cemetery in Buenos Aires. When this effort was unsuccessful, due to a series of strange and violent events, the president called on an Italian priest to take the body out of the country to an unspecified location. In order to further confuse future efforts to locate the corpse, he also sent empty coffins—and this is the source of the fiction that Martínez circulates that proposes Evita's body was copied—to Argentina's embassies in Germany, Italy, and Belgium. He left strict instructions that no one in the government, including himself, was to know the location of the body until the political climate had cooled.[2] The personal cost to Aramburu of the removal of Eva Perón's body from the country would be high, however. In 1974, four years after his assassination by the Montoneros—this in apparent retribution for the 1956 José Léon Suárez massacre documented by Rodolfo Walsh in *Operación masacre*—the insurgent group would steal the president's corpse and hold it captive until Isabel Perón brought her husband's second wife's body back to Argentina. The history that Martínez reorganizes and reimagines in *Santa Evita* is already, then, a history of disappearance.

All of the preceding is well documented and part of verifiable historical record. What history cannot account for, however, is the cult of memory that sprung up around Eva Perón's corpse and its whereabouts. Aramburu cultivated a highly organized gap in what he, or anyone else, knew of the body and its global itineraries; he then covered over for that lack of knowledge by dissimulating, in the three empty caskets he sent around the world, that he was in possession of the corpse in the first place. Instead of emptying the country of the most powerful remaining Peronist signifier, Aramburu fomented a charged and unwieldly cultural and political myth about the location and fate of Evita's corpse. Martínez uses this myth—its genesis, propagation, circulation, and diffuse historic parameters—to comment on the legacies of Peronism that have fractured Argentina as well as, in the metonym of the corpse, to represent the country's recent history of enforced disappearance as a tool of authoritarianism. The cult of Evita itself divided between those more fervent members who revered her—and proposed, as she lay dying, her canonization—and a more measured and general recognition of the meaningful policy changes she implemented and other good works she spearheaded to improve the condition of the Peronist *descamisados*. What Eva Perón signified or might signify, if after her death but more pointedly under the strict platforms of deperonization, multiplied. Martínez engages that excess—although his work of fiction both compounds and directs it—as a central narrative mode and oblique historical intervention. Where Evita became in death the politically and culturally superabundant, Martínez recasts the excess in meaning afforded by her corpse as container for those murdered by the anti-Peronist campaigns installed under Videla and the following years of dictatorship. Her fictional corpse becomes not only the embodiment of "Volveré y seré millones" ("I will return and I will be millions")—the apocryphal phrase attributed to her by Martínez that became part of incorruptible historical record—but a way to acknowledge the place of the tens of thousands disappeared in Argentina's recent history. This is a narrative effort that includes troubling, as did *La novela de Perón*, the abiding expectation that history and literature perform separate tasks. But where in his earlier novel Martínez openly announces his account of the private life of Perón as fiction, in *Santa Evita* he constructs what reads as a work of literary journalism out of largely spurious biographical and historical documents. In this last, he participates in the long legacy—whose beginnings are marked as early as 1845 in the publication of the *Facundo*—of blurring the boundaries between history and fiction in Argentine letters. But he also responds more specifically to the many dangerous historical distortions perpetrated by the recent Videla government.[3] The dead body confirms that there are ethical stakes to how we understand the pressures history and fiction exert on one another. Brokered by the unexpected possibility that it serve as cipher or placeholder for the disappeared in particular, the corpse of one of Argentina's most divisive historical figures functions as a significant metonymic site of resistance in the postdictatorship.

The author's choice to draft Evita Perón's body—hypervisible in life as much as death—in this role is not without either precedent or complications. Eva Perón, even before her death, was defined in many ways by her body, which came to stand in for the national project of Peronism. Her early history as a pinup and actress of radio melodramas—many of these historical in theme—was hypersexualized; her detractors saw her as the poor, illegitimate, and illiterate child who worked her way first into entertainment and then into government by way of questionable means. Evita compensated for this by declaring herself the Spiritual Head of the Nation, a role that required she desexualize herself to be mother to her nation of *descamisados*. She never had children, which rendered her, in the semiotics of nation-building, an empty vessel available to take on this part. But the contradictions continue. Her husband sent her on tour around Europe as surrogate body of the state but then denied her the opportunity—one he would later afford to his third wife, whose presidency gave way to Videla—to serve as his vice president when the masses clamored for her.[4] Eva Perón already participated while alive in a cultural and political economy in which she functioned as excess, cipher, or surrogate. In the preservation of her corpse after her death, Perón only compounds and materializes this role. Martínez, for his part, both capitalizes on and repurposes this history such that the emptiness or surrogacy assigned to Evita in life and acquired by her in death comes to take on new meaning, and ethical capacity, when recast as a work of fiction.

Martínez offers up a rebellious body that throughout the novel resists ownership, burial, historical emplacement, and seems to carry out private acts of vengeance and provoke public displays of reverence as it escapes every attempt by the military to control and disappear it. Evita will not be manhandled, contained, or hidden. But several characters' obsessions with the corpse and the displays of male ownership and violence they enact against it have their counterpart in history. Martínez adapts or reimagines real-life aggressions carried out against or on behalf of the body; the violence it suffers throughout the book also replicates the damage found done to the body when finally returned, after buried for almost two decades under an assumed name in Italy, to Perón. Evita's sisters, upon viewing the body, found it had been beaten, stabbed, maimed, partially decapitated, and dipped in tar and quicklime.[5] Martínez reanimates some of these aggressions in his novel—the body is the synergist throughout of both latent and overt acts of national and private violence and obsession—but at every turn Evita rebels against, repays, or otherwise resists the attempts to control or harm her. This push-and-pull between control and resistance makes up the novel's central storyline, which is interrupted by, among other things, spurious descriptions of historical events that read as factual, dubious accounts of personal reflections, invented autobiographical and biographical accounts, references to literary texts and conversations that never occurred, and fragments from diaries, songs, and film scripts.

When *Santa Evita* begins, on the afternoon of Saturday, July 26, 1952, Eva Perón is on her deathbed. Not seven pages into the book, Evita dies, and her body is handed over directly to Dr. Ara. Martínez condenses the passage of the next three years in order to introduce the reader to his fictional version of Colonel Moori Koenig, who as history dictates, has been charged with getting rid of Evita's embalmed corpse. He goes to the headquarters of the CGT to visit Dr. Ara, who balks at being asked to give back this body that he has come to love beyond proportion.[6] He has, in the preceding three years, constructed three wax and fiberglass copies of the original body that serve, in the novel, as both simulacra of Eva Perón's embalmed corpse and simulated content of the empty coffins that Aramburu devised to dissimulate his possession of the body. Colonel Koenig seeks custodianship of her daughter's corpse from Evita's mother so that he might give it and its copies a clandestine burial,[7] but as they part she cautions him not to bury one of the copies by mistake. He assures her that he has marked—branded, actually—the original body so that he will always be able to identify it, and here begins the story of his efforts, on behalf of the state, to bury the corpse and its three copies.

What follows is an itinerary marred with violence, exile, and death. The Colonel drafts three men to help him, yet all of the burials are cursed with complications. He hides the body behind a movie screen in a cinema, in a military storeroom, and in vans, buses, cellars, and kitchens around Buenos Aires. An officer will take possession of the body, but his obsession with it will lead him to shoot his wife before moving the corpse to his attic. Colonel Koenig soon recovers it and hides it in a radio equipment packing box in his office. At the same time, an anonymous Peronist group named the Comando de la Venganza (Commando of Vengeance) leaves lighted candles, flowers, and threatening notes wherever the Colonel leaves the body. He fears that the body will be taken from him, so he moves his family to his ancestral Bonn and puts the corpse first in a shed in the garden of the city's Argentine embassy and then in an ambulance that he parks outside his house. The Colonel's wife leaves him. He then loses Evita in the city's red light district before burying her body in the garden of his grandparents' house in Eichstatt. When he later tries to dig it back up, he finds it has been washed away in a storm. He is finally called back to Argentina, where his superiors inform him he has from the beginning been in possession of one of Evita's copies, which provokes his final descent into madness. But the military had already much earlier declared him insane and charged another colleague to take the allegedly real body to Milan by boat. Here Evita is buried under the name María de Magistris in the Monte Grande cemetery. At the end of the novel, our author is contacted in the middle of the night by the Army Intelligence Service, who claims to want to share with him the real story of the fate of the corpse. Martínez meets up with several officers who correct the details they believe the author has gotten wrong in his novel, which they have already read. They tell him there were no copies and give him the deed to Evita's grave in Milan and the release signed by Perón when his wife's body was finally exhumed and returned to him in Madrid in 1973. They claim the corpse now rests safely in the mausoleum erected to Eva Perón in La Recoleta Cemetery in Buenos Aires. After their conversation, Martínez begins to write a novel about the afterlife of Eva Perón's dead body and the book ends where it began,[8] with Evita on the brink of death and the reader poised to reread everything that has come before. This narrative feedback loop enacts in one final gesture the possibility that Evita's corpse and the history it embodies participates in a kind of eternal return from which neither the reader nor Argentine history will soon escape. But in so doing, it also confirms that the memory of the disappeared—here actualized in the allegorical form of a corpse also gone missing, excised by the state from a public national consciousness, and denied from official history—will endure. And where every new reading is necessarily transformed by the one that precedes it, this memory will be recast over and over again as agent of new sequences or possibilities of narrative unfolding.

Null Intersection

Where Roman Jakobson gives us, as is well known, metaphor and metonym as prevailing forces of language in, respectively, poetry and prose,[9] the metonym of the corpse operates in *Santa Evita* as the central force that drives narrative emplotment. Here metonymy takes on outsized proportions as an embodied, copied, and rebellious historical remainder that both motivates and shapes the novel. The forms of absence the corpse comes to represent function—if in a more visible and material way than what we see in *La novela de Perón*—as both the object or raw material of the story (fabula) and the way the story is organized or progresses (syuzhet). The corpse serves throughout the novel as an empty vessel, receptacle, container, or blank slate for different versions of past or future historical possibilities, gaps, erasures, and unfulfilled desires. And these metonymic operations exert pressure on the novel's narrative emplotment: its sequences, configurations, spatial organization, and subsequent ethical capacity.

As a figure of speech, metonymy expresses a relation of contiguity in which either a thing or concept is referred to by the name of something closely associated with it or a part of some thing or idea comes to represent its whole. But this contiguity, Paul Ricoeur proposes in his discussion of Jean Cohen's work, "rests on a void." Metonymy does not participate in semic intersection—as does metaphor—such that its two halves do not internalize the smaller parts of what each intends; instead, it manifests an association without conceptual overlap, transgression, or borrowing. Objects and ideas abut one another and signal past one another to new associations that make up new polysemic variations; but the initial association is premised on "a null intersection." Ricoeur explains, again drawing from Cohen: "[in metonymy] there is a common inclusion, but of the two terms in a larger domain, whether of semes in the case of conceptual decomposition or of things in the case of material decomposition. In short, 'in metaphor the intermediate term is encompassed, whereas in metonymy it is encompassing.'"[10] Metonymy, then, works to expand a semic field even at the same time this expansion is premised on an absent space where related things or ideas do not overlap, and do not, as in metaphor, become one. Insomuch as prose manifests the propagation of time and space on the page, this internal and inherent drive at expansion renders metonymy, per Jakobson, the proper agent of narrative. Metonymy offers up a "change of name" or moves "beyond the name," as its etymology suggests, such that it might either rename or reclassify objects or ideas or take its work even further to construct larger metaleptic chains of association. These operations of reidentification, transformation, or generation endow metonymy with particular ethical capabilities; as both figure of speech and force of language, it reaches outward, moves beyond itself, and forges associations to broker connotations or cognitive expectations where none have previously existed. That it does so by overcoming a constitutive gap or breach in possible relationship renders metonymy—and then also narrative, which depends upon metonymy's impulse and momentum to function—fundamentally equipped to represent ethical gestures or encounters on the page or, true to name, beyond it. Metonymy as such, as well as its more specialized form of metalepsis, may be the trope par excellence to identify and reach out to the selfsame other, forge new meeting spaces, and build community.

Martínez activates these possibilities when he drafts Evita's preserved corpse as an empty vessel capable of taking in and giving shape to the historical absences that have haunted Argentina. He names Eva Perón as historical cipher capable of assimilating these absences but then also, as is proper to the metonym, transforming them into something else. As a cipher, on loan to Latin from the Arabic *sifr*, "empty, nothing," the corpse is a null space, a void, a placeholder that can give its space over to any waiting value. It also assumes the properties of the lesser-used meaning of "nonentity," "someone of no consequence or power" but then, in a process of metonymic regeneration or transformation, reidentifies Eva Perón in death as a dynamic agent of resistance and memory. As a null space, the corpse is flexible as to the properties it can take on. The fact of an empty, waiting female body ready to be inscribed with meaning is charged and difficult, and Martínez engages with these complications, which I discuss at greater length later. But its primary task throughout the novel is to serve as semic—if at once satirical and ethical—placeholder for that which has been left out, discarded, or excised in Argentina's history. As metonymic structure, the corpse—whose properties are only strengthened by embalming as a form of encasing and preserving—encompasses and houses the various semantic associations it takes on. It opens up its own field of meaning as well as foments new relationships between potentially divergent connotations. In this way, the disappeared might come to signal still other ethical breaches in Argentine history; and failures, laments, regrets or other missed opportunities—again, Benjamin's definition of tragedy—in their turn still other tragedies. Here the metonymy gains in meaning but the corpse serves to contain its proliferating significance as it travels around Buenos Aires and abroad as the novel advances.

Because metonymy works to offer another name, here the breaches and absences manifest in Argentine history are signaled by Eva Perón and what the name Evita signifies in history also comes to take on new properties. Martínez does not resolve the first lady's complicated persona; instead, his presentation of spurious or invented historical material only further galvanizes the myths that sprung up around her in life and redoubled in death. But without coming down on one side or another of the virgin/whore complex attributed to Evita while alive, he does afford her in death significant redemptive properties. While not a saint, and certainly not a savior, he positions her as capable of recalibrating and recasting certain historical possibilities. The decision is risky, given her charged and controversial role in recent Argentine history, but Martínez makes of her a fitting, if complicated, narrative cipher. The spatial connotations inherent here and in the idea that Evita's body allows what she represents to *take place* is fundamental to the possibility that I lay out in the coming pages that the corpse provide for a new form of community. Metonymy, as Ricoeur confirms, is an inherently spatial construct. It is predicated on a void that then provides for new or reconfigured associations that themselves work to make up and annex new cognitive or imaginative space. As a figure of speech and as a narrative force, metonymy works to build new worlds whose various components accrete and take up their own particular space. Martínez renders this spatialization hypervisible in selecting Evita's corpse as the receptacle for what has been discarded or excised from official history. But in doing so he allows these absences and the disappeared, in this complex operation, to take up a well-defined, tangible space that becomes both literary theme and place, a true *topos*.[11]

In one of the most explicit examples of this transformation, Koenig and his men prepare to bury the bodies' copies in cemeteries around Buenos Aires. One of the officers asks the Colonel: "Algo me intriga . . . esa mujer, el cuerpo. Es una momia, ¿no? Hace tres años que ha muerto. ¿Para qué la queremos? La podríamos tirar desde un avión, en el medio del río. La podríamos meter dentro de una bolsa de cal, en la fosa común. Nadie está preguntando por ella. Y si alguien pregunta, no tenemos por qué contestar"[12] (There's something that puzzles me . . . That woman, the body: it's a mummy, right? She's been dead for three years. What do we want her for? We could throw her out of a plane into the middle of the river. We could put her inside a sackful of quicklime, in a common grave. Nobody's asking about her. And if anyone does ask, we don't have to answer). Eva Perón has at this point been dead for three years and the government that deposed the General has forbidden any mention of the Peróns or their political party; as Galarza says, nobody has been asking after Evita's body. It has been stored quietly on the second floor of the CGT since 1952, so he wants to know why the government wants the body kept intact and in their sight. He proposes multiple scenarios in which they might dispose of the body and deny their knowledge of its whereabouts, all of which recall the techniques of enforced disappearance used by the military during the dictatorship. But his colleague Arancibia tells him that it is too late to just get rid of the corpse:

Tal vez ya es tarde—dice Arancibia, el Loco—. Hace dos años se podía. Si hubiéramos matado al embalsamador, el cuerpo se habría corrompido solo. Ahora es un cuerpo demasiado grande, más grande que el país. Está demasiado lleno de cosas. Todos le hemos ido metiendo algo adentro: la mierda, el odio, las ganas de matarlo de nuevo. Y como dice el Coronel, hay gente que también le ha metido su llanto. Ya ese cuerpo es como un dado cargado. El presidente tiene razón. Lo mejor es enterrarlo, creo. Con otro nombre, en otro lugar, hasta que desaparezca.

—Hasta que desaparezca—repite el Coronel, que no cesa de fumar. Se inclina sobre el mapa de Buenos Aires.[13]

"It might be too late," Arancibia, the Madman, says. "Two years ago it could have been done. If we'd killed the embalmer, the body would have decomposed all by itself. It's too big a body now, bigger than the country. It's too full of things. We've all kept putting something into it: shit, hatred, wanting to kill it again. And as the Colonel says, there are people who have put their tears into it too. That body is like loaded dice now. The president is right. The best thing to do is bury it, it seems to me. Under another name, in another place, till it disappears."

"Till it disappears," the Colonel repeats, still chain-smoking. He bends over the map of Buenos Aires.

Martínez here lays bare and comments upon, within the action of the novel, his own strategies of metonymic substitution and expansion. Arancibia—the officer who, besides the Colonel, will become most obsessed with the corpse—recognizes that the embalmed body has become a receptacle for expressions of national belonging, longing, shame, and fury. It is a tinderbox full of things that never did, could have differently, or might still happen, which render it too politically charged to be left out in public. As the Colonel tells Dr. Ara at the beginning of the novel, "Al embalsamarlo, usted movió la historia de lugar. Dejó a la historia dentro. Quien tenga a la mujer, tiene al país en su puño"[14] ("By embalming it, you made history change place. You left history inside. Whoever has the woman has the country in the palm of their hand"). If the state had laid Eva Perón to rest when she died, never permitted Dr. Ara to preserve her symbolic function, then her body and all of its potential to generate new meaning would have decomposed. But by embalming the corpse and letting it remain above ground it became a null intersection, "an ellipsis of the very relation of reference"[15] disposed to receive the country's laments, regrets, hopes, and desires. Aramburu's new government cannot stabilize while this vestige, from both the past and the future, still circulates. Arancibia sees burying it under another name—somewhere else, until it disappears—as the only way to rid the country of the body.

Like Addie Bundren before her—if here at the level of the political instead of the personal—Evita's corpse contains and catalyzes the darkest parts of a national unconscious. The excesses of a repressed national imaginary are displaced onto and condensed into this body that will, at every turn, resist burial. Displacement and condensation are both, per Jakobson and the wider reading of language's capacity to push against its own limits that Ricoeur performs in *The Rule of Metaphor*, metonymic operations.[16] They each, if in different ways also elucidated by Freud in his principles of the unconscious, enact the contiguity that defines the work of metonymy.[17] Here what has been repressed historically—the fractured legacy of Peronism, the crimes of the military dictatorship, the ensuing campaigns of impunity, the tens of thousands disappeared—finds its oblique expression in the double-loaded metonymic figure of the dead body. The scores of corpses that buttress and bear out the nation's history are here condensed and displaced into a single angry body animated by everything that did not take place or might have differently.

Arancibia recognizes that these latent processes, once activated, pose a mortal threat to the nation. His desire to disappear the body in which they converge reenacts the Videla government's efforts to contain and control death even as they manufacture it, a critical component of the program of widespread social schizophrenia carefully crafted by the junta to cover over for the fact of enforced disappearance. As Admiral Emilio Massera pronounced in a November 1976 speech to the military at the Navy Mechanics School (ESMA), "We will not allow death to roam unconstrained in Argentina. . . . We are not going to fight unto death, we are going to fight beyond death, unto victory."[18] The title of the speech, "Los Muertos por la patria" (The dead for the fatherland), confirms already both the system of exchange wherein Massera expects death to circulate and the possibility of an animate dead. For here, via a well-placed preposition, the victims of guerilla violence exchange their lives for their nation. But the title also offers up the secondary possibility that the dead actively support, buttress, or fight for the country. In either case, death is not static but a force of national belonging and nation-building, which provides an oblique justification for the systematic disappearances the junta is carrying out. But in the words he offers up at the ESMA—in proffering a backhanded pretext for the wildly disproportionate military response to isolated acts of urban guerrilla violence[19]—Massera declares that the junta "will not allow death to roam unconstrained." Death is something to be tamed and constrained, staunched by the government and here, in this rallying cry, the nation. A program of enforced disappearance that denies death—here not mentioned outright but in Massera's characteristic double-speak—fits the bill. Disappearance does not allow death, in the skewed logic of the junta, to proliferate in a national consciousness. He goes on: "We are not going to fight unto death, we are going to fight beyond death." Death is not here a stopping point but rather a threshold that leads to the junta's vision of the "Western, Christian" nation that lies beyond. Massera here offers up in condensed version the skewed arguments that underpin an authoritarianism that submits disappearance as a natural course of events in a teleologically driven history instead of a gaping ethical breach. He also, in stripping death of its power, necessarily denies the grief and mourning that serve as an a priori premise of our precarious lives and, as I discuss in this work's introduction, one of the gravest consequences of enforced disappearance. Martínez responds, in *Santa Evita* and in the metonymic figure of Evita's corpse, to this official and overt denial, rejection, displacement, and dismantling of death. He brings back death, and with it his country's history of disappearance, as a narrative force capable of relating history otherwise. The embodied historical remainder that he gives us in Evita's preserved body—at once cipher and container for a national unconscious—is the narrative mode of disappearance that drives Martínez's novel.

Simulacra, Site, and the Superabundant

If Evita's original, embalmed corpse functions as a metonymic force of form throughout the novel, its copies serve as simulacra and simulation of this indexical power. In history, Evita's body was not copied but instead simulated when Aramburu sent the three empty caskets around the world to dissimulate the government's possession of the corpse. The political calculation recalls, if by way of an advance hyperinvisibility, Massera's later efforts to simultaneously produce and deny death under the dictatorship. Martínez turns Aramburu's empty indexes into simulacra when Dr. Ara's fictional counterpart enlists a sculptor to help him manufacture three copies of Evita's corpse so that the government and insurgents will be unable to identify the original body should either come to claim it. Throughout the novel, Martínez emphasizes both the emptiness of the original corpse and the multiplication of this emptiness so that despite the proliferating bodies, the novel produces a network of mobile, null spaces. By embalming his wife's body, Perón vacates what Evita might have come to signify in death and covers over this gap with an enduring simulacrum of her life. She is relegated to a permanent state of suspension that enters into a system of circulation that in exchanging the currency of death for that of the nation are both unmasked as voids.

Martínez renders this empty space tangible and hypervisible by conceiving of three simulacra to accompany the original body. Where the simulacrum is the copy without an original, these copies reveal Evita's corpse to be already an empty signifier. The copies are both proliferations of this originary absence and work to distract from and cover over for it, as Jean Baudrillard predicts in the third stage of his successive phases of the image: "[the image] masks the absence of a basic reality." But the copies are as much a threat as the original corpse, for in the image's fourth and final stage "[the original] bears no relation to any reality whatever: it is its own pure simulacrum." Here "simulation envelops the whole edifice of representation as itself a simulacrum,"[20] such that Martínez's copies reveal Eva Perón's body to be itself a body without an original, in death an empty referent. The move parlays, upon close reading, a subtle resistance—and this resistance will prove an important fundament to the ethical significance the corpse will take on—to official attempts to deny death insomuch as it recognizes Evita as dead and gone. But the copies do more to emphasize the corpse as the center of a network of signification that bolsters, propagates, and traffics in absence. Within this complex system, Eva Perón comes to enact the polysemic endpoint of metonymy and mean many things all at once. As the novel progresses—and as the original corpse and its copies are confused for one another to the point where it is impossible to tell who is in possession of which and which is responsible for the action it engenders—the body and its protheses become a vast metaleptic structure that generates from absence a fiction capable of recalibrating how we come to historical knowledge and what we expect it to include. Because from this network of invented simulation and propagating associations excised historical forms begin to take shape.

The copies that Dr. Ara fabricates, however, are not—and never could be—exact. But when the doctor shows them to Evita's mother, she cannot tell them apart. One lies on a glass table, a second reclines on pillows on the floor, and the third sits reading a postcard Evita sent from Madrid seven years earlier. All the copies are dressed in the same white tunic as the embalmed corpse and are such perfect replicas that not even Doña Juana, as Martínez describes, could have given birth to them. Each imitation—the first two made of wax and vinyl, the last of fiberglass—is more perfect than the next. She who reads, Coppelius's Olympia refashioned, is the doctor's magnum opus.

Doña Juana worries that she will not be able to recognize her own daughter. But Dr. Ara assures her:

> Hay que exponerlas a los rayos X. A la genuina se le notan las vísceras. En las demás sólo se ve la nada. ¿Qué hacen los físicos cuando quieren interrumpir la fluencia natural de las cosas? Algo muy simple: las multiplican.—El embalsamador, excitado, había subido una o dos octavas el timbre de la voz.—A un olvido hay que oponerle muchas memorias, a una historia real hay que cubrirla con historias falsas. Viva, su hija no tenía par, pero muerta ¿qué importa? Muerta, puede ser infinita.²¹

> They must be x-rayed. The internal organs of the genuine one can be seen. The only thing that can be seen inside the others is emptiness. What do physicists do when they wish to interrupt the natural flow of things? Something very simple: they multiply them. In his excitement, the embalmer had raised the pitch of his voice one or two octaves. "Oblivion must be countered by many memories, a real story must be covered up by false stories. Alive, your daughter had no equal, but once dead, what difference does it make? Once dead, she can be infinite."

The real Dr. Ara includes in his memoir the film of an X-ray of Evita's cranium, pointing out a gray shadow that appears within as an infallible element of identification should it ever be needed.²² But the fictional doctor emphasizes instead that the real corpse can be distinguished from its copies because these are empty inside. Martínez here renders in physical terms, if with a slippage in valence, the power of the simulacra to signal absence. Their physical emptiness is a faithful reproduction of the semiotic emptiness of Evita's original corpse. This original void is both the oblivion and the real story the doctor refers to here, the copies its many memories and false stories. Martínez suggests here, as did Walsh in "Variaciones en rojo" and Cortázar in *Fantomas*, that imitation and art are in a position both to cover over and to unmask absence or disappearance. Evita's copies cover up for her embalmed corpse's originary emptiness and serve to deflect meaning from it, enacting Baudrillard's "strategy of the real, of the neoreal, and the hyperreal that everywhere is the double of a strategy of deterrence."[23] For the copies of Evita's corpse, proliferating evidence of the hyperreal, manifest the fact that the original corpse is in its incorruptibility itself already a strategy of deterrence. It interrupts and deters death and turns Eva Perón's body into the first copy of the first lady. While still alive, she was singular and inimitable and participated in "the natural flow of things." But as a preserved corpse, Evita requires copies to serve as "the difference fiction,"[24] which masks her own irreality and substantive lack of meaning.

This necessary plurality, alongside the central metonymic force of the corpse, is the narrative mode of disappearance that drives the action and intrigue of the novel. But it also instantiates and multiplies, in real physical terms, the fact that Evita's corpse is already in excess—of life, death, and the nation. The preserved dead body, in Baudrillard's reading of the mummy, proves the value of our culture of accumulation wherein we "stockpile the past in plain view" at the same time that its hypervisibility distracts us from the emptiness of our own origin myth.[25] The possibility is important, especially given the devastation that neoliberalism will come to wreak on Argentina in the ensuing years. But in Martínez's version of events, the corpse is a structure of excess whose full and originary absence serves as an empty vessel, container, and finally place or placeholder for contiguous excesses: that which has been left out of, excised from, exceeds, or pushes back against history or historical record.

As the corpse takes shape throughout the novel as an embodied remainder of these historical absences or absencing, it comes to also *take place*—and here the temporal meets the spatial—or become a site in its own right. The evolution is significant, for in concretizing the metonymic operations by which the corpse, already in excess, becomes a container for the disappeared, the body becomes also place, shelter, or refuge for those who were denied precisely this. The process inverts Aristotle's conception of place as receptacle, a premise that underpins fundamental, Western ideas about how space occurs and who gets to take it up. Where in Plato, place is derivative of an omnireceptive, a priori, and fluid *chōra*, Aristotle gives us place that functions as a vessel that contains and surrounds a body or object, so that the limits of this receptacle "are together with what is limited."²⁶ Boundary here provides for content such that place, for Aristotle, is a border that accommodates what it holds within, moves with it, and in the last analysis, allows what it withholds to manifest or take place.

But the model is problematic, and not only for its structural limitations. Elizabeth Grosz elucidates its difficult ramifications when she argues for new notions of community predicated on a concerted, organized attempt to produce what she calls "architectures of excess" that controvert traditional concepts of space and place. She reviews the possibility, via Georges Bataille and Luce Irigaray, that Aristotle's dominant model of space gives us a feminized and passive interior space that allows for its own conquest or appropriation. Without a reordering of space that might provide for sexual difference, woman, Irigaray observes, is both "the space, or better, *the matrix*, of male self-unfolding" and a ready abyss or void.²⁷ Within this paradigm a "perverse exchange [occurs] at the origin of space" in which, to paraphrase, woman gives man a world and man confines woman in his.²⁸ This process strips the maternal and the feminine of its own interiority so that, turned inside out, it serves as a passive, empty space waiting to be colonized, constructed upon, and inhabited. But the conception of place, as Grosz argues, as "any notion of order, system, community, knowledge, and control . . . entails a notion of excess, expenditure, and loss that can be associated with those elements of femininity and of woman that serve to distinguish women as irreducible to and not exhausted in the masculine and the patriarchal."²⁹ Here the possibility that woman-as-place is neither interior nor exterior and not defined or limited by her relation to a smooth, male space serves to identify a feminized and dynamic notion of excess. Correspondences with Evita's embalmed corpse quickly multiply.

Irigaray proposes a way loose from the double-bind of ex/interiority when she envisions the female body in place as, in Edward S. Casey's description, "*doubly engaging*."³⁰ Here, writes Irigaray,

> she is able to move within place as place. Within the availability of place. Given that her issue is how to trace the limits of place herself so as to be able to situate herself therein and welcome the other there. If she is to be able to contain, to envelope, she must have her own envelope. Not only her clothing and ornaments of seduction, but her skin. And her skin must contain a receptacle. She must lack neither body, nor extension within, nor extension without.³¹

The female body takes place and becomes place when she is—here in skin—an envelope for the receptacle—here in womb—of her body. She contains a body that is both selfsame and double that provides for its own extension in space. This body does not depend on an inside or an outside—extension within or without—but in woman's double engagement of envelope and receptacle takes up its own room (perhaps a version of Heidegger's *einräumen*, or making room). Woman is here not double, but in Casey's estimation, doubly engaged with herself and others and always an open, porous container, or "open/enclosure."[32] The female body escapes the double-bind of Aristotelian emplacement by being herself already doubly engaging and always, despite her capacity to contain, open and moving.[33]

Grosz writes, "space itself needs to be reconsidered in terms of multiplicity, heterogeneity, activity, and force. Space is not simply an ether, a medium through which other forces, like gravity, produce their effects: it is inscribed by and in turn inscribes those objects and activities placed within it."[34] Reconceiving of space in this way—following Irigaray's model of woman-as-place and with a nod to the rhizomatic contributions of Deleuze and Guattari—allows us, in Grosz's formulation, to "actively strive to produce an architecture of excess"[35] that will make a space for new forms of community. Grosz defends excess as a politically charged space or site and the superabundant as its necessary question. She explains:

> The concept of excess, or more, enables the question of the superabundant—that which is excluded or contained because of its superabundance—to be raised as a political, as much as an economic and an aesthetic, concept. This excess, that which the sovereign, clean, proper, functional, and self-identical subject has expelled from itself, provides the conditions of all that both constitutes and undermines system, order, exchange, and production. What preconditions and overflows that thin membrane separating the outcast from the community, the container from the contained, the inside from the outside, is the embeddedness of the improper in the proper, the restricted within the general economy, the masculine within the feminine body, architecture within the body of space itself.[36]

Following in the tradition of others also rethinking community—Nancy, Derrida, Agamben, Rancière—Grosz identifies that which requires exclusion from the sovereign body as constitutive to, here embedded within, that system. When its superabundance overcomes attempts at exclusion or containment, then it becomes an excess whose constitutive viability Grosz imagines as fundament for other forms of community that require other kinds of architecture. Martínez gives us this in the embalmed corpse of Eva Perón; it becomes here another kind of architecture, a structure capable of housing and doing justice to those who have been historically excised or discarded. Where Evita's body is the originary void turned dwelling, its copies are the visible manifestation of the superabundance or excess that it houses. These copies are the necessary question that provide for the politically—and following Grosz also aesthetically—charged space of excess of Evita's corpse. The novel formulates throughout the questions they precipitate—where do I belong and how?—and offers up the corpse as answer.

Grosz and Irigaray function as lenses through which to read Eva Perón's corpse as "doubly engaged," a selfsame space that contains multitudes and is itself excess and representative of those who have been deemed in excess to the national body. Irigaray tells us that woman is, down to her very skin, her own container capable of serving as envelope for another, and Grosz proposes that the multiplicity and dynamism inherent in this design is the premise for a new model of community that gives place to the other, the discarded, or the left out. Martínez not only gives us a model for these possibilities in *Santa Evita* but activates them as the driving force of the novel's narrative emplotment such that its subject is also the mode of its unfolding, *doubly engaging*. Here the corpse of Eva Perón is a highly visible, reified, and itinerant version of Irigaray's female body. She is both envelope and receptacle, selfsame and double of the historical excisions and unrealized historical possibilities that she encloses. She also—and this provides for the arc of the novel's action to which I turn later—never occupies a stable place. Even when the body remains in one location long enough that it might be found—behind the movie screen at the Rialto, for example, or in Arancibia's attic—it remains definitively unidentifiable because its copies obscure its clear trajectory. Martínez's version of Evita is, if in death, the female body that both functions as her own, proper place while resisting at every turn the male—here represented largely by the military—effort to emplace, situate, and contain her. The corpse functions as its own container model and as a site of resistance to other models of the traditionally male, historical, and authorial that attempt to limit her capacity to represent that which has not been or cannot be, in the modes most readily available to us, represented. The embodied remainder makes room for this superabundance as a narrative mode of disappearance that drives emplotment and configuration toward their necessary ethical limits.

Chapter Four

Burial Plots in the Bardo

Evita's corpse functions in *Santa Evita* as metonym, structure, and site. But, insomuch as it also acts out Irigaray's conception of woman-as-place—she who takes up a fluid place of her own—the body is also always on the move, fluid, itinerant. Here everything that the corpse represents becomes the driving narrative force of the novel even as it enacts a kind of nomadism that ultimately confirms both the necessary diffuseness of the memory of the disappeared and that memory as a site of ethical resistance. The only proper place that woman occupies in Irigaray, after she comes into her double engagement, is herself. Evita's proper place—and here, particularly as it relates to metonym, the ethical capacity of the proper name to name both body and place is also critical—is coincident throughout the novel with wherever she is, and she is everywhere. She will not submit, in death, to emplacement; she will not be buried or emplotted. *Santa Evita* is a burial plot, if I might here take advantage of the double valence. The novel's plot—at least the primary narrative world in which action moves forward—is about the military's attempts to bury Evita's corpse and rid the country of the threat she poses to national stability. But Evita is herself already, metonymically, a burial plot. She is the final resting place—although a restless one—of what has been left out of or excised from the official history of nation-building. The second burial plot animates and drives the first such that together they manifest the work's narrative emplotment, or the ways that it comes together and its ethical capacity. The possibility does not turn on a felicitous coincidence of etymology but rather lays bare the constitutive intimacies between emplacement, storytelling, and death.

As David Sherman writes, "A burial plot is not simply a corpse's resting ground, but also its story, the arc of time between perishing and final disposal."[37] But Martínez's novel gives us a burial plot that balks against these natural engagements with death, forcing new answers to a new set of questions: What kind of burial plot, or story, does the embalmed corpse require? What kind of stories emerge to narrate the life of the corpse that is both denied burial and becomes its own final resting place? What do the unburied dead have to tell us, about their own complicated afterlives and our remaining life? And how might they, like the epic's honored dead, participate in and precipitate the rise and fall of family and nation? Martínez gives us answers to some of these questions in *Santa Evita*. The embalmed corpse is rebellious and resistant in its materiality. It disorders—variously foreshortens, prolongs, reverts, confuses, or entirely empties out—the narrative time that we construct to emplace the dead and explain death. The preserved body does not stay put, or at least has the potential to not do so. This errancy renders fluid the meaning that we assign it, that it acquires, or that it generates, as well as threatens the possibility of settling into a cohesive narrative. The narratives that we construct to understand, if not contain, the life of the corpse require other forms of emplotment, as Faulkner confirms in his epic of modernist experiment. But the embalmed corpse compounds these needs to the point of resistance, or at least until the point at which resistance becomes itself the narrative, as happens in *Santa Evita*. Martínez's postmodern techniques of recursivity, embedded ontologies, hyperintertextuality, metafiction, and hybridity foreground, rather than attempt to cancel out, this resistance. The novel gives way to the demands of the corpse. For our narrative approaches toward the dead body—perhaps especially to those bodies that remain missing—illustrate how we understand our ethical obligation, bond, and debt to the dead.

Martínez does not strive to contain or fix Evita's corpse. The metonymic function he affords it allows it to only gain in meaning, its structure and preservation permit it to serve as itinerant memory site, and it resists—as exemplified in the repeated, failed attempts to bury it—narrative emplotment throughout the novel. The burial plot will not, in short, be buried when dealing with those whose death we have forestalled, denied, or withheld. Martínez both emphasizes and reflects on the difficulties of this emplotment by foregrounding the visual and spatial terms that are so crucial to how we understand narrative unfolding. These find their corollary in the many locations, itineraries, and maps that populate *Santa Evita*; but where they should work to concretize the corpse's location—and therein contain its threat to Argentina—they instead fail, are not decipherable, lead nowhere, turn back on themselves, are hidden or just plain exhausted. Martínez's reliance on spatial specificity and destination—while bearing out Walsh's claim decades earlier that Buenos Aires functions on a par with other global metropolises as a favorable setting for detective stories—serves not to properly emplace the corpse but rather to highlight the fact that it will be not buried, emplotted, or forgotten in either fiction or memory.

The double signification of emplotment is crucial here. Where *plot* is first a small piece of ground, then a map, chart, and only later the set of events in a story, *emplotment* retains both its roots' spatiality and the possibility that this ground provides for the unfolding of the action of a story. This action is necessarily predicated on spatiality even as it organizes a work's temporal configuration such that it makes sense and, per Paul

Ricoeur—"narrative emplotment" is his term—gives us causality, necessity, believability, intelligibility, and coherence. Emplotment reveals an internal logic to the moving parts of a text whose conceptual relations—ones we might understand either outright or partially—are capable of galvanizing certain ethical responses in the reader.[38] We move here from space to time to ethics wherein McHale's postmodern ontological questions—where am I? what world is this? what makes it possible?[39]—become ethical concerns that demand a ready answer from the novel and its intersection with the lived world. The use of maps in Martínez's novel allows us—or at least gives us the illusion we are doing so—to track the movement of Evita's bodies, which is also a history of the futile attempts to contain, constrain, and rein in the corpse and its metonymic value. The map becomes a record of the corpse's resistance to emplotment, which Martínez illustrates, not at all incidentally, by way of the labyrinths that Borges uses to structure his own detective stories. Ultimately, the impossibility of emplotment comes to exemplify Martínez's larger authorial concerns about the work of both history and fiction, and their possible shared ethical endpoint.

In chapter 6, "El enemigo acecha" ("The Enemy Is Lying in Wait"), Martínez claims to reveal his sources for his historical novel. He reports that he collected the majority of the information that he uses to construct the novel from interviews with Moori Koenig's widow and the Colonel's confidant, Aldo Cifuentes. The Colonel left to Cifuentes the letters and notes in which he describes his attempts to get rid of Evita's body. Cifuentes shares these with Martínez, who also records their conversations on seven audiotapes.[40] On side A of the first cassette, Cifuentes narrates how Koenig devised his plan to bury the copies of Eva Perón in various cemeteries around Buenos Aires. The Colonel seeks out three officers—Arancibia, Galarza, and Fesquet—to help him complete the job. But before Koenig gathers his team, he has to decide where to bury the copies of Eva Perón's body. He spreads out a map of greater Buenos Aires and places on top a sheet of tracing paper on which he has drawn a picture of Paracelsus's trident. Buenos Aires, Cifuentes tells Martínez, is shaped like a pentagon: a trident comprised of three isosceles triangles atop a base and handle. Acting out the mysticism of the cult of Eva Perón that much of the novel satirizes, the Colonel tries to reconcile the trident to the pentagon in the hope that the operation will reveal the most auspicious locations in which to bury the likenesses of Evita. But, warns Cifuentes, attempting to harmonize these contrary symbols is a dangerous endeavor proper to the uncertainties of alchemy. The map that the Colonel turns to in order to contain the body's simulacra is itself already an object of mysticism and is here overlaid with symbols that work to communicate more than what the map might on its own. There is no possibility of containment here; to the contrary, the map proves a source of expanding signification, propagating more meaning as each of the subsequent attempts at burying the copies fails, and with fatal consequence.[41]

When he lays the trident atop the map of the pentagon—here pointed satire that also recalls López Rega's very real and dangerous affinity for occultism—Koenig attempts to harmonize incongruous symbols in order to bury the copies of Eva Perón's corpse. But according to Cifuentes, the Colonel's manipulations engendered an even more complex hermeneutics:

«Cuando Moori Koenig hizo coincidir el mango del tridente con el Dock Sur, las puntas sobresalieron del mapa y quedaron apuntando hacia los tambos y tierras para ganado que se perfilan mas allá de San Vicente, Cañuelas y Moreno. De nada le servían esos campos remotos. Desplazó entonces el mango sobre el mapa hasta situarlo en la esquina de Buenos Aires donde él estaba, de pie, bajo una lámpara. Miró la hora, me dijo, porque en el filo de la realidad a la cual se asomaba todo era vértigo. Eran las seis menos seis minutos. La distracción de su mirada duró menos de un segundo. Eso bastó para que el tridente se contrajera y sus flechas se clavaran en tres sitios increíblemente precisos: la iglesia de Olivos, a orillas de una estación ferroviaria llamada Borges; el Recinto de Personalidades en el cementerio de la Chacarita; el mausoleo blanco de Ramón Francisco Flores en el cementerio de Flores. Ésa era la brújula del azar que había esper . . .»
Fin de la ci(n)ta.[42]

When Moori Koenig placed the handle of the trident so that it exactly coincided with the South Dock, the ends of it went off the map and lay there pointing toward the milking yards and cattle ranges that can be seen in the distance beyond San Vicente, Cañuelas, and Moreno. These remote fields were of no use to him. He then moved the handle over the map until it was exactly at the corner of Buenos Aires, where he was standing underneath a lamppost. He looked at the time, he told me, because on the cutting edge of the reality he glimpsed, everything was a dizzying whirl. It was six minutes to six. His gaze was distracted for less than a second. This was enough time for the trident to contract and for the points of it to bury themselves, with incredible precision, in three specific places: the church in Olivos, alongside a railway named Borges; the Celebrities Corner in Chacarita cemetery; Ramón Francisco Flores's white mausoleum in Flores cemetery. That was the compass of chance that he had hope—"

End of the record(ing).

Cifuentes here continues his account of how Koenig decided on the locations where he would bury the copies. The Colonel, according to his friend, starts out in his office where he stands above the map of Buenos Aires and tries the trident out in various positions to see where it might point. At first its tines land nowhere of note, on empty space beyond the city's boundaries. But then he moves the handle of the trident to the corner of Buenos Aires—a corner that corresponds to the eastern edge of the city, along the Río de la Plata, given the location of the three cemeteries—where he stands beneath a lamppost within the map. Martínez here situates the Colonel within a reported and embedded narrative world (the recording/citation) in which he finds himself on the edge of the represented world before him. Martínez places Koenig within the narrative that awaits him as he begins to plot where he will bury the bodies. But he also confirms the impossibility that this future narrative, insomuch as it is directed and subsumed by the map, will be anything but tropological. For Martínez recalls here the map's inherent failure to ever function as more than trope that Borges reminds us of in his essay "Del Rigor en la ciencia" ("On Exactitude in Science") when he gives the Colonel a map to work out where he will bury Evita's simulacra. When Koenig uses it to plot the burial plots of these copies, he plans how to bury "the difference fiction" that protects the originary absence of Eva Perón's corpse within a trope made possible by pseudo-alchemy. The corpse and its copies, as well as the Colonel, are here well on their way to being lost to us: Koenig is trapped within a trope within which he seeks to enact the simulated burial of simulacra that are being used to minimize the threat of an originary simulation that covers up for the vacuity of the national body. The complications do not end here.

As soon as Cifuentes recounts Koenig's report that the trident contracts to reveal the ideal burial plots, the cassette cuts off. Martínez interrupts the story in the middle of the word *esperado* (hoped), which leads the reader to conclude that there is little hope for a successful end to the Colonel's project. The author goes on to note: "Fin de la ci(n)ta" such that we have reached the end of both the citation and the cassette. Martínez here cuts off Cifuentes, who is giving a secondhand account of Koenig's exploits, and reinstates himself as narrator. He leaves behind the embedded worlds of the map and of the tape and returns his reader to the primary narrative world, in which he goes on to tell the story of the Colonel's disastrous attempts to hide Eva Perón's body and his men's dangerous mission to bury the copies that will not be buried.

Martínez prefaces the preceding passage, however, with a parenthetical aside in which he reflects on his surprise at the extent to which the Argentine military has made use of the occult sciences. He tells us, however, that Koenig's cartographical exercise must have been influenced more by literature than the occult. He proposes to Cifuentes that the Colonel's map-reading operation shares uncanny similarities with Borges's short story "La muerte y la brújula" ("Death and the Compass"), but Cifuentes corrects him: "El ingenioso juego del detective Lönnrot en 'La muerte y la brújula' es un juego mortal, pero sólo sucede dentro de un texto. Lo que el Coronel tramó debía suceder en cambio fuera de la literatura, en una ciudad real por la que se desplazaría un cuerpo abrumadoramente real"[43] ("Detective Lönnrot's ingenious game in 'Death and the Compass' is a deadly one, but it takes place only within a text. What the Colonel was plotting was to happen, however, outside of literature, in a real city through which an overwhelmingly real body was to be transported"). Martínez here lays bare his own narrative strategy; he buries within a bit of autofiction a nod to Borges, whose work serves as a paradigm for the impossible cartographical operation he sets up in the novel. Yet even as he protects the reliability of his source in his own voice, he counters it when Cifuentes rejects the Colonel's application of the story. Martínez reveals and covers up his own use of Borges's story as a model for his own narrative. For, as Cifuentes points out, Lönnrot's game is a fatal one, but only in literature; the Colonel's plot would take place in a real city that would host a real body. Here Martínez folds the lived, and historical, world into an imagined real world that takes its own cues from literature in order to bury its simulated dead. The center does not hold here even as Cifuentes insists that the body to be emplotted is "overwhelmingly real."

Martínez's reference to Borges here is brief but telling. The comparison it provokes gives us clues that help parse his recursive worlds, but more importantly it provides insight into the theories of space and time that underpin the novel's emplotment and communicate, in a final analysis, the body as a site of ethics and resistance. In "Death and the Compass," as is well known, the detective Erik Lönnrot is murdered by his nemesis Red Scharlach in the labyrinth of a murder investigation in which the former gets trapped. Lönnrot tells Scharlach, who is about to kill the detective:

> —En su laberinto sobran tres líneas—dijo por fin. Yo sé de un laberinto griego que es una línea única, recta. En esa línea se han perdido tantos filósofos que bien puede perderse un mero detective. Scharlach, cuando en otro avatar usted me dé caza, finja (o cometa) un crimen en A, luego un segundo crimen en B, a 8 kilómetros de A, luego un tercer crimen en C, a 4 kilómetros de A y de B, a mitad de camino entre los dos. Aguárdeme después en D, a 2 kilómetros de A y de C, de nuevo a mitad de camino. Máteme en D, como ahora va a matarme en Triste-le-Roy.
> —Para la otra vez que lo mate—replicó Scharlach—le prometo ese laberinto, que consta de una sola línea recta y que es invisible, incesante.[44]

> "In your labyrinth there are three lines too many," he said at last. "I know of one Greek labyrinth which is a single straight line. Along that line so many philosophers have lost themselves that a mere detective might well do so, too. Scharlach, when in some other incarnation you hunt me, pretend to commit (or do commit) a crime at A, then a second crime at B, eight kilometers from A, then a third crime at C, four kilometers from A and B, half-way between the two. Wait for me afterwards at D, two kilometers from A and C, again halfway between both. Kill me at D, as you are now going to kill me at Triste-le-Roy."
> "The next time I kill you," replied Scharlach, "I promise you that labyrinth, consisting of a single line which is invisible and unceasing."

Lönnrot, returned at the end of the story to where he began, knows he is caught in his nemesis's trap but attempts a final escape. His last wish is that next time they meet, Scharlach kill him in the labyrinth that Borges cites as the most complicated of all: the single straight line. But as the detective describes it, he sets himself up to be Scharlach's eternal foe. For Zeno's Paradox ensures that they will be trapped in an infinite regress, the trajectory to their meeting point being continuously halved and their final destination always just out of reach.

What Martínez borrows from Borges here is the construction of a temporospatial labyrinth reduced to its most basic fundament: a single line of experience from which there is no escape. The author sets Koenig and the cadaver of Eva Perón on a similar trajectory: one that leads nowhere, but whose singular contours the two are doomed to follow. Martínez foregrounds this failed trajectory, as well as returns it to history, when he writes, "Lo que el Coronel *tramó* debía suceder en cambio fuera de la literatura" ("What the Colonel *was plotting* was to happen, however, outside of literature"). What Koenig plots—in a plan and on a map—is proper, Cifuentes tells Martínez, to the lived world but not to literature precisely because it cannot be emplotted. But the attempt to return the body to history fails as it meets the confines of the novel that narrates its resistance to the Colonel's burial plots. If the corpse's trajectory is here represented in the infinite regress of Borges's labyrinth, the fate of the copies are the "three lines too many" that the detective observes. They are failed leads that only serve to distract from identifying the location of the real corpse. At the end of the novel, Koenig returns to where he started; his belief that he had been in possession of the real body all along confirms that he will be forever trapped in the labyrinth into which Eva Perón's corpse disappears. Martínez uses Borges to illustrate the impossibility that he sets up over the course of the novel of ever definitively knowing where the body is located and what it contains. He here protects the body and the absences that it gives form to. In so doing, he affords that which has been historically excised, excluded, or denied a narrative agency to operate beyond the confines of traditional epistemological systems that might try to rein them in.

At the end of Cifuentes's recording, Martínez returns the reader to the first-level narrative, where the narrator recounts the Colonel's attempts to bury Evita's corpse and its copies. Arancibia, Fesquet, and Galarza come to Moori Koenig's office at the appointed time. The Colonel briefs them on the state of the corpse, explains that they will each be assigned a copy to bury, shows them on his map where they are to go that night, and emphasizes the strict secrecy of their mission. Each officer will be assigned four enlisted men, a noncommissioned officer, and a truck in order to carry out his task. None of the men will know each other; the enlisted men will be brought in from different provinces and discharged from the military the next morning. The Colonel has provided for every possibility, every calculable error or uncertainty, in order to ensure his plan work. Arancibia will bury his copy in Chacarita cemetery, Fesquet his in a newly dug flowerbed at the church in Olivos, and Galarza will take the third copy to the cemetery at Flores. The Colonel alone will be responsible for "ridding the country" of Eva Perón's body.

Major Arancibia starts off in the direction of Chacarita cemetery. But on the way he takes a small detour to stop the van, show the body to his sergeant, undress and abuse it. He finds that the body is missing the tip of its left ear and a part of the middle finger of its right hand. These are marks the Colonel had left on the real corpse in order to distinguish it from the others so that already the confusion about who is carrying Evita's real body, and where it is buried, begins. Arancibia goes on to bury his copy in Chacarita, under the name of María M. de Magaldi, just a few plots over from where Evita's first lover is buried. The watchman writes the name on the small, wooden cross that adorns the grave. Meanwhile, the nervous Fesquet buries his copy at the church in Olivos under the name María M. de Maestro. He is so relieved to have carried it off, however, that he lets his sergeant drive on the way home, therein disobeying the Colonel's orders and precipitating the trouble that ensues. Lastly, Galarza's exploits are more complicated and more public than he planned. He blows a tire out on the van on the way to the cemetery in Flores and when he gets there, the watchman will not bury the coffin without Galarza's signature and the dead person's name. Galarza tells him the dead man's name is NN, *non nominatus* or "no name," the name they give to bastards in the army, and also to the disappeared.

At the same time as the Colonel's men are burying their copies, Koenig's own efforts to store Evita's body are foiled. The building opposite the Waterworks where he had planned to leave her has caught fire, and he cannot gain access to the street. He consults her astrological profile for guidance and decides to take her to the east toward the river. He attempts to leave her parked at the docks of the naval station or on a ship, but is refused both. The Colonel then decides he will leave the corpse in the van that he will park next to the sidewalk outside Intelligence Services, where he can keep an eye on it. He drives in circles around the city, takes unnecessary detours on his way back to headquarters to thwart anyone who is following him, and then pulls up in front of the building only to find a row of lighted candles and flowers on the sidewalk, an altar presumably left by the Comando de la Venganza, who best him every time. His enemies have gotten to his impromptu destination before him.

Here Martínez traces for us the ways in which the Colonel falls victim to Zeno's Paradox. He imagines his mission as a straight shot but, like Lönnrot and Scharlach, will never catch up with his enemies. The straight line he envisions does not allow him to ever reach his destination—wherever that is—but it also does not provide for chance and redirection. Similarly to the ways in which the teleologically based conceptions of history that buttress all dictatorship actively work to mute or cancel out accident or happenstance, here the Colonel's plans to fulfill his historical purpose do not take into account the possibility that other factors or events may and do intervene. But the chance and redirection that history strives to mute, as Cifuentes knows, is what fiction turns into Ricoeur's "concordant discordance," perhaps a tensive unity, but still intelligible and cohesive. In this instance, the Colonel's repeated failures to bury the body prove the final logic of the whole novel: Evita Perón's embalmed corpse, and what it represents, resists straightforward narrative. The dead body requires of its narration obliquity, ways out, and also ways back in.

"Fue el azar," the Colonel would tell Cifuentes years later after he learns that the body he buried was not Eva Perón's corpse, "La realidad no es una línea recta sino un sistema de bifurcaciones. El mundo es un tejido de ignorancias" (Reality is not a straight line but a system of forking paths. The world is a fabric woven of unknown threads).[45] He falls here into another Borgesian trap, the same one that ensnares Stephen Albert in "El jardín de senderos que se bifurcan" ("The Garden of Forking Paths"). In this alternate labyrinth, the sinologist is killed by Ts'ui Pên, who strives to "imponerse un porvenir que sea irrevocable como el pasado" (impose upon himself a future as irrevocable as the past).[46] To be successful in his own atrocious task, to cheat what reads as chance but is really the rhizomatic logic of the corpse, Koenig has to imagine the future as an unchangeable past, which is to say, accept that history is static. This possibility is part of Borges's—if with a wink—refutation of time, but it also finds its expression in his rejection of the capacity of the map to accurately represent the world. Here the failures of the map are also the failures of emplotment. In "La muerte y la brújula," Lönnrot finds Scharlach waiting for him at Triste-le-Roy, his final destination that is also the missing point of the diamond-shaped map across which he has been tracking his enemy. In Martínez's rewriting of the story, Koenig plays the part of Lönnrot when he shows up at the Intelligence Services to find that his own enemy has beaten him there. But in his final revelation—that reality is a system of forking paths—he reveals that he has not learned much. His forking paths, which here recall the burial of the corpse's copies, lead nowhere. And Borges's metaphysical rhomb, here Koenig's pentagon, collapses into a straight line that allows for no escape and that corresponds, throughout the novel, to Benjamin's conception of history as "one single catastrophe."[47]

Martínez uses the map in *Santa Evita* both to give us the Borgesian philosophies of space and time that confirm Evita's corpse is the historical excess that will not be contained and to play with the capacity of dominant forms of discourse, such as two-dimensional cartography, to communicate what gets left out of or muted by historical record. The burial plot of the unburied dead, Martínez reveals, requires in the first instance alternate strategies of emplotment, such as those techniques of postmodern fiction might provide. But even these, insomuch as narrative emplotment always strives to communicate sense, causality and believability, fall short. Eva Perón's corpse is here in excess of emplotment. She is its embodied remainder in the same way that Argentina's disappeared evade, escape, and most importantly exceed representation. In building his novel out of recursive structures, characteristic hypo- and hyperdiegetic ontologies, a vast network of intertextual references and intermedial forms, and auto/biographical metafiction, Martínez affords the corpse a lot of narrative play. But in his adoption of Borges—buried within other failed metaphysical and cartographical operations—he confirms the infinite regress, and return, of Evita's corpse. It recedes, disappears, eludes or escapes us. But it also always comes back into view and reveals itself to have been there all along. As a burial plot, Martínez confirms, Evita Perón's body is the narrative remainder: the excess, the superabundant, and what remains.

Aesthetic Justice

Ten years before the publication of *Santa Evita*, we get a distant view of Evita in *La novela de Perón*. In a final tour around Madrid before he flies out for Argentina, Perón visits the sites that his wife visited during her tour of Spain in 1947; his memories of her are intercalated with excerpts of their life together from the memoir that López Rega is transcribing for him. Leaving aside the unreliability of this fictional memoir—despite its content having been published and commented upon in acclaimed biographies of Eva Perón—we here get a first glimpse of Evita. Martínez recounts the apocryphal story of how she met her husband—"Gracias por existir" (Thanks for existing) are words she never spoke to him[48]—and Perón gives us this description of his now long dead wife: "En su cuerpo esmirriado, de marfil, había más fósforo que carne. El que no sabía tocarlo se quemaba" (In her scrawny, ivory-colored body, there was more inflammable phosphorus than flesh. A man who didn't know how to handle her got burned).[49] He remembers her—and here he remembers her still alive—as more light than flesh, difficult to handle, "un sol líquido" (a liquid sun). Here, buried deep within heavily rewritten transcriptions of the memoirs of an aging man with a faulty memory, Martínez gives us an early look at the Eva Perón that already seems to occupy his imagination. She is fiery, fluid, rebellious. And too much.

Martínez builds on this image when he writes *Santa Evita*. He harnesses the possibility that she is reactive, incendiary, unmanageable, and excessive—phosphorus, the morning star that comes out too early and stays too long—such that she might represent in her excess what has been remaindered in Argentina's history. The corpse gives a place to Argentina's unexpressed fears, latent desires, and unfulfilled hopes as well as everything the country's recent governments worked to diminish, hide, excise, and deny from its history and national imaginary. In doing so, Martínez proves their gross error. For in the same way that Grosz identifies the improper, disordered, and broken Other as constitutive to the sovereign body, what official history has left out is also fundamental to the nation. Martínez proposes in his work that we look elsewhere for its traces, to fiction instead of to history, even if only to confirm the limits of its discursive capacity. Here he can propose the essential vacuity of Argentina's most well-known sovereign body as cipher, container, and site for all the other bodies violently and illegally excised from the country's history and then use the full force of that collective body both to wreak havoc and to tell a story. While some of that damage includes Martínez's concerted efforts to reveal the artifice of the archive, historical record, the map, or auto/biography, the greatest and most fruitful disruption comes in what he reveals about the limits of fiction. For in *Santa Evita*, he constructs a work that gives us a history of what the novel cannot contain or adequately represent. And by representing that which cannot be properly represented, he performs, if there is such a thing, a particular kind of aesthetic justice.

Diana Taylor reflects in *Disappearing Acts* on the difficulty of representing the disappeared. As disembodied images or ideas that enter and circulate in the public sphere, she writes, they function as "pure representation."[50] She goes on to consider the complexities of representing the disappeared in art and literature: "artists (and scholars) are left holding the bag of their signifiers. The signified, banished to some offstage or off-scene, lies beyond their realm of visibility. We have no access to the signified, who will forever prove inaccessible to representation."[51] The absent signifier, she concludes, cannot be represented. The concerns she articulates are crucial and will not be soon resolved. But I would ask, as I have done throughout this book, what happens when the absent, the disappeared, and the withheld appear to us not as subject but as form? Are we any better poised to see the signified here function as form, as a force of form, or a form in force?

Martínez allows us to consider these possibilities when he gives us the corpse of Eva Perón as a metonym that acts out and exerts pressure on his work's narrative emplotment. Here the historical absences that the body takes on are recast as agents of the novel's unfolding. They become the work of fiction: what it attends to, reinterprets, provokes. Martínez uses Evita's unburied body as a narrative mode of disappearance such that what cannot be represented—that absent signifier—takes up form in the novel and helps to shape it. In so doing, he confirms that what has been absented will not be easily emplaced or emplotted, does not conform to a straight narrative, and will not be either buried or forgotten. *Santa Evita* proposes that contiguity—the speaking otherwise that the metonym takes on and the new literary spaces and historical imagination it provides for—is a form of resistance and the basis for a new kind of community. Through it, what cannot represent itself takes shape before us and points us past the limits of fiction to the future. Martínez writes:

> Fictions about history reconstruct stories, oppose power and, at the same time, point the way ahead. . . . One of the most original aspects of historical fiction is its attempt to recuperate a community's myths, without invalidating or idealizing them, but by acknowledging them as tradition, as a force that has left its sediments in the collective imagination. Every myth ultimately expresses communal desire. And nothing so clearly belongs to the future as desire. . . . Fiction about history are writings about the future.[52]

In *Santa Evita*, Martínez acknowledges the myth, communal desire, and imagination that accumulated for decades around Eva Perón's dead body. But he also suggests that these are themselves forms of absence that cannot give way to future historical possibilities without also making space for what they have silenced, left out, and absented. Martínez assigns this task to Evita's corpse, where she becomes placeholder, at the limits of the literary, for a coming community.

Conclusion

The Disappearance of Literature

This book begins with the nautical coordinates that mark the location of Claudia Fontes's *Reconstrucción del retrato de Pablo Míguez*, seventy meters from the northern Buenos Aires shoreline amid the gray and turbulent waters of the Río de la Plata. Here Pablo Míguez is at times more visible than at others. Sometimes the surface of his reconstructed body so perfectly reflects the color of the river's water that he disappears from view, vanished for a moment into the refracting prism of the natural world around him. Pablo Míguez's disappearance on the horizon is caused by the conditions that surround him and the perspective from which we view him. That he comes in and out of sight serves as a dynamic reminder that the disappeared remain even in those lapses when we cannot see them, making Fontes's reconstruction among the most eloquent memorials to the victims of the Argentine dictatorship erected in Buenos Aires's Parque de la Memoria. But this movement rooted in fixity also reminds us that form, structure, and technique are always present, even when not wholly visible, and that they actively work to shape memory, history, and how we see.

I have sought, in the preceding chapters, to elucidate how disappearance functions as a fundamental literary device, mode, and preoccupation in a specific corpus of Argentine fiction that emerges in tandem with the use of systematically enforced disappearance as a mechanism of state terror. Like Fontes's statue, these tools and strategies appear and disappear, often according to what changes in the text occur around them or how, as readers, we engage with the work. I have aimed to get as close as possible to these narrative techniques and forms, to show how we might read them at work in the text as well as decipher their still latent potential, and to offer up these instantiations of disappearance as critical catalysts for the production of new historical knowledge in the face of state terror and its insidious sociocultural legacies. In their dynamic interpellation of a careful reader, capacity to house encoded patterns in and between texts, and reformulation of how we organize and access knowledge, the narrative modes of disappearance at work in the fiction of Walsh, Cortázar, and Martínez also function as a crucial ethical commons for the work of witnessing, storytelling, and imagination required to act in a time of catastrophe and in rebuilding a social infrastructure devastated by the state. Modes of disappearance take up space, open up space, and build new spaces on the page that, read together and over time, become a narrative common place defined by new forms of cognitive and imaginative engagement itself transferable to other spheres of aesthetic, political, and judicial action. The space of disappearance in the form of fiction compels not only empathy—this one of the fundamental tasks of fiction—but also action, and future calls to action, in the lived world.

Disappearance, signaled in the first place by dissimulation, takes shape in our literary corpus as doubling and displacement, suspension, and an embodied superabundant. In each of these instances, what is missing, forcibly expelled, suspended, and excised appears in the narrative fabric of the novel as both the raw material of the work and as a broker of its organization. In this way, and in these given forms, disappearance is at once the story being told and the agent of its telling. It gives us, in Cortázar's *Fantomas*, two worlds in order to return us to one in which catastrophe might disappear, if only we read it otherwise, on our historical horizon. It shows up in *La novela de Perón* as a form of suspension that allows Martínez to rewrite what we know of Perón, certainly, but more importantly proffers abeyance, the withheld, and the removed as spaces or catalysts capable of offering up alternative historical possibilities. And in *Santa Evita*, if in its most visible metonymic incarnation, disappearance takes shape in the remaindered body of Eva Perón wherein what is left out or left over takes over a historical imaginary that resists emplacement or emplotment, and in so doing troubles the capacities of both memorialization and fiction. Read together, and subsequent to Walsh's narrative world where art is the necessary means and ends of disappearance, these three novels confirm the mode of disappearance—how it appears, takes form or place in literature—as fiction's own object. They also give us the moving parts of a history of narrative disappearance that comes together to take up its own space in Latin American literary history. But they also signal, well before we get to the new millennium, a history of aesthetic engagement in which, in addition to functioning as crucial indexes of a particular political reality, Argentina's modes of disappearance are symptom and product of a larger disappearance of literature on the horizon.

The work of narrative does not here find its necessary end in fiction. It actualizes rather the possibility, put forth by Maurice Blanchot already in the 1950s, that literature's future belongs to disappearance. When asked about the future of literature and its contemporary tendencies, Blanchot identifies disappearance as a surprising, and surprisingly easy, answer to the question. In his estimation, this receding, vanishing, or dissolution is the moment at which literature becomes most properly art by moving beyond itself to speak *otherwise*. The ways in which the modes of disappearance I identify in this book speak or mean otherwise have been a critical part of working out how they provide for new historical possibilities; read through Blanchot, these become defining characteristics of the literary. Here at the end of this book—both as conclusion to this study and as placeholder that looks forward to future work on the materialization of disappearance—I examine the aesthetic and ethical stakes of Blanchot's disappearance of literature, particularly as it takes shape as a defining characteristic of the literary on either side of the new millennium. The modes of disappearance in late twentieth-century Argentine fiction, and the spaces and forms of knowledge they stake a claim to, catalyze, most immediately, the political and the historical. But they also prepare us to engage with the larger disappearance of literature as a dynamic, generative, and wholly receptive common place of aesthetic production that allows for new ways of thinking about art—and if obliquely, also the human—and what these might communicate and how.

In his short essays "The Disappearance of Literature" and "Death of the Last Writer," Blanchot offers up evidence of a coming disappearance of literature in a series of symptoms that describe how we think about art, its production, and its value in the twentieth century. Each of these symptoms, surely the product of a specific Western cultural moment trying to find its footing in the aftermath of the trauma of the Second World War, reveal one of two possibilities that trouble our human engagement with art. Art either escapes us, insomuch as it communicates something that we cannot grasp, or we turn away from what it most wants to tell us. Adorno's maxim about the barbarism of writing poetry after Auschwitz might serve as ready example in each case, but Blanchot is concerned rather with the more general and never satiated striving of literature to enunciate or communicate something essential. He notes that where art is necessarily the representation of some "concern that demands expression in work,"[1] artists as distinct in their aims as Valéry and Kafka affirm their "entire work is only an exercise." In this proposition that a life's work is only an attempt and always unfinished, the work of art slips out of grasp. Not unrelatedly, he writes, we suffer from a proliferation of mass-produced texts or documents that "ignore any literary intention" that should alert us, in relief, to what literature wants most to say. In a moment that recalls, if avant la lettre, the status of the text in the coming digital world, Blanchot asks, "This anonymous, authorless language, which does not take the form of books, which soon disappears and wants to disappear, couldn't it be alerting us to something important, about which what we call literature also wants to speak?"[2] Here the daily tide of text and texts that envelops us—in Blanchot's moment "documents or reports"[3] but in our contemporary moment the twenty-four-hour news cycle, the internet's billion-plus web pages, advertising tucked into every possible corner of our lives—performs brazenly and wantonly its own disappearance and is indeed designed to dissipate so that it might immediately reappear again in some new configuration of itself. Perhaps, observes Blanchot, this authorless language signals some parallel striving in literature, a move toward a place where "only impersonal neutrality seems to speak," a "non-literature"[4] where inspiration reveals itself to us, if only fleetingly, in its wholeness. The movement seems to be the thing here in Blanchot for whom disappearance is always an active becoming, never a static condition or end point. Where literature works to shed what it aims to narrate or tell—what Benjamin calls its "transmitting function"[5]—it moves toward the most properly literary. What literature most expressly aims to communicate, Blanchot proposes after Benjamin, is opposed to what we understand as literature, "a late word, a word without honor, which is helpful mostly just to reference books," a phenomenon that emerges to reveal an ongoing preoccupation with something "essential"—but not essentialist—that escapes, or is concealed by, the genres and literatures of our age.

Each of these instances that Blanchot cites understands the literary by way of what it is not or can never be, at first glance a negative theology of sorts, but in the end rather a productive paraontology—here closely aligned with the structure of Agamben's future thought on both text and the human—that asks us to think beyond literature in order to get to the literary. Blanchot writes, "what is called into question is perhaps literature, but not as a definite, certain reality, an ensemble of forms, or even a mode of perceptible activity: rather as what is not discovered, is not verified, and cannot be directly justified, to which we come close only by turning away from it, which we grasp only when we go beyond it, through a quest that must not be preoccupied with literature . . ."[6] This *thinking beyond* is not so much a slippage as the enacting of obliquity or a view that allows us to see before us two things at once, one directly and one out of the corner of our eye. To get at what is most literary, and what the literary is capable of, we need to look just a little displacedly at or how we think literature. This oblique view allows the literary to come into focus, even if that focus means that literature escapes us in the meantime. This doubled vision is the same mode of looking that enables us, as I work out in chapter 2 of this book, to see catastrophe on the horizon or, like Benjamin's Angelus Novus, at our feet. Blanchot's literature is not Cortázar's historical catastrophe—although perhaps the historical crisis disappears into the present in not unsimilar ways to Blanchot's coming book—but they each require we read for obliquity. What we understand to be both literary and a historical present are defined by looking a little bit off, askance, elsewhere. Blanchot's proposition is in the end itself catastrophic, in the most original sense of the word: it signals an overturning, a sudden end, a reversal of what is expected where "non-literature" takes the place of, and then becomes, the literary and a future that gives way to art.

This coming catastrophe, the book to come, is a historical affair. In both structure and in what it promises, it functions as a historical question and marker that, read after the fact, only raises the stakes of what Argentina's narrative modes of disappearance might communicate to us about history, absence, and the experience of literature. Blanchot writes:

> Even "the absence of time" toward which the literary experience leads us is hardly the region of the timeless, and if by the work of art we are reminded of the weakening of an actual initiative (a new and unstable appearance of the fact of existing), this beginning speaks to us in the intimacy of history, in a way that perhaps gives a chance to the initial historical possibilities. All these problems are obscure.[7]

The instantiation of writing, or what writing instantiates, is a moment with the potential to shape history, or in Blanchot's vision, what the future might bring. Writing is itself the event that becomes historical because it marks human time. Where disappearance is written already into writing, as we find in contemporary works of Argentine fiction, it announces or enacts its own future history, in this case both literary and political, or more specifically, the political function of the literary. If Rilke, Hölderlin, and Char each manifested in their work a "form of experienced time [*durée*] very different from the time that simple historical analysis grasps,"[8] this experience of time that exceeds or goes beyond becomes a kind of Benjaminian "*weak messianic power to which the past has a claim.*"[9] Here unrealized or unfinished potential becomes a phenomenon proper to a particular moment in time and also a marker of historical time insomuch as what is left undone, or still to come, comes to define how we understand our past, and as Koselleck tells us in his own claims to a nontotalizing totality of historical time, also our present. Literature is evidence of a present absence that will alter the future and the "absence of time" that literature allows us to enter into—this form of experienced time one of the surest markers that literature is happening or happening to us—is not in Blanchot's formulation a nonhistorical event. To the contrary, the instantiation of the literary, the attempt, the fact of its undertaking even where it does not arrive, crafts already human time, event, and action. Literature's earliest moment is the possibility of expression that might help us to make sense of where we are in time and how we are embedded in it. All literature, whatever its future, is in its inception a now-time, a *Jetztzeit*, the time of innervation and action that marks—signals the space of and measures—the possibility of the historical moment experienced as an instant freed from a continuum of time. For Blanchot, the literary makes this version of the historical possible, where both are marked by some opening outward whose future does not come but that nevertheless allows us to measure where we have been. The narrative devices and modes of disappearance from which Walsh, Cortázar, and Martínez craft their works actualize, if on a much smaller scale, the historical questions inherent to Blanchot's disappearance of literature: they enact on the page writing's dissolution and history's craft, both of which exert pressure on the lived present by requiring that a reading public come to terms with this productive and fundamental irreconciliation.

In Blanchot's estimation, "non-literature" is the goal of each book, even as "every single book determines absolutely what literature is."[10] Every book necessarily fails or falls short in what it wants to achieve or communicate, although not every work faces this catastrophe—the overturning or sudden end of the aesthetic that it enacts—head on. Because "a work can never take as its subject the question that sustains it,"[11] literature enacts a necessary looking away, or looking otherwise, that makes the literary possible. Blanchot insists: "Never could a painting even begin if it set out to make painting visible. It is possible that every writer feels called to answer alone, through his own ignorance, for literature, for its future, which is not only a historical question but, through history, the movement by which, while necessarily 'going' outside of itself, literature nonetheless tries to 'come' to itself, to what it essentially is."[12] Literature's attempt to speak itself into being over and over, while also activating its own historical stance or capacity, is the movement that points us to the literary. This initial enunciation and the possibilities that it signals are the realm of the literary, which remains a future moment visible only, as we have seen, by looking indirectly. The writer might, "at the very most, through his work, give an *indirect* answer" to the question that sustains the literary. This question, Blanchot concludes, is the "work of which [the writer] is never master, never certain, which does not want to answer to anything but itself and which makes art present only there where it hides itself and disappears."[13] Every work of literature, which is to say, the work of literature, proffers an indirect or oblique answer to both the quest of the artist and the question that Blanchot responds to, with a hint of exhaustion, in his brief essays: "Where is literature going?" In every instance the answer is toward disappearance, which is also to say, "toward itself."[14] Disappearance is in Blanchot's formulation a precondition of the literary, its future, and the history that it accounts for that in its turn finds its limits in the impossibility of speaking anything beyond itself.

The work of fiction that I have been concerned with throughout this book offers up disappearance as a mode of representation at the same time that it gives us representation, in its very smallest parts, as a mode of disappearance. In both instances, as it does in Blanchot's formulation, disappearance holds. It emerges in specific, repeatable, and transferable forms that hold up throughout and across texts such that even as representation threatens to dissolve, come undone, or recede, we can witness the process take shape and see what it leaves in its stead. And from these forms of disappearance, in a process of inverse generation, are constructed whole works of fiction that signal the future state of literature, wherein what is most properly literary speaks where literature cannot. This textual question, however, is a wholly human affair. Where the human need to create performs the disappearance of its own evidence, we are left still with the initial striving that shapes our world and our experience of that world before it begins to recede before us. The work of disappearance that Blanchot locates at the core of the literary thus defines both the human and the text and indeed cannot understand one without the other. The coming disappearance that he observes is in the end his optimism that literature will speak for itself and in so doing represent what is most fully, properly, and rightfully human. Disappearance is here the force of form, our literary future, and the promise of the human on the page and beyond.

The modes of disappearance at work in Walsh, Cortázar, and Martínez also attend to the demands of both the textual and the human. Walsh gives us disappearance as a crucial hinge to knowledge production, Cortázar shows us what larger crimes against humanity disappearance signals on the horizon, and Martínez offers it up as a tool for constructing counterhistories and as a memorial container. In each of these endeavors, the relationship between the text and the human is porous, so that one generates the other, and what we know of it. Disappearance here binds the text to the human, even as it also returns each to its own in a radically futural movement forward that we arrive at by understanding literature otherwise. The works of fiction brought together in this book offer up new stakes for this optics of obliquity: locating the points of convergence between the literary and the human that emerge when we read beyond, at the limits of text and form, gives us a roadmap for moving through and beyond the consequences of state terror to a place where disappearance might take on new valences in new contexts. The community of forms that doubling and displacement, suspension, and the embodied remainder make up in their juxtaposition, overlap, intersection, and collective striving toward shared aesthetico-ethical aims provides for this space of disappearance. It emerges, finally, as the title of this book signals, as a narrative commons in the last quarter of the twentieth century but continues to function still decades later as fundament to future narrative experimentation that works with absence as a raw material of fiction and as one of its most ethical possible articulations.

The modes of disappearance at work in Walsh, Cortázar, and Martínez model, individually and collectively, a community of forms and the possibility of community that these forms engender. They demonstrate the ways in which blank spaces, interstice, and belonging apart are not instantiations of emptiness, devoid of purchase or power, but rather generate their own system of meaning within a collective space that exerts pressure on and articulates the possibility of that collective. Where the possibility of belonging, and thus community, is an appearing together, that appearance, exposition, or coming forward is predicated on or depends on these spaces and what they aim to communicate. The space of disappearance—that space where disappearance manifests and the forms it takes—enacts and activates its own kind of coming forward, that first step of community, in which what is not expressly manifest is a constitutive part of being-with. It bears out in form and function the dynamic and singular plurality—whose import redoubles in the face of state terror—of Rancière's "Separés, on est ensemble," as well as other late twentieth-century conceptions of community in which the negated, excised, or excluded are galvanized as fundamental not to the construction of an inviolate whole but a meaningful coming or belonging together.[15] Here doubling and displacement, suspension, and the embodied remainder model modes of belonging such that disappearance does not accomplish excision from a political or social community but rather, in alignment with Arendt and Lyotard, signals its own foundation. These literary modes at work in fiction allow us to see the excised at work where, if the novel functions as a motivator and barometer of democracy, these become useful corollaries—examples that we can map and study on the page—to vital forms of belonging otherwise. Here the novel undoes the double-bind of belonging, takes apart the distinction between inside/outside, interiority/exteriority, inclusion/exclusion, to reveal the spaces of disappearance as the free and raw material of both fiction and community at the literary limits contemplated by Blanchot.

While I have studied in each chapter what I perceive to be the principal narrative tool or mode in each of the preceding novels, these appear together—where this juxtaposition and conjoining is its own ethical stance—across late twentieth-century Argentine literature in diverse and flexible combination. So doubling works, for example, in tandem with suspension, displacement with embodiment, and the remainder with dissimulation, and so on in every possible merger. That they exert pressure on each other in different ways means the demands they make upon the reading process and the ways the novel intersects with political and cultural history are also varied and mutable. The possibility, however, that they show up together in various combination—giving us, for example, the reader's suspension between diegetic worlds in *Fantomas*, Perón's simulated and dissimulated political double in *La novela de Perón*, the continuous displacement of Evita's corpse in *Santa Evita*—confirms that while these modes each perform specific tropic or rhetorical functions, together they comprise a community of forms. And while the forms of stories, as McClennen and Slaughter emphasize, "enable forms of thoughts, forms of commitment, forms of being, and forms of justice,"[16] these forms are not limited to literary format or genre but also include the rhetorical and tropic forms *within* stories that have, of course, been the focus of this book. Whatever work in the lived world story forms accomplish, the forms that shape them from the inside out—these necessarily bound up with plot and content—are tasked with similar responsibilities or felicities. Doubling and displacement, suspension, and embodiment are a community of forms but also a means of belonging, being, and acting in the world that bear out the fundament of community.

In this way—wherein literature explicates the human world that returns again to literature—they also open up in the novel a mode and space of coming together that serves as a ballast for future narrative that might take on the difficult work of disappearance.

The modes and forms of disappearance come together to function as a narrative commons, a shared space built out of the capacity of disappearance to tell a story, build new worlds, and provide for new structures of knowledge. This site is variously a repository, reference point, and point of departure for new works of literature that draft disappearance as a fundamental literary device or narrative strategy, but also for a more general understanding of the work disappearance is capable of undertaking and taking on. This space of disappearance teaches us that what is absent, missing, gone, or silenced *takes form* and is an active and dynamic agent in reforming both fictional and lived worlds; more than a remainder or a memory, disappearance is, as I have argued, rather constitutive to what we know of the modern world and how we know it. Neither the political nor ethical ramifications of what narrative disappearance might enact have lessened as the decades beyond the end of Argentina's last military dictatorship advance. To the contrary. The literary commons that disappearance here provides for serves, on both sides of the millennial marker, as an important model of constellation, contingency, entanglement, simultaneity, interruption, suspension, instability, and obliquity. Attending to how disappearance functions and what it makes possible in the case of Argentina also prepares us to better engage with what is, for the time being, a lived world still defined by versions of these states or conditions. As this book goes to print, for example, the refugee crisis worsens worldwide, children separated from their families by order of law languish in indefinite detention in pens at the United States border, our northern ice sheets lose 12.5 billion tons of ice in a single day, and Amazonia burns; the commons this book identifies is a collective space that opens up to global writers confronted with the task of responding to new and various forms of disappearance and reading publics taxed with understanding and making space for the difficult stories and worlds they represent.

In the meantime, other works of Argentine fiction contemporary to the ones this book studies also participate in this narrative commons. These include, among others, Ricardo Piglia's novels—whose absence from this present study leaves its own gap that begs attention from future scholarship—*Respiración artificial* (1980) and *La ciudad ausente* (1992), Juan José Saer's *Nadie nada nunca* (1980), Tununa Mercado's *En estado de memoria* (1990), and Liliana Heker's *El fin de la historia* (1996). These works also deploy disappearance as narrative device or end and investigate its aesthetic and political limits, these last necessarily changing shape as the close of the century comes closer into sight. Those written after Argentina's return to democracy in 1983 also exemplify more recent notions of the limits of the literary, such as Idelber Avelar's proposition that "literature's postdictatorial mourning already implies mourning for the literary." Here the fiction of postdictatorship struggles against, and finally assimilates, the possibility that "writing is no longer possible and that writing's only remaining task is to account for that impossibility."[17] It becomes record and custodian of literature's central aporia or blind spot, wherein the human need for expression—here Blanchot's literary attempt, enunciation, instantiation—eclipses the success or fidelity of that expression, functioning in its striving in the face of this knowledge as an ethical proposition.

The spaces of disappearance negotiated throughout this book have been those opened up by the work Argentine fiction undertakes at a particular moment in time. But this task of world-building in the face or in the aftermath of a systematic program of enforced disappearance is also shared both by late twentieth-century narrative from Argentina's neighboring Chile and Uruguay—each beset by their own long legacies of authoritarian rule—and the more recent narrative projects undertaken by younger first and second generations of authors who came of age or were born during their respective countries' dictatorships. In Argentina, the aesthetic and political legacies of disappearance continue to appear in works of this first generation of authors, including César Aira's *Los fantasmas* (1990)—and here Aira serves as a bridge between this new generation and its precursors—Elsa Osorio's *A veinte años, Luz* (1998), Sergio Chejfec's *Los planetas* (1999), and Alan Pauls's pointed *El pasado* (2003) and his trilogy of *Historias* (2007–2013). The newest generation of fiction by Argentine writers has often turned its attention to other, more immediate concerns: coming of age during economic crisis; the destructive force of globalization both at home and abroad; transnational movement and identity; new dystopic or fantastic forms; and if on a less expansive scale, making sense of family, the everyday, the mundane, and the interior complexities of our smaller lived worlds. What is not or no longer present seems to remain, however, if reimagined or reinvented, an active narrative agent. For there is a sense that cuts through much of this work of the necessity of escape or at least its attempt, of conversations or reflections that obscure what is most immediate, of the difficulty of building a life or knowing a world made out of moving parts secured to a receding or vanishing fundament. There is a future in which Argentine literature might escape the shadow of its historical past, but that future has not yet arrived. It is difficult to read the work of this most contemporary generation without finding ways in which its fiction is still informed by the modes of narrative that first tried to make sense of Argentina's most recent past. There is also, among this generation of writers—the last to be born into the dictatorship—those who are pointedly engaged in dealing with the events of the dictatorship, the legacies of disappearance, and the facts of a past still under construction in a way that earlier generations, still living the immediate consequences of a state of terror, were not quite able to. Andrés Neumann's *Una vez argentina* (2003); Félix Bruzzone's *Los topos* (2008) or his collection of short stories, *76* (2013); and Raquel Robles's *Pequeños combatientes* (2013), for example, each offer up direct representations of the dictatorship in works where disappearance is fully formed—or as fully as it might be—as a site of inquiry and narrative catalyst.

The narrative commons that the space of disappearance provides for will expand to meet the narrative needs of a public still engaged in making sense of the legacies of Argentina's military dictatorship and its systematic program of enforced disappearance. Where Walsh served as necessary precursor to Cortázar and Martínez and then these in their turn to newer generations of fiction writers in the Southern Cone, the modes of disappearance that these first enact on the page make space for this commons that houses the diverse and urgent attempts to see and attend to what is before us even when it is gone. This narrative commons is a space to which fiction, its authors, and its readers might return as they need to make sense of how disappearance works upon both the text and the human. It is a radically futural space, one still very much coming together, that takes us past both literature and the human in order that we might return to what is most proper—most our own, most right, most just, most fitting, most becoming—to each. The space of disappearance is, in the end, the common place that survives—open, dynamic, evolving, and inclusive—amid the enduring ruins of state terror.

Notes

Introduction

1. Claudia Fontes, "Reconstruction of the Portrait of Pablo Míguez," n.d., accessed 18 March 2018, http://claudiafontes.com/project/reconstruction-of-the-portrait-of-pablo-miguez/.

2. Fontes, "Reconstruction." For more on Fontes's sculpture, which took her from 1999 to 2010 to plan, build, and emplace, see the artist's statement on her website at http://claudiafontes.com. This statement accompanied her 1999 application to the international competition for artwork to be included in the Parque de la Memoria that also houses the Monumento de las Víctimas del Terrorismo de Estado. She here describes her project: "Este es mi proyecto: nominal, explícito, particular, figurativo, descriptivo, personalizado, oportuno y puntual, fechado, anclado a una hora y lugar, y es en ese metro cuadrado de río donde puede adquirir significado. Participo en este concurso con este proyecto porque anhelo que al recordar que el día 12 de mayo de 1977 a las 3 de la mañana Pablo Míguez, de catorce años de edad, fue privado de su libertad y de su futuro, se mantenga en pie la verdad irreductible de que por lo menos esta tremenda injusticia sí tuvo y sigue teniendo lugar. Participo porque quisiera que nadie se atreviera a desvirtuarlo." Fontes offers up an English translation of the proposal on her website, as well as detailed and photographed descriptions of the process of performing the reconstruction of Pablo Míguez and its placement in the Río de la Plata. For more on the life and death of Míguez, see Alejandra Dandan, "No se sabe nada de lo que pasó con Pablo," *Página/12*, 11 October 2010, accessed 18 March 2018, https://www.pagina12.com.ar/diario/elpais/1-154722-2010-10-11.html. For an analysis of Fontes's sculpture as a memorial object, see Bridget V. Franco, "Floating Statues and Streams of Consciousness: Memory Work in Argentina's Río de la Plata and Río Salí," in *Written in the Water: The Image of the River in Latin/o American Literature*, ed. Jeanie Murphy and Elizabeth G. Rivero (Lanham, MD: Lexington Books, 2018), 35–54. For more on the planning of the Parque de la Memoria, see Andreas Huyssen, "Memory

Sites in an Expanded Field: The Memory Park in Buenos Aires," in *Present Pasts: Urban Palimpsests and the Politics of Memory* (Stanford: Stanford University Press, 2003), 94–109.

    3. Uki Goñi, "Blaming the Victims: Dictator Denialism Is on the Rise in Argentina," *The Guardian*, 29 August 2016, accessed 3 October 2016, https://www.theguardian.com/world/2016/aug/29/argentina-denial-dirty-war-genocide-mauricio-macri.

    4. Macri's refusal to recognize the victims of state terror is just one symptom of a larger conservative platform that aims to vacate the history of Argentina's military dictatorships and curtail efforts to bring those responsible to justice. Shortly after taking office at the end of 2015, he closed down the government's human rights websites and slashed the national budget for human rights programs. Since then, the number of federal convictions for gross human rights abuses have fallen sharply; petitions granted to convicted repressors for house arrest instead of prison time, as well as for treatment in military hospitals instead of prison hospitals, are rising steadily; and he repeatedly appears in public with known repressors and their families. These actions fulfill Macri's promise in 2014, while still mayor of Buenos Aires, to put a stop to "el curro de los Derechos Humanos" (the work of Human Rights). See https://www.eldestapeweb.com/todos-los-retrocesos-las-politicas-derechos-humanos-que-asumio-macri-n19820; https://www.perfil.com/noticias/politica/las-medidas-pro-contra-el-curro-de-los-derechos-humanos.phtml; and https://www.lanacion.com.ar/1750419-mauricio-macri-conmigo-se-acaban-los-curros-en-derechos-humanos.

    5. For more on the history of the dictatorship and its aftermath, see David Rock, *Argentina, 1516–1987: From Spanish Colonization to Alfonsín* (Berkeley: University of California Press, 1987); Iain Guest, *Behind the Disappearances: Argentina's Dirty War Against Human Rights and the United Nations* (Philadelphia: University of Pennsylvania Press, 1990); Horacio Verbitsky, *El vuelo* (Buenos Aires: Planeta, 1995); Marguerite Feitlowitz, *A Lexicon of Terror: Argentina and the Legacies of Torture* (New York: Oxford University Press, 1998); and Susana Kaiser, *Postmemories of Terror: A New Generation Copes with the Legacy of the "Dirty War"* (New York: Palgrave Macmillan, 2005). Relevant works of testimonial literature include Alicia Partnoy, *The Little School: Tales of Disappearance and Survival*, trans. Alicia Partnoy et al. (San Francisco: Cleis Press, 1986); Eric Stener Carlson, *I Remember Julia: Voices of the Disappeared* (Philadelphia: Temple University Press, 1996); Jacobo Timerman, *Prisoner without a Name, Cell without a Number*, trans. Toby Talbot (Madison: University of Wisconsin Press, 2002); and Mario Villani and Fernando Reati, *Desaparecido: Memorias de un cautiverio. Club Atlético, El Banco, El Olimpo, Pozo de Quilmes, y ESMA* (Buenos Aires: Editorial Biblos, 2011). Films and documentaries that elucidate the years of the dictatorship and the legacies of disappearance include *La historia oficial*, dir. Luis Puenzo (Port Washington, NY: Koch Lorber Films, 1985); *La noche de los lápices*, dir. Héctor Olivera (New York: Latin American Video Archives, 1986); *Buenos Aires vice-versa*, dir. Alejandro Agresti (Buenos Aires: SBP, 1996); *Garaje olimpo*, dir. Marco Bechis (México D.F.: Zima Entertainment, 1999);

Botín de guerra, dir. David Blaustein (Buenos Aires: Cinemateca, 2000); *Cautiva*, dir. Gastón Biraben (Buenos Aires: Primer Plano Film Group, 2003); *Our Disappeared/Nuestros desaparecidos*, dir. Juan Mandelbaum (Newburgh: New Day Films, 2008); *El secreto de sus ojos*, dir. Juan José Campanella (Buenos Aires: Distribution Company, 2009); and Jonathan Perel's *El predio* and *Los murales*, released at the 2010 and 2011 Buenos Aires Film Festival.

6. For more on the history of Argentina's torture and detention centers, see *Nunca Más: Informe de la Comisión Nacional sobre la Desaparición de Personas* (Buenos Aires: EUDEBA, 1984); Munú Actis et al., *Ese infierno: Conversaciones de cinco mujeres sobrevivientes de la ESMA* (Buenos Aires: Editorial Sudamericana, 2001); Pilar Calveiro, *Poder y Desaparición: Los campos de concentración en Argentina* (Buenos Aires: Ediciones Colihue, 2001); Marcelo Brodsky, *Memoria en construcción: El debate sobre la ESMA* (Buenos Aires: La marca editora, 2005); Susana Draper, *Afterlives of Confinement: Spatial Transitions in Postdictatorship Latin America* (Pittsburgh: University of Pittsburgh Press, 2012); and Karen Elizabeth Bishop, "The Architectural History of Disappearance: Rebuilding Memory Sites in the Southern Cone," *Journal of the Society of Architectural Historians* 73, no. 4 (December 2014): 556–578.

7. Feitlowitz, *A Lexicon of Terror*, 6. Feitlowitz specifies further: "Over the entire decade of the 1970s, the leftist groups carried out a total of 697 assassinations, killing 400 policemen, 143 members of the military, and 54 civilians, mostly industrialists."

8. Feitlowitz, *A Lexicon of Terror*, 36.

9. See Feitlowitz, *A Lexicon of Terror*; David M. K. Sheinin, *Consent of the Damned: Ordinary Argentinians in the Dirty War* (Gainesville: University of Florida Press, 2012).

10. See Feitlowitz, *A Lexicon of Terror*, particularly chapter 3; Calveiro, *Poder y Desaparición*; and Paul Ryan Katz, "A New 'Normal': Political Complicity, Exclusionary Violence and the Delegation of Argentine Jewish Associations during the Argentine Dirty War," *The International Journal of Transitional Justice* 5, no. 3 (November 2011): 366–389.

11. Diana Taylor, *Disappearing Acts: Spectacles of Gender and Nationalism in Argentina's "Dirty War"* (Durham, NC: Duke University Press, 1998), 123–124. For an earlier description of "perceticide," see Juan Carlos Kusnetzoff, "Renegación, desmentida, desaparición y percepticido como técnicas psicopáticas de la salvación de la patria (Una visión psicoanalítica del informe de la CONADEP)," *Psicoanálisis, represión, política*, ed. Oscar Abudara et al. (Buenos Aires: Ediciones Kargieman, 1986), 95–114.

12. Taylor, *Disappearing Acts*, 119.

13. Taylor, *Disappearing Acts*, 123.

14. Feitlowitz, *A Lexicon of Terror*, 13.

15. Feitlowitz, *A Lexicon of Terror*, 40. "To those who *disappeared themselves* [we say] return, show your face if your conscience permits." Emphasis in the original.

16. Taylor, *Disappearing Acts*, 148. Emphasis in the original. Camps quoted in interview on the junta's practice of trafficking the babies of alleged subversives in Jo Fisher, *Mothers of the Disappeared* (Boston: South End Press, 1989), 102.

17. Judith Butler, *Frames of War: When Is Life Grievable?* (New York: Verso, 2009), 14. Here Butler builds on her previous study, *Precarious Life: The Powers of Mourning and Violence* (New York: Verso, 2004).

18. For more on the societal impact of the state-sanctioned denial of death, see Annette H. Levine, *Cry For Me, Argentina: The Performance of Trauma in the Short Narratives of Aída Bortnik, Griselda Gambaro, and Tununa Mercado* (Madison, NJ: Fairleigh Dickinson University Press, 2008), 18–19; and Fernando Reati, *Nombrar lo innombrable: Violencia política y representación literaria en la novela argentina, 1975–1985* (Buenos Aires: Editorial Legasa, 1992), 26. Levine's and Reati's larger studies offer up critical readings of Argentine narrative in the dictatorship and postdictatorship.

19. See Angus Fletcher, *Allegory: The Theory of a Symbolic Mode* (Princeton: Princeton University Press, 1964). Avelar's incisive study on mourning in postdictatorial Latin American fiction also does important work on the significance of allegory in late twentieth-century literature of the Southern Cone. See Idelber Avelar, *The Untimely Present: Postdictatorial Latin American Fiction and the Task of Mourning* (Durham, NC: Duke University Press, 1999).

20. Gérard Genette, *Figures of Discourse*, trans. Alan Sheridan (New York: Columbia University Press, 1982), 143. Emphasis in original.

21. Genette, *Figures of Discourse*, 133. Emphasis in original.

22. Brian McHale, *Postmodernist Fiction* (New York: Routledge, 1987), 10.

23. McHale, *Postmodernist Fiction*, 9.

24. McHale, *Postmodernist Fiction*, 9.

25. This argument is not new. Marjorie Perloff offers up the claim in her *21st-Century Modernism: The "New" Poetics* when she observes at work a "second-wave of modernism" that picks up where the avant-garde of the early twentieth century left off, then interrupted by the First World War and that only now, almost a hundred years later, reveals its full and latent potential. See Marjorie Perloff, *21st-Century Modernism: The "New" Poetics* (Oxford: Wiley-Blackwell, 2002). I remain grateful to Perloff for her generous conversation about this project in its earliest incarnation, as well as to lively conversations of the same with Thomas Hines. Julio Premat makes similar claims to a literary contemporaneity and history that, despite its best efforts, is neither wholly new nor fully present. See in particular Julio Premat, "Contratiempos. Literatura y época," *Revista de estudios hispánicos* 48, no. 1 (2014): 201–217, and *Non nova sed nove: inactualidades, anacronismos, resistencias en la literatura contemporánea* (Macerata: Quodlibet Elements, 2018).

26. Nelly Richard, *The Insubordination of Signs: Political Change, Cultural Transformation, and Poetics of the Crisis*, trans. Alice A. Nelson and Silvia R. Tandeciarz (Durham, NC: Duke University Press, 2004), 21.

27. Richard offers up this analysis as explanation for why Ariel Dorfman's play *La muerte y la doncella* was not well received in Chile despite its acclaim abroad, particularly in the United States and Britain.

28. Andrew C. Rajca's recent work proposes the very timely possibility of working outside the binary of hero/victim not in art but in the political landscape of the late Southern Cone postdictatorships. His book seeks "to open a critical space for a nonethical transformation with postdictatorial culture that allows for moments of political subjectification outside the parameters of liberal humanitarianism and the visible hero/victim of dictatorship." See *Dissensual Subjects: Memory, Human Rights, and Postdictatorship in Argentina, Brazil, and Uruguay* (Evanston, IL: Northwestern University Press, 2018), 9.

29. The figure of the blind spot also appears as a vital site of meaning in twentieth-century philosophy. Blanchot offers up obliquity as marker of the literary and locates a rich, refractory blind spot as the endpoint of all meaningful literary effort. De Man valorizes it as a critical site of insight in a text that manifests, if not for the author, for the reader keen enough to recognize his own blindness as a particular hermeneutic phenomenon. Derrida identifies the dynamic production of blind spots—ambiguities, deferrals, paradox—as fundamental to the deconstructive project and indeed the very task of reading. And blind spots, if by a different name, are integral to Rancière's exposition of dissonance, dissensus, and disruption as fundamental to his theories of politics and community. Most recently, and I reflect on this work further in chapter 2, Janet Roitman galvanizes the inherent paradox at work in the blind spot to parse the global economic crisis of 2008 and how we conceive more generally of crisis and history. In every one of these iterations, blind spots are productive sites of meaning-making that point reader, text, history, and culture in another direction by other means.

30. See Paul de Man, *Blindness and Insight: Essays in the Rhetoric of Contemporary Criticism*, 2nd ed. (Minneapolis: University of Minnesota Press, 1983), 106.

31. In the US academy, at least, this growing interest surged after the avowed, systematic implementation of torture as a morally and legally justified method of interrogation after the World Trade Center terrorist attacks of September 11, 2001. In a slightly longer view, these preoccupations also build upon the groundwork laid by the so-called "ethical turn" of the 1990s. See, among others, Ian Balfour and Eduardo Cadava, eds., "And Justice for All? The Claims of Human Rights," *South Atlantic Quarterly* 103, nos. 2–3 (2004): 277–588; Domna C. Stanton, ed., "The Humanities in Human Rights: Critique, Language, Politics," *PMLA* 121, no. 5 (October 2006): 1518–1661; James Dawes, *That the World May Know: Bearing Witness to Atrocity* (Cambridge, MA: Harvard University Press, 2007); Joseph R. Slaughter, *Human Rights, Inc.: The World Novel, Narrative Form, and International Law* (New York: Fordham University Press, 2007); Elizabeth Swanson Goldberg, *Beyond Terror: Gender, Narrative, Human Rights* (New Brunswick, NJ: Rutgers University Press, 2007); James Dawes, "Human Rights in Literary Studies," *Human Rights*

Quarterly 31 (2009): 394–409; Sophia A. McClennen and Joseph R. Slaughter, "Introducing Human Rights and Literary Forms; Or, The Vehicles and Vocabularies of Human Rights," *Comparative Literature Studies* 46.1 (2009): 1–19; Alexandra Schulteis Moore and Elizabeth Swanson Goldberg, *Teaching Human Rights in Literary and Cultural Studies* (New York: The Modern Language Association of America, 2015); and Elizabeth S. Anker, *Fictions of Dignity: Embodying Human Rights in World Literature* (Ithaca, NY: Cornell University Press, 2017). Other relevant works include Crystal Parikh, *Writing Human Rights: The Political Imaginaries of Writers of Color* (Minneapolis: University of Minnesota Press, 2017), and James Dawes, *The Novel of Human Rights* (Cambridge, MA: Harvard University Press, 2018). The number of conference panels and roundtables dedicated to the intersection of human rights and literary studies in particular has also multiplied in the past two decades, as is evidenced in the programs of the annual meetings of the Modern Language Association, the American Comparative Literature Association, and the Latin American Studies Association, as well as in the proliferation of more regional and local symposia on the subject.

32. Steve J. Stern and Scott Strauss have identified as "the human rights paradox" the ways in which the tensions that emerge between theories of human rights and their lived realities work upon how we understand human rights more generally. For more, see Steve J. Stern and Scott Strauss, eds., *The Human Rights Paradox: Universality and Its Discontents* (Madison: University of Wisconsin Press, 2014). For a keen discussion of how this paradox shows up in Argentine fiction, see the introduction in Nancy J. Gates-Madsen, *Trauma, Taboo, and Truth-Telling: Listening to Silences in Postdictatorship Argentina* (Madison: University of Wisconsin Press, 2016).

33. Avelar, *Untimely Present*, 232–233. Emphasis in original.

34. See Theodor W. Adorno, "Cultural Criticism and Society," in *Prisms*, trans. Samuel and Shierry Weber (Cambridge, MA: MIT Press, 1967), 34.

35. Jean-François Lyotard, "The Other's Rights," in *The Politics of Human Rights*, ed. The Belgrade Circle (London: Verso, 1999), 181.

36. McClennen and Slaughter, "Introducing Human Rights and Literary Forms," 11.

37. McClennen and Slaughter, "Introducing Human Rights and Literary Forms," 11.

38. Caroline Levine, *Forms: Whole, Rhythm, Hierarchy, Network* (Princeton: Princeton University Press, 2015), 3.

39. Levine, *Forms*, 3.

40. Levine, *Forms*, 3.

41. Levine, *Forms*, 9.

42. At the time of this book's writing, Argentina is immersed in the denunciation of the disappearance of Santiago Maldonado, the young activist detained on August 1, 2017, during a protest for indigenous rights in the southern province of

Chubut. Enforced disappearance has thus been thrust back into national and international headlines, only buttressed by the continued Megacausa ESMA, the series of trials seeking justice for crimes committed at the ESMA during the dictatorship, and the ongoing work of the Madres and Abuelas de Plaza de Mayo in their search for missing grandchildren born in captivity or trafficked during the dictatorship. The United Nations Committee on Enforced Disappearance is currently overseeing an international investigation into Maldonado's disappearance even as the Argentine public demands his "aparición con vida." On October 20, 2017, the family of Santiago Maldonado announced that his body had been found in the Rio Chubut; they are now seeking justice for his death. See "Comunicado de la familia," accessed 20 October 2017, http://www.santiagomaldonado.com/comunicado-la-familia-2010/.

43. See the essays by Sarah Winter, Aryn Bartley, and Paul Gready in McClennen and Slaughter's special issue.

44. Dawes, *The Novel of Human Rights*, 5.

45. Levine, *Forms*, 19.

46. J. Hillis Miller's incisive work on community and fiction in the aftermath of state-sponsored violence is particularly relevant to the thinking I develop here about the ways in which a community of forms provides for a larger narrative commons. See J. Hillis Miller, *The Conflagration of Community: Fiction before and after Auschwitz* (Chicago: University of Chicago Press, 2011).

47. See the introduction to Hayden White, *Tropics of Discourse: Essays in Cultural Criticism* (Baltimore: Johns Hopkins University Press, 1978).

48. Rancière proposes the idea of an aesthetic break in which the continuity enjoyed, in his example on the stage, between a language of natural signs (*poiesis + aisthesis*) and the mimetic's ability to provoke an ethical response is ruptured. This break is the foundation of Rancière's dissensual community. See Jacques Rancière, *The Emancipated Spectator*, trans. Gregory Elliott (New York: Verso, 2011), 60.

49. See Jean-Luc Nancy, *Le partage des voix* (Paris: Éditions Galilée, 1982), and Miller, *The Conflagration of Community*, 18.

50. Jacques Rancière, "Aesthetic Separation, Aesthetic Community: Scenes from the Aesthetic Regime of Art," lecture delivered June 20, 2006, at the symposium Aesthetics and Politics: With and Around Jacques Rancière, held at the University of Amsterdam, *Art and Research: A Journal of Ideas, Contexts, and Methods* 2, no. 1 (Summer 2008): http://www.artandresearch.org.uk/v2n1/pdfs/Rancière.pdf.

51. Rancière, *The Emancipated Spectator*, 59.

52. Rancière, *The Emancipated Spectator*, 59.

53. Blanchot, "The Disappearance of Literature," in *The Book to Come*, trans. Charlotte Mandel (Stanford: Stanford University Press, 2003), 200.

54. Blanchot, "The Disappearance of Literature," 198.

55. Blanchot, "The Disappearance of Literature," 198.

56. See Cathy Caruth, *Literature in the Ashes of History* (Baltimore: Johns Hopkins University Press, 2013), xi. Caruth proposes a history that disappears,

eliminates "the very possibility of its own remembrance," and recedes upon the horizon. "History," she writes, "emerges . . . as the performance of its own disappearance." The modes of disappearance I identify in this work intersect with the disappearing history that Caruth observes. They seek to make visible, seen, and known a tenuous history predicated on the traumatic legacy of disappearance; reveal the mechanisms by which disappearance manifests; and offer them up otherwise. Where in Caruth's discerning study the theorists and literary characters that she deals with "struggle . . . to claim a new mode of conceptual and historical survival in the face of a history that seems constantly about to disappear," I examine how disappearance becomes constitutive to history and to literature on the very cusp of their shared and coming disappearance. The task here—which also functions as a reply to Caruth—is to engage with disappearance as a particular historical and literary form that reforms the world as we know it. The rhetorical and literary modes of disappearance that this work examines—the ways and means of narrative production—also strive to make history legible, and thereby open to future recuperation and a future *acting out*, here a reaction ethical in principle, judicial in nature, and full of aesthetic potential. Caruth takes apart the trace, the dream, repetition, the stammer—all things or events that signal an absence—as evidence of a receding history. The history of literary disappearance that I propose deals inversely in the narrative spaces that are opened up by what is gone or vanishing, even as it keeps in sight the receding historical horizon that Caruth points us toward.

57. Blanchot, "The Disappearance of Literature," 198.

58. For further discussion of the stakes and pedagogies of close reading and human rights, see Karen Elizabeth Bishop, "On Teaching the Close Reading of Torture Literature: An Approximation," in *Teaching Human Rights in Literary and Cultural Studies*, ed. Alexandra Schulteis and Elizabeth Swanson Goldberg (New York: Modern Language Association, 2015), 178–188.

59. Nancy J. Gates-Madsen's recent book on the representation of silence in postdictatorship Argentina offers an important, in-depth study of what is not spoken or heard and how these silences show up in a variety of cultural texts. See Gates-Madsen, *Trauma, Taboo, and Truth-Telling*.

60. Jean Baudrillard, *Simulacra and Simulation*, trans. Sheila Faria Glaser (Ann Arbor: University of Michigan Press, 1994), 3.

61. Juan Pablo Neyret, "Novela significa licencia para mentir," *Espéculo: Revista de estudios literarios* (2002): http://www.ucm.es/info/especulo/numero22/t_eloy.html.

62. Tomás Eloy Martínez, "Ficción e historia en *La novela de Perón*," *Hispamérica: revista de literatura* 17, no. 49 (1988): 41–49.

63. These interviews were published first in April 1970 in the Argentine magazine *Panorama* and then in 1996 brought out in book form as *Las memorias del general*. See Tomás Eloy Martínez, *Las memorias del general* (Buenos Aires: Planeta, 1996), and "Las memorias del general," 29 March 2016, accessed 17 March 2018, http://fundaciontem.org/las-memorias-del-general/.

64. Martínez, "Ficción e historia," 42.

Chapter One

1. Walsh was sympathetic, if not fully aligned, with Peronism during the 1950s. In the early 1970s, he became affiliated with the Fuerzas Armadas Peronistas that later merged with the radical leftist organization the Montoneros. Walsh's work as an intelligence official for the group would last only a few years, however, coming to an end when its leadership took the organization underground in 1974. In early 1976, Walsh founded ANCLA, Agencia de Noticias Clandestinas, which disseminated clandestine information about the operation of the new military dictatorship, including its use of systematic disappearance, concentration camps located around Argentina, and the death flights used to dispose of the disappeared in the Río de la Plata, the ocean, or desert. Toward the end of 1976, however, Walsh realized that he would need to create an even more revolutionary news network, and he formed Cadena Informativa to operate parallel to ANCLA. At the bottom of the network's circulations appeared the following: "Cadena Informativa es uno de los instrumentos que está creando el pueblo argentino para romper el bloqueo de la información. Cadena Informativa puede ser USTED MISMO, un instrumento para que usted se libere del terror y libere a otros del terror. Reproduzca esta información, hágala circular por los medios a su alcance: a mano, a máquina, a mimeógrafo. Mande copias a sus amigos: nueve de cada diez las estarán esperando. Millones quieren ser informados. El terror se basa en la incomunicación. Vuelva a sentir la satisfacción moral de un acto de libertad. DERROTE AL TERROR. HAGA CIRCULAR ESTA INFORMACION" (Cadena Informativa is one of the instruments that the Argentine people are creating in order to break open the blocks on information. Cadena Informativa can be YOU, an instrument so that you are free from terror and free others from terror. Reproduce this information, circulate it by the means at your disposal: by hand, by machine, by mimeograph. Send copies to your friends: nine out of ten of them are waiting for it. Millions want to be informed. Terror is based on incommunication. Feel once again the moral satisfaction of an act of freedom. DEFEAT TERROR. CIRCULATE THIS INFORMATION). Natalia Vinelli, *ANCLA: Una experiencia de comunicación clandestina orientada por Rodolfo Walsh* (Buenos Aires: La Rosa Blindada, 2000), 98. This last effort would cost Walsh his life.

2. Michael McCaughan, *True Crimes: Rodolfo Walsh, the Life and Times of a Radical Intellectual* (London: Latin American Bureau, 2002), 280–284.

3. Edgar Allan Poe, "The Philosophy of Composition," in *The Norton Anthology of Theory and Criticism* (New York: W.W. Norton & Co., 2001), 742–750.

4. My understanding of the relationship between disappearance and space is indebted here to Poe's short story "The Purloined Letter." See Jacques Lacan, "Seminar on 'The Purloined Letter,'" in *The Poetics of Murder: Detective Fiction and Literary Theory*, ed. Glenn W. Most and William W. Stowe (San Diego: Harcourt Brace Jovanovich, 1983), 21–54; Anthony Vidler, "X Marks the Spot: The Exhaus-

tion of Space at the Scene of the Crime," in *Warped Space: Art, Architecture, and Anxiety in Modern Culture* (Durham, NC: Duke University Press, 2000), 123–132.

5. See Ricardo Piglia's and Juan José Saer's remarks about Walsh's evolution as a writer in their conversation on "Literatura y política hoy." Ricardo Piglia, *Por un relato futuro: Conversaciones con Juan José Saer* (Barcelona: Editorial Anagrama, 2015), 94–129.

6. While two of the men arrested were Peronist rebels, the others were either just friends gathered at a house in the outskirts of Buenos Aires to listen to a boxing match or passersby on the street. A group of city police and army officers raided the house, detained the men they found there, and ordered their immediate execution.

7. McCaughan, *True Crimes*, 80–83.

8. McCaughan, *True Crimes*, 83. Cited in English. Emphasis added.

9. Rodolfo Walsh, *Ese hombre y otros escritos personales*, ed. Daniel Link (Buenos Aires: Seix Barral, 1996), 206. Translations are mine unless otherwise noted.

10. Rodolfo Walsh, *Un oscuro día de justicia/Zugzwang* (Buenos Aires: Ediciones de la Flor, 2006), 64–65.

11. Walsh here aligns himself with Genette's reflections on the future of fiction in his 1966 *Figures of Discourse*, which I take up in conjunction with Blanchot's theory of the disappearance of literature in this work's introduction.

12. Walsh, *Un oscuro día*, 61–63.

13. Walsh's position here both anticipates and goes beyond Saer's remarks on the form of the novel, per Adorno's theories of immanence, as agent for the production of literary content and the politicization of both. Piglia, *Por un relato futuro*, 118.

14. Carlos Gamerro comes to a similar conclusion in "Rodolfo Walsh: Prólogo a una edición nonata de sus *Obras escogidas*," *Hispamérica* 123 (2012): 3–14.

15. McCaughan, *True Crimes*, 55. Borges and Bioy Casares, both of whom influenced Walsh's detective fiction, set many of their own works in Latin America. In the "Noticia" to his 1953 collection *Diez cuentos policiales argentinos*, Walsh avers that the *porteño* reading public is ready to accept the city as an appropriate setting for detective fiction, which Argentine writers are "singularly talented" in producing.

16. There is not an extensive body of scholarship dedicated to Walsh's *Variaciones en rojo*. Michael McCaughan dedicates just shy of two pages of his biography of Walsh to discussing the works; Aníbal Ford spends two pages of a lengthy article on what he sees as the literary defects of the trilogy; Victoria Cohen Imach published the only article dedicated entirely to the story "Variaciones en rojo" in 1991. Other criticism includes references to *Variaciones en rojo* in various articles from the important 1993–1994 special issue of *Nuevo Texto Crítico* dedicated to Walsh; of these, the essays by Eduardo Romano and Jorge Lafforgue spend the most time with Walsh's detective fiction. Daniel Link, Walsh's most important posthumous editor, alludes to Walsh's early work in his introductions to *El violento oficio de escribir* (1995) and in *Ese hombre y otros escritos personales* (1996). David

Viñas writes lucidly on the relationship between Walsh's detective fiction and the evolution of his politics, and later work by José Fernández Vega and Carlos Gamerro also offer up readings of *Variaciones en rojo*. These references make up the body of scholarship on Walsh's only original collection of detective fiction. The majority of Walsh criticism focuses on his works of literary journalism, most notably *Operación masacre*. See Aníbal Ford, "Walsh: la reconstrucción de los hechos," *Nueva novela latinoamericana*, vol. 2, ed. Jorge Laffogue (Buenos Aires: Editorial Paidos, 1972), 272–322; Victoria Cohen Imach, "Las máscaras o el pintor de paredes: Asunción de la periferia en 'Variaciones en rojo' de Rodolfo Walsh," *Hispamérica* 58 (1991), 3–15; Jorge Lafforgue, ed., *Nuevo Texto Crítico* 12–13 (July 1993–June 1994); David Viñas, "Rodolfo Walsh, el ajedrez y la guerra," *Literatura argentina y política: De Lugones a Walsh* II (Buenos Aires: Editorial Sudamericana, 1996), 167–173; José Fernández Vega, "De la teología a la política: El problema del mal en la literatura policial de Rodolfo Walsh," *Hispamérica: revista de literatura* 83 (1999): 5–15; and Carlos Gamerro, "Rodolfo Walsh: Prólogo a una edición nonata de sus *Obras escogidas*," *Hispamérica* 123 (2012): 3–14.

17. W. H. Auden, "The Guilty Vicarage," *Harper's*, May 1948, accessed 7 March 2017, http://harpers.org/archive/1948/05/the-guilty-vicarage/.

18. Rodolfo Walsh, *Variaciones en rojo* (Madrid: Espasa Calpe, 2002), 9.

19. McCaughan, *True Crimes*, 48.

20. Walsh, *Variaciones*, 11.

21. Cf. Gaston Leroux's "Le Mystère de la chambre jaune."

22. Michel Foucault, *The Order of Things: An Archaeology of the Human Sciences* (Vintage: New York, 1994), 16.

23. Foucault, *The Order of Things*, 16.

24. Walsh, *Variaciones*, 115–116.

25. Walsh, *Variaciones*, 117.

26. Note the location of the weapon—a dagger, *puñal*—found at the bottom of the stairs. Walsh, *Variaciones*, 126.

27. Walsh, *Variaciones*, 127.

28. Walsh, *Variaciones*, 128. Emphasis in original.

29. Walsh, *Variaciones*, 131.

30. Umberto Eco, *The Limits of Interpretation* (Bloomington: Indiana University Press, 1991), 160.

31. This is how Eco describes the mechanism that Borges employs in writing his detective fiction, if not all his fiction. He relies here on Spinoza's dictum "ordo et connexio rerum idem est ac ordo et connexio idearum," or "the movements of our mind that investigates follow the same rules of the real." Eco, *The Limits of Interpretation*, 156, 160.

32. Foucault, *The Order of Things*, 8.

33. Walsh, *Variaciones*, 158.

34. Walsh, *Variaciones*, 164.

35. For an elegant study of the significance of topological thinking in the Western imagination, see Angus Fletcher, *The Topological Imagination: Spheres, Edges, and Islands* (Cambridge: Harvard University Press, 2016).

36. Walsh, *Variaciones*, 164.

37. Walsh, *Variaciones*, 166. Emphasis added.

38. Baudrillard, *Simulacra and Simulation*, 3.

39. Baudrillard, *Simulacra and Simulation*, 3.

40. Walsh, *Variaciones*, 238.

Chapter Two

1. Taylor, *Disappearing Acts*, 119.

2. Ernesto González Bermejo, *Conversaciones con Cortázar* (Barcelona: EDHASA, 1978), 119.

3. González Bermejo, *Conversaciones con Cortázar*, 119.

4. Julio Cortázar, *Obra crítica*, vol. 3, ed. Saúl Sosnowski (Madrid: Alfaguara, 1994), 167. Published in English by John Incledon, "The Fellowship of Exile," *Review: Literature and Arts of the Americas* 15, no. 30 (1981): 14–16.

5. Cortázar, *Obra crítica* 3, 169.

6. Julio Cortázar, *Cartas*, vol. 2, ed. Aurora Bernárdez (Buenos Aires: Alfaguara, 2000), 1136, 1141. Translations are my own throughout unless otherwise noted.

7. See particularly pages 120–122 of Ricardo Piglia's and Juan José Saer's conversation about Cortázar's internal and public struggle to merge political action with literature. Of particular interest is when Piglia notes that "todas las posiciones públicas de Cortázar en relación con la literatura son defensivas" (all of Cortázar's public positions in relation to literature are defensive) (121). The fact that Cortázar always seemed to have to defend his literature from attacks that it was not politically engaged enough very much fueled this internal debate. Ricardo Piglia, "Literatura y política hoy," in *Por un relato futuro: Conversaciones con Juan José Saer* (Barcelona: Editorial Anagrama), 94–129.

8. Fantomas, an evil genius of crime, was the protagonist of a series of thirty-two short novels written by Marcel Allain and Pierre Souvestre and published in France from 1911 to 1913. The novels were widely popular at the time, hailed by Blaise Cendrars as "the modern *Aeneid*," by Guillaume Apollinaire as "one of the richest works that exist," and by Jean Cocteau as "absurd and magnificent lyricism." Merle Rubin, book review of *Fantomas*, *Los Angeles Times*, 10 August 1986, accessed 10 November 2017, http://articles.latimes.com/1986-08-10/books/bk-2030_1_marcel-allain. For more on the history of the work's reception, see John Ashbery's introduction to the translation of a novelized version of the serial published in 1986. Ashbery recognizes the work's vast popularity even while he puzzles over its literary flatness and inferiority to other more developed works of crime fiction;

he writes, as Rubin notes, "With Fantomas, terror becomes almost monotonous." Both Ashbery and this book's reviewer agree that the most interesting thing about the work is its curious reception, particularly among France's influential avant-garde. See John Ashbery, Introduction to *Fantômas* (New York: Penguin, 2006), 1–7. For more on the history of *Fantômas*, see chapter 2 of Robin Walz, *Pulp Surrealism: Insolent Popular Culture in Early Twentieth-Century Paris* (Berkeley: University of California Press, 2000), 42–75.

9. For more on the origin and publication history of *Fantomas*, see "Three Booklets of 1975," David Kurnick's afterword to his excellent translation into English of *Fantomas* in Julio Cortázar, *Fantomas versus the Multinational Vampires: An Attainable Utopia*, trans. David Kurnick (Los Angeles: Semiotext(e), 2014), 81–87, as well as two articles that inform Kurnick's research, Carlos Gómez Carro, "La amenaza elegante: *Fantomas*, Julio Cortázar y Gonzalo Martré," *Revista replicante*, 10 April 2011, accessed 10 November 2017, http://revistareplicante.com/la-amenaza-elegante/; Marie-Alexandra Barataud, "Del texto y de la imagen: la escritura transgenérica en *Fantomas contra los vampiros multinacionales de Julio Cortázar*," n.d., accessed 10 November 2017, www.crimic.paris-sorbonne.fr/actes/sal4/barataud.pdf. I am indebted to Kurnick's thoughtful conversations on *Fantomas* and his translation. For a useful overview of Gonzalo Martré's work on *Fantomas*—including his 2013 *Fantomas: El regreso de la amenaza elegante*—and Cortázar's appropriation of the character, see also Ricardo Vigueras-Fernández, "El regreso de Fantomas: la conspiración Cortázar-Martré contra el neoliberalismo," *Polifonía: Revista académica de estudios hispánicos* 4 (2014): 38–50, http://www.apsu.edu/polifonia/v4/2014-fernandez_0.pdf.

10. González Bermejo, *Conversaciones con Cortázar*, 122.

11. Compared to the fifty-thousand-copy print runs that other works of the Boom enjoyed, this was a relatively small print run but still not unsubstantial in scope. The book has been long out of print.

12. In addition to the introductions to the work of the tribunal or to *Fantomas* that Cortázar offers to Basso, Jonquières, and Retamar in the preceding passages, he sends the work to Ariel Dorfman in a letter of September 24, 1975, and mentions the work of the next tribunal, which Cortázar attended for ten days in Lisbon in January 1976, to Lida Aronne de Amestoy.

13. Julio Cortázar, *Cartas*, vol. 4, ed. Aurora Bernárdez y Carles Álvarez Garriga (Buenos Aires: Alfaguara, 2012), 522. Emphasis in original.

14. Cortázar, *Cartas* 4, 523. Emphasis in original.

15. Cortázar, *Cartas* 4, 540.

16. The principal scholarship on *Fantomas* includes Ellen McCracken, "*Libro de Manuel* and *Fantomas contra los vampiros multinacionales*: Mass Culture, Art, and Politics," in *Literature and Popular Culture in the Hispanic World: A Symposium*, ed. Rose S. Minc (Gaithersburg, MD: Hispamérica, 1981); Jean Franco, "Comic Stripping: Cortázar in the Age of Mechanical Reproduction," in *Julio Cortázar: New Readings*, ed. Carlos J. Alonso (Cambridge: Cambridge University Press, 1998), 36–56; a

discussion of the book in Peter Standish, *Understanding Julio Cortázar* (Columbia: University of South Carolina Press, 2001), 121–150; Ellen McCracken, "Hybridity and Postmodernity in the Argentine Meta-Comic: The Bridge Texts of Julio Cortázar and Ricardo Piglia," in *Latin American Literature and Mass Media*, ed. Edmundo Paz-Soldán and Debra A. Castillo (New York: Garland, 2001), 139–151; and the more recent scholarship by Gómez Carro, Barataud, Kurnick, and Vigueras-Fernández. I am grateful to Ellen McCracken for many lively and incisive conversations about Cortázar's work, which were fundamental to this chapter's evolution.

17. McCracken, "*Libro de Manuel*," 75–76.
18. Kurnick, "Three Booklets of 1975," 86.
19. Kurnick, "Three Booklets of 1975," 86.
20. I use throughout Kurnick's translation into English of *Fantomas*.
21. Julio Cortázar, *Fantomas contra los vampiros multinacionales* (México D.F.: Excelsior, 1975), 13–14.
22. The *fotonovela* does not quite have an equivalent for a North American reading public. These were cheap books comprised of black-and-white photographs of movie stills published on newsprint and unaccompanied by captions sold in Latin America to viewers who could not afford to go to the movies. The *fotonovela* allowed them to "see" the movies they could not access. Cortázar here places *Fantomas* somewhere on a spectrum between a work designed for a lower-class reading public and the more highly educated readers of *Peanuts* and *Mafalda*, whose often self-reflexively ironic texts appeared first in newspapers and then in book form.
23. Emphasis added. Julio Cortázar, "Continuidad de los parques," in *Los relatos 2: Juegos* (Madrid: Alianza Editorial, 2004), 7–8; Julio Cortázar, "Continuity of Parks," in *Blow-Up and Other Stories*, trans. Paul Blackburn (New York: Pantheon Books, 1967), 64.
24. Cortázar, *Fantomas*, 29.
25. Cortázar, *Fantomas*, 40–41.
26. Cortázar, *Fantomas*, 41.
27. Cortázar, *Fantomas*, 37.
28. See note 7 in this chapter.
29. Cortázar, *Fantomas*, 7.
30. Cortázar, *Fantomas*, 17.
31. Cortázar, *Fantomas*, 18.
32. Cortázar, *Fantomas*, 19–20.
33. Cortázar, *Fantomas*, 66.
34. Reinhart Koselleck, "The Unknown Future and the Art of Prognosis," in *The Practice of Conceptual History: Timing History, Spacing Concepts*, trans. Todd Samuel Presner et al. (Stanford: Stanford University Press, 2002), 135.
35. Koselleck, "The Unknown Future," 133. Citation from Immanuel Kant, *Anthropology from a Pragmatic Point of View*, trans. Robert Louden (Cambridge: Cambridge University Press, 2006), 79.
36. Koselleck, "The Unknown Future," 131.

37. Reinhart Koselleck, "History, Histories, and Formal Structures of Time," in *Futures Past: On the Semantics of Historical Time*, trans. Keith Tribe (Cambridge, MA: MIT Press, 1985), 104.

38. See Reinhart Koselleck, "Some Questions Regarding the Conceptual History of 'Crisis,'" in *The Practice of Conceptual History*, 236–247.

39. Janet Roitman, *Anti-Crisis* (Durham, NC: Duke University Press, 2014), 10.

40. Roitman, *Anti-Crisis*, 13.

41. Roitman, *Anti-Crisis*, 13.

42. My reflections on Roitman's work are also indebted to the keynote address on *Anti-Crisis* that she delivered for the symposium on Visual Culture in and out of Crisis, organized by Rhiannon Noel Welch, at Rutgers University, New Brunswick, October 19, 2017.

43. Roitman also recognizes the political potential inherent to the form of the comic when she ends her work with a possible alternate version of events as parsed by Umberto Eco in his 1984 "The Myth of Superman." Roitman, *Anti-Crisis*, 96.

44. Scott McCloud, *Understanding Comics: The Invisible Art* (New York: HarperCollins, 1993), 65.

45. McCloud, *Understanding Comics*, 67.

46. Walter Benjamin, "On the Concept of History," in *Selected Writings*, vol. 4: 1938–1940, trans. Edmund Jephcott et al. (Cambridge, MA: Belknap Press, 2006), 395.

47. Jorge L. Catalá Carrasco, Paul Drinot, and James Scorer, ed., *Comics and Memory in Latin America* (Pittsburgh: University of Pittsburgh Press, 2017).

48. Cortázar, *Fantomas*, 44.

49. Cortázar, *Fantomas*, 44–46.

50. Cortázar, *Fantomas*, 46.

51. Cortázar, *Fantomas*, 57.

52. Cortázar, *Fantomas*, 58.

53. Cortázar, *Fantomas*, 59–60.

54. Thomas Pavel, *Fictional Worlds* (Cambridge: Harvard University Press, 1986), 43–72.

55. Pavel, *Fictional Worlds*, 89.

56. Cortázar, *Fantomas*, 66.

57. Kurnick's translation of this phrase allows it to serve as well-placed emphasis—"I'm telling you"—to the speaker's entreaty that we come together to fight for political change. But it elides in English the proposition that she seems to be about to make.

Chapter Three

1. Martínez, *Las memorias del general*, 9–15. Translations are my own unless otherwise noted.

2. Marily Martínez-Richter, ed., *La caja de escritura: diálogos con narradores y críticos argentinos* (Madrid: Iberoamericana, 1997), 36.
3. Martínez-Richter, *La caja de la escritura*, 42.
4. Martínez, "Ficción e historia," 42.
5. Avelar, *The Untimely Present*, 11.
6. Scholarly works on the relationship between history and fiction in *La novela de Perón* include: Silvia Ganduglia, "La representación de la historia en *La novela de Perón*," *Ideologies and Literature* 4, no. 1 (1989): 271–297; Keith McDuffie, "*La novela de Perón*: historia, ficción, testimonio," in *La historia de la literatura iberoamericana*, comp. Raquel Chang Rodríguez and Gabriella de Beer (Hanover, NH: Ediciones del Norte, 1989), 295–305; Cristina Parodi, "Ficción y realidad en *La novela de Perón* de Tomás Eloy Martínez," *Nuevo Texto Crítico* 4, no. 8 (1991): 39–43; María José Punte, "Perón: Personaje de Novela," *RILCE: Revista de Filología Hispánica* 20, no. 2 (2004): 223–239; Karen Elizabeth Bishop, "Myth Turned Monument: Documenting the Historical Imaginary in Buenos Aires and Beyond," *Journal of Modern Literature* 30, no. 2 (2007): 151–162; and Gerald Martin, "Tomás Eloy Martínez, Biography and the Boom: *La novela de Perón* (1985) and *Santa Evita* (1995)," *Bulletin of Latin American Research* 31, no. 4 (2012): 460–472.
7. Hayden White, *The Content of the Form: Narrative Discourse and Historical Representation* (Baltimore: Johns Hopkins University Press, 1987), 3.
8. Tomás Eloy Martínez, "Myth, History and Fiction in Latin America," trans. Marguerite Feitlowitz, lecture presented at the Inter-American Development Bank Cultural Center, Washington, DC, May 1999. Reprinted in *Encuentros* 32 (May 1999): 6.
9. The historical stakes of Martínez's project serve as introduction to the novel's first appearance in serialized form in the weekly publication *El Periodista de Buenos Aires*. Published from September 1984 to May 1989—although from 1988 to 1989 in a smaller format—*El Periodista* announced the first installment of *La novela de Perón* on the cover of its inaugural issue (September 15–21) and ran the first chapter of the novel, "Adiós a Madrid," on pages 23–28. On the cover of the inaugural issue, the magazine offered up this introduction to the novel: "Desde hace más de diez años, Tomás Eloy Martínez teje y desteje un vasto empeño: un libro sobre la vida de Juan Domingo Perón. El apasionante resultado de su trabajo, que comienza a publicar hoy en forma exclusiva EL PERIODISTA, está lejos de constituir una pura ficción; la caudalosa masa de documentos y testimonios personales que aporta iluminan de manera definitiva la figura del líder justicialista" (For over ten years, Tomás Eloy Martínez has woven and unwoven a vast undertaking: a book about the life of Juan Domingo Perón. The exciting result of his work, which *El Periodista* begins exclusively publishing today, is far from constituting a pure fiction; the expansive mass of documents and personal testimony that it offers up illuminates for us, once and for all, the figure of the leader of the Justicialist Party).

This text differs slightly from the cut-out that accompanies the first page of the installment, which reads toward the end: "Desechados así, por insuficientes, el camino de la transcripción anotada de las memorias y el de la biografía ortodoxa, el escritor optó por el cauce que consideró más amplio para contener, si no la verdad, al menos las diversas verdades que surgieron en la investigación de la vida de Perón, para que éstas jugaran entre sí, libremente, sus propias dialécticas. El apasionante resultado de su trabajo—cuyos tramos fundamentales comienza a publicar hoy en forma exclusiva EL PERIODISTA DE BUENOS AIRES—participa de muchos de los rasgos de una novela. Sin embargo, está lejos de constituir una pura ficción. Por el contrario, sus fulgores iluminan, con más rigor y autencidad que muchos tratados de la historia, la figura de Juan Domingo Perón" (Rejecting as insufficient the detailed transcribing of memoirs and the traditional biography, the writer chose the course he thought ample enough to contain, if not the truth, then at least the many truths that arose in his investigation into the life of Perón so that these might come together to freely manifest their own dialectics. The thrilling result of his work—whose essential plots we begin to exclusively publish today in *El Periodista de Buenos Aires*—feature many of the same characteristics as a novel. But this is far from a pure fiction. On the contrary, its brilliance illuminates, more rigorously and authentically than many works of history, the figure of Juan Domingo Perón).

Both introductions recognize the possibility that *La novela de Perón* is not "a pure fiction," but the more extended cut-out emphasizes the hybrid generic nature of the novel when it states that the work "share[s] many of the same features as a novel," and that it might function as a more rigorous and authentic portrait of Perón than "many works of history." The magazine here reveals the stakes of Martínez's project: a work of fiction that might do the work of history, except better and otherwise. The political significance of this project is amplified by the fact that *El Periodista de Buenos Aires* emerged in the early days after the fall of the dictatorship and the magazine was invested in documenting the sociopolitical complexities of the transition. The headline for Martínez's novel, for example, appears between stories dedicated to the school of dictators and another to abortion in Argentina, and next to the main story on Henry Kissinger's recent visit to Mar de Plata and Buenos Aires, "Kissinger: Al rescate de la patria financiera" (Kissinger: To the rescue of the investment nation). Martínez's novel headlines as a significant sociopolitical event alongside other defining concerns in Argentina's return to democracy. This introduction to an Argentine reading public lays out the significance of the novel as well as reveals the political context in which it appears as one where traditional historiographic methods are already compromised. I am grateful to Marcy Schwartz for providing me with the copies that Tomás Eloy Martínez gave her of *El Periodista* in which Martínez's novel first appeared.

10. Rock, *Argentina*, 358.
11. See Rock, *Argentina*, 358–362.

12. Neyret, "Novela significa," n.p.
13. Rock, *Argentina*, 259–261.
14. Neyret, "Novela significa," n.p.
15. What has come to be known as the Ezeiza massacre occurred near the Ezeiza International Airport outside of Buenos Aires on June 20, 1973, as both left- and right-wing factions of Perón's supporters gathered to meet the flight that returned the exiled general, accompanied by then-president Héctor Cámpora, from Madrid to Buenos Aires. From the dais where Perón was to have addressed the crowd, snipers hired by representatives from the conservative trade unions—these organized by José López Rega—opened fire on the left-wing Montoneros, the Juventud Peronista (Peronist Youth), and their allies, killing at least thirteen people and injuring hundreds more. While no official inquiry confirmed the number of casualties, it is thought to be much higher than reported. The massacre ended confidence in Cámpora's capacity to serve as president, thus making way for Perón to take his place, as well as fractured former alliances between the left- and right-wing Peronist factions. For more, see Rock, *Argentina*, 360; and Horacio Verbitsky, *Ezeiza* (Buenos Aires: Editorial Contrapunto, 1985).
16. Tomás Eloy Martínez, *La novela de Perón* (New York: Vintage, 1985), 11. Tomás Eloy Martínez, *The Perón Novel*, trans. Helen Lane (New York: Knopf, 1998). I use Lane's translations of the novel throughout.
17. See in particular chapter 1 of Richard, *The Insubordination of Signs*.
18. Martínez, *La novela de Perón*, 16–17.
19. Martínez, *La novela de Perón*, 12.
20. See Taylor, *Disappearing Acts*, 148–150 and this book's introduction for a more detailed discussion.
21. See Taylor, *Disappearing Acts*, chapter 5.
22. Martínez, *La novela de Perón*, 351.
23. Martínez, *La novela de Perón*, 351.
24. Martínez, *La novela de Perón*, 352.
25. Martínez, *La novela de Perón*, 354.
26. Martínez, *La novela de Perón*, 354–355.
27. Martínez, *La novela de Perón*, 354.
28. Baudrillard, *Simulacra and Simulation*, 25–26. Emphasis in original.
29. See Michel Foucault, *The Order of Things: An Archaeology of the Human Sciences* (Vintage: New York, 1994), René Girard, *Violence and the Sacred*, trans. Patrick Gregory (Baltimore: Johns Hopkins University Press, 1977), and Giorgio Agamben, *Homo Sacer: Sovereign Power and Bare Life*, trans. Daniel Heller-Roazen (Stanford: Stanford University Press, 1998).
30. Baudrillard, *Simulacra and Simulation*, 26. Emphasis in original.
31. Martínez, *La novela de Perón*, 357.
32. Martínez, *La novela de Perón*, 360.
33. See Baudrillard, *Simulacra and Simulation*, 3.

34. White, *The Content of the Form*, 4.

35. White, *The Content of the Form*, 4.

36. I refer here to the distinctions that Brian McHale makes between the epistemological as proper to modernism and the ontological as product of postmodern thought and experience. Already in this last question—"what am I in this world"—the overlap of the two is clear. See my introduction for a more thorough discussion of the difference.

37. See McHale, *Postmodernist Fiction*, 112–130. For more on "Chinese boxworlds," see also Genette, *Narrative Discourse*, 237–243.

38. Martínez, *La novela de Perón*, 259–260.

39. Martínez does not become in this chapter, per James Phelan's model of character construction, more than character as idea (thematic) or artificial construct (synthetic). Despite giving us a double of himself in the novel, this gesture toward the mimetic keeps Martínez at an auto-metafictional remove and functions rather as example of the narrative correspondences in the construction of history and fiction. It also allows the author to serve as a foil for Perón, who does not ever quite manage to become a fully fledged protagonist of his own story. See in particular the introduction of James Phelan, *Reading People, Reading Plots: Character, Progression, and the Interpretation of Narrative* (Chicago: University of Chicago Press, 1989) and *Narrative as Rhetoric: Techniques, Audiences, Ethics, Ideology* (Columbus: Ohio State University Press, 1996), 29.

40. Martínez, "Myth, History and Fiction in Latin America," 9.

41. These examples are arranged not as they appear in the novel, but chronologically, working up until the evening of June 20, 1973, which is where the novel leaves off. The passages are drawn from chapters 14, 9, 17, 1, 10, and 19.

42. Martínez, *La novela de Perón*, 265.

43. Cf. Tomás Eloy Martínez, *Santa Evita* (Buenos Aires: Editorial Planeta, 1995), 192, specifically the passage that begins, "He reconstruido cada línea de ese diálogo más de una vez . . ."

44. For more on the construction of this rhetoric, see in particular the introduction and chapter 1 of Feitlowitz, *A Lexicon of Terror*.

45. Avelar, *The Untimely Present*, 187.

46. Martínez, *La novela de Perón*, 170.

47. For more on Benedetti's notion of "desexilio," or "dis-exile," see Frans Weiser, "Lost Between Past and Future: Mario Benedetti's Geography of Return," in *Cartographies of Exile: A New Spatial Literacy*, ed. Karen Elizabeth Bishop (New York: Routledge, 2016), 173–190.

48. Martínez, *La novela de Perón*, 308.

49. Martínez, *La novela de Perón*, 17.

50. As I discuss in other chapters, the missed opportunity is Benjamin's definition of catastrophe as a basic historical concept. Here the fact that Perón never lands at Ezeiza provides for the massacre that this non-event, or missed opportunity,

opens up. See Walter Benjamin, *The Arcades Project*, trans. Howard Eiland and Kevin McLaughlin (Cambridge, MA: Belknap Press, 2002), 474.

51. Martínez, *La novela de Perón*, 210–211.

52. Martínez, *La novela de Perón*, 338–339.

53. Bighead, who is a part of Nun's group, entered into a deal with one of López Rega's lieutenants to send off the shot that would allow his boss's Peronist faction to fire on the Montoneros. Throughout the story, Bighead has been working with Nun and Diana, and they do not anticipate his betrayal. When he shoots, he does not take aim at anyone in particular but fires into the air and shouts, "Perón o muerte!" (Perón or death!) Seconds later the snipers shoot off the nape of his neck, and the action of the narrative resumes, more frenzied than before. The divisive gap in time that prefaces this action is also the uncrossable divide that opens up between the divergent Peronist factions that have been waiting for an excuse to break out in violence.

Chapter Four

1. For more on Aramburu's efforts at "deperonización," see Rock, *Argentina*.

2. A broad historical overview of the handling of Evita's preserved corpse can be found in chapter 11 of Nicholas Fraser and Marysa Navarro, *Evita: The Real Life of Eva Perón* (New York: W.W. Norton, 1996).

3. For more on these distortions, particularly Emilio Massera's orchestration of public rhetoric in support of the junta, see this book's introduction and the introduction of Feitlowitz's *A Lexicon of Terror*.

4. Eva Perón's principal biographies include Fraser and Navarro, *Evita*; Alicia Dujovne Ortiz, *Eva Perón: La biografía* (Madrid: Santillana Ediciones Generales, 1996); Fermín Chávez, *Eva Perón en la historia* (Buenos Aires: Ediciones Oriente, 1986); and *Eva Perón: Sin mitos* (Buenos Aires: Editorial Fraterna, 1990).

5. Perón is said to have exclaimed "¡qué atorrantes!" (those bastards!) upon opening his late wife's coffin after sixteen years. See Ortiz, *Eva Perón: La biografía*, 522–533.

6. Dr. Ara's published memoirs are also evidence of his outsized dedication to the corpse. See Pedro Ara, *El caso Eva Perón: (apuntes para a historia)* (Madrid: CVS Ediciones, 1974).

7. Martínez also narrates Dr. Ara's attempt to secure this same authorization from Doña Juana, but she refuses to give it to him or to help him bury the copies he has made of her daughter's body. On this point, as on countless others, Martínez's account detours from historical record. In his auto/biography, Dr. Ara includes a facsimile of a copy of a letter apparently given to him by Eva's mother, in which she names him protector of her daughter's corpse should Perón neglect to offer up any instructions of his own for the care of Evita's body. The letter is written on

stationery engraved with the initials of Juana Ibarguren de Duarte and signed by her on September 20, 1955, during the political turmoil that ensued shortly after Perón was unseated as president. See Ara, *El caso Eva Perón*.

8. Martínez reports that an earlier version of the novel went on for another fifty pages. I am indebted to Margo Persin for sharing with me her comments and line edits on an early draft of the novel that the author asked her to read.

9. Roman Jakobson, "The Metaphoric and Metonymic Poles," in *Modern Criticism and Theory: A Reader*, 3rd ed., ed. David Lodge and Nigel Woods (New York: Routledge, 2013), 165–168.

10. Paul Ricoeur, *The Rule of Metaphor: The Creation of Meaning in Language*, trans. Robert Czerny (London: Routledge, 2003), 194. Ricoeur cites from Jean Cohen, *Structure du langue poétique* (Paris: Flammarion, 1966), 117–118.

11. Aristotle's understanding of *topos* is intimately connected to describing the relation of bodies in space. Luce Irigaray, as I discuss later, will both build on and complicate this possibility. For more, see Edward S. Casey, *The Fate of Place: A Philosophical History* (Berkeley: University of California Press, 1997); and Rebecca Hill, *The Interval: Relation and Becoming in Irigaray, Aristotle, and Bergson* (New York: Fordham University Press, 2012).

12. Martínez, *Santa Evita*, 154. I use throughout Helen Lane's translations of the novel. See Tomás Eloy Martínez, *Santa Evita*, trans. Helen Lane (New York: Vintage, 1996).

13. Martínez, *Santa Evita*, 154.

14. Martínez, *Santa Evita*, 34.

15. Ricoeur, *The Rule of Metaphor*, 214.

16. Ricoeur, *The Rule of Metaphor*, 210.

17. In his work on dreams and the unconscious, Freud understands condensation as a synecdochic operation and displacement as properly metonymic. See Sigmund Freud, *The Interpretation of Dreams*, trans. Joyce Crick (Oxford: Oxford University Press, 1999), particularly section 6 on "The Dream-Work." Lacan will later revise this when he aligns condensation with metaphor.

18. Emilio Massera, the navy's representative in the Videla junta, delivered this speech at the Navy Mechanics School (ESMA) on November 2, 1976, eight months after the coup d'état that ushered in the dictatorship. See Emilio E. Massera, *El Camino a la democracia* (Caracas: El Cid Editor, 1979), 15–18. Cited by Feitlowitz, *A Lexicon of Terror*, 25–26.

19. See note 7 in this work's introduction.

20. Baudrillard, *Simulacra and Simulation*, 6.

21. Martínez, *Santa Evita*, 55.

22. Ara, *El caso de Eva Perón*, 203.

23. The full passage reads: "When the real is no longer what it was, nostalgia assumes its full meaning. There is a plethora of myths of origin and of signs of

reality—a plethora of truth, of secondary objectivity, and authenticity. Escalation of the true, lived experience, resurrection of the figurative where the object and substance have disappeared. Panic-stricken production of the real and of the referential, parallel to and greater than the panic of material production: this is how simulation appears in the phase that concerns us—a strategy of the real, of the neoreal and that hyperreal that everywhere is the double of a strategy of deterrence." Baudrillard, *Simulacra and Simulation*, 7.

24. Baudrillard, *Simulacra and Simulation*, 9.

25. Baudrillard, *Simulacra and Simulation*, 10.

26. Quoted by Casey, *The Fate of Place*, 57. This summary draws from Aristotle's later formulations on the conception of place.

27. Elizabeth Grosz, "Architectures of Excess," in *Architecture from the Outside: Essays on Real and Virtual Space* (Cambridge, MA: MIT Press, 2001), 157.

28. Grosz, "Architectures of Excess," 158.

29. Grosz, "Architectures of Excess," 156–157.

30. Casey, *The Fate of Place*, 325. Emphasis in original.

31. Luce Irigaray, *An Ethics of Sexual Difference*, trans. Carolyn Burke and Gillian C. Gill (New York: Continuum, 2005), 32. This last sentence appears as a vertical list in the text. Where also cited by Casey, this key sentence is omitted.

32. Casey, *The Fate of Place*, 325.

33. Casey, *The Fate of Place*, 326. My reflections on Irigaray are indebted to Casey, whose reading of the pressures that Irigaray exerts on Aristotle is more nuanced and extensive. But my brief reading will help to elucidate one of Grosz's proposals for thinking about space otherwise, and then also the communities that excess might provide for.

34. Grosz, "Architectures of Excess," 162–163.

35. Grosz, "Architectures of Excess," 162.

36. Grosz, "Architectures of Excess," 162.

37. David Sherman, "Joyce, Faulkner, and the Modernist Burial Plot," in *In a Strange Room: Modernism's Corpses and Mortal Obligation* (Oxford: Oxford University Press, 2014), 108. I am indebted to David Sherman's many generous conversations and collaborations about dead bodies and the stories they demand.

38. See in particular the first two volumes of Ricoeur's series on time and narrative. Paul Ricoeur, *Time and Narrative*, vols. 1–2, trans. Kathleen McLaughlin and David Pellauer (Chicago: University of Chicago Press, 1984; 1985).

39. I refer here to my discussion of McHale in this work's introduction. See McHale, *Postmodernist Fiction*, 10.

40. This is also the number of cassette tapes that Martínez recorded in his interview with Perón in 1970. See Martínez, *Las memorias del general*, 14.

41. In the end, the copies will be hastily buried only to be later dug back up and sent to Lisbon, Rotterdam, and Hamburg or Rotterdam, Brussels, and Rome, depending on whose account we most trust, and several people will die in the

process. The former is Colonel Corominas's version of events, the latter Koenig's. See Martínez, *Santa Evita*, 78.

42. Martínez, *Santa Evita*, 151–152.

43. Martínez, *Santa Evita*, 151.

44. Jorge Luis Borges, "La muerte y la brújula," in *Ficciones* (Madrid: Alianza Editorial, 1997), 171–172. I use here Donald Yates's translation into English from Jorge Luis Borges, "Death and the Compass," in *Labyrinths: Selected Stories and Other Writings*, ed. and trans. Donald A. Yates and James E. Irby (New York: New Directions, 1964).

45. Borges, "La muerte y la brújula," 177.

46. Jorge Luis Borges, "El jardín de senderos que se bifurcan," in *Ficciones* (Madrid: Alianza Editorial, 1997), 105. I use here Donald Yates' translation into English from Jorge Luis Borges, "The Garden of Forking Paths," in *Labyrinths: Selected Stories and Other Writings*, ed. and trans. Donald A. Yates and James E. Irby (New York: New Directions, 1964).

47. Benjamin, "On the Concept of History," 392.

48. For a more extensive discussion of genre and the genealogy of this apocryphal phrase, see Bishop, "Myth Turned Monument," 151–162. For further scholarship on Martínez's larger project to trouble the boundaries between history and fiction in *Santa Evita*, see Caleb Bach, "Imagining the Truth," *Américas* 50, no. 3 (May/June 1998): 15–21; Graciela Michelotti-Cristóbal, "Eva Perón: Mujer, personaje, mito," *Confluencia* (Spring 1998): 135–144; Rita De Grandis, "Evita / Eva Perón: entre la Evita global y la local," *Revista Canadiense de Estudios Hispánicos* 23, no. 3 (Spring 1999): 521–528; Olga Steimberg de Kaplán, "El problema de la verdad en la nueva novela histórica: la obra de Tomás Eloy Martínez," *Alba de América* 17, no. 32 (Spring 1999): 187–195; Lloyd Hughes Davies, "Portraits of a Lady: Postmodern Readings of Tomás Eloy Martínez's *Santa Evita*," *Modern Language Review* 95, no. 2 (April 2000): 415–423; Alma Guillermoprieto, *Looking for History: Dispatches from Latin America* (New York: Pantheon Books, 2001); Neyret, "Novela significa"; and Lloyd Hughes Davies, *Projections of Peronism in Argentine Autobiography, Biography and Fiction* (Cardiff: University of Wales Press, 2007).

49. Martínez, *La novela de Perón*, 300.

50. Taylor, *Disappearing Acts*, 140.

51. Taylor, *Disappearing Acts*, 145.

52. Martínez, "Myth, History and Fiction in Latin America," 12.

Conclusion

1. Blanchot, "The Disappearance of Literature," 199.
2. Blanchot, "The Disappearance of Literature," 199–200.
3. Blanchot, "The Disappearance of Literature," 199–200.

4. See Aaron Hillyer, *The Disappearance of Literature: Blanchot, Agamben, and the Writers of the No* (New York: Bloomsbury, 2013), for more on the "non-literature" that Blanchot proposes and its iterations in later theory and literature.

5. Walter Benjamin, "The Task of the Translator," in *Illuminations*, trans. Harry Zohn (New York: Schocken Books, 1969), 69.

6. Blanchot, "The Disappearance of Literature," 200.

7. Blanchot, "The Disappearance of Literature," 198.

8. Blanchot, "The Disappearance of Literature," 198.

9. Benjamin, "On the Concept of History," 390. Emphasis in original. See Michael G. Levine, *A Weak Messianic Power: Figures of a Time to Come in Benjamin, Derrida, and Celan* (New York: Fordham University Press, 2014), for a more extensive meditation on Benjamin's observation. I am grateful to Michael Levine's generous comments on an early version of this conclusion.

10. Blanchot, "The Disappearance of Literature," 201.

11. Blanchot, "The Disappearance of Literature," 201.

12. Blanchot, "The Disappearance of Literature," 201.

13. Blanchot, "The Disappearance of Literature," 201. Emphasis added.

14. Blanchot, "The Disappearance of Literature," 195.

15. These include Giorgio Agamben's "coming community," Maurice Blanchot's necessary "absence of community," Jean-Luc Nancy's "unworked community" (*communauté désouvrée*)—this not quite inoperative, per J. Hillis Miller, but deconstructed—and Georges Bataille's "negative community."

16. McClennen and Slaughter, "Introducing Human Rights and Literary Forms," 11.

17. Avelar, *The Untimely Present*, 232.

Works Cited

Actis, Munú, Cristina Aldini, Liliana Gardella, Miriam Lewin, and Elisa Tokar. *Ese infierno: Conversaciones de cinco mujeres sobrevivientes de la ESMA*. Buenos Aires: Editorial Sudamericana, 2001.
Adorno, Theodor W. "Cultural Criticism and Society." In *Prisms*, translated by Samuel and Shierry Weber, 17–34. Cambridge, MA: MIT Press, 1967.
———. *Minima Moralia: Reflections on a Damaged Life*. Translated by E. F. N. Jephcott. New York: Verso, 2006.
Agamben, Giorgio. *Homo Sacer: Sovereign Power and Bare Life*. Translated by Daniel Heller-Roazen. Stanford: Stanford University Press, 1998.
Agresti, Alejandro, dir. *Buenos Aires vice-versa*. Buenos Aires: SBP, 1996.
Anker, Elizabeth S. *Fictions of Dignity: Embodying Human Rights in World Literature*. Ithaca, NY: Cornell University Press, 2017.
Ara, Pedro. *El caso Eva Perón: (apuntes para la historia)*. Madrid: CVS Ediciones, 1974.
Ashbery, John. Introduction, 1–7. *Fantômas*. New York: Penguin, 2006.
Auden, W. H. "The Guilty Vicarage." *Harper's*. May 1948 (accessed 7 March 2017). http://harpers.org/archive/1948/05/the-guilty-vicarage/.
Avelar, Idelber. *The Untimely Present: Postdictatorial Latin American Fiction and the Task of Mourning*. Durham, NC: Duke University Press, 1999.
Bach, Caleb. "Imagining the Truth." *Américas* 50, no. 3 (May/June 1998): 15–21.
Barataud, Marie-Alexandra. "Del texto y de la imagen: la escritura transgenérica en *Fantomas contra los vampiros multinacionales de Julio Cortázar*." N.d. (accessed 10 November 2017). www.crimic.paris-sorbonne.fr/actes/sa4/barataud.pdf.
Baudrillard, Jean. *Simulacra and Simulation*. Translated by Sheila Faria Glaser. Ann Arbor: University of Michigan Press, 1994.
Balfour, Ian, and Eduardo Cadava, eds. "And Justice for All? The Claims of Human Rights." *South Atlantic Quarterly* 103, no. 2/3 (2004): 277–588.
Bechis, Marco, dir. *Garaje olimpo*. México D.F.: Zima Entertainment, 1999.
Benjamin, Walter. *The Arcades Project*. Translated by Howard Eiland and Kevin McLaughlin. Cambridge, MA: Belknap Press, 2002.

———. "On the Concept of History." In *Selected Writings*, vol. 4: 1938–1940, translated by Edmund Jephcott et al., 389–400. Cambridge, MA: Belknap Press, 2006.

———. "The Task of the Translator." In *Illuminations*, translated by Harry Zohn, 69–82. New York: Schocken Books, 1969.

Beverley, John. *Against Literature*. Minneapolis: University of Minnesota Press, 1993.

Biraben, Gastón. *Cautiva*. Buenos Aires: Primer Plano Film Group, 2003.

Bishop, Karen Elizabeth. "The Architectural History of Disappearance: Rebuilding Memory Sites in the Southern Cone." *Journal of the Society of Architectural Historians* 73, no. 4 (December 2014): 556–578.

———. "Myth Turned Monument: Documenting the Historical Imaginary in Buenos Aires and Beyond." *Journal of Modern Literature* 30, no. 2 (2007): 151–162.

———. "On Teaching the Close Reading of Torture Literature: An Approximation." In *Teaching Human Rights in Literary and Cultural Studies*, edited by Alexandra Schulteis and Elizabeth Swanson Goldberg, 178–188. New York: Modern Language Association, 2015.

Blanchot, Maurice. "The Disappearance of Literature." In *The Book to Come*, translated by Charlotte Mandel, 195–201. Stanford: Stanford University Press, 2003.

———. *The Space of Literature*. Translated by Ann Smock. Lincoln: University of Nebraska Press, 1989.

Blaustein, David. *Botín de guerra*. Buenos Aires: Cinemateca, 2000.

Borges, Jorge Luis. *Ficciones: relatos*. Madrid: Alianza Editorial, 1997.

Brodsky, Marcelo. *Memoria en construcción: El debate sobre la* ESMA. Buenos Aires: la marca editora, 2005.

Butler, Judith. *Frames of War: When Is Life Grievable?* New York: Verso, 2009.

———. *Precarious Life: The Powers of Mourning and Violence*. New York: Verso, 2004.

Calveiro, Pilar. *Poder y Desaparición: Los campos de concentración en Argentina*. Buenos Aires: Ediciones Colihue, 2001.

Carlson, Eric Stener. *I Remember Julia: Voices of the Disappeared*. Philadelphia: Temple University Press, 1996.

Caruth, Cathy. *Literature in the Ashes of History*. Baltimore: Johns Hopkins University Press, 2013.

Casey, Edward S. *The Fate of Place: A Philosophical History*. Berkeley: University of California Press, 1997.

Catalá Carrasco, Jorge L., Paulo Drinot, and James Scorer, eds. *Comics and Memory in Latin America*. Pittsburgh: University of Pittsburgh Press, 2017.

Chávez, Fermín. *Eva Perón en la historia*. Buenos Aires: Ediciones Oriente, 1986.

———. *Eva Perón: Sin mitos*. Buenos Aires: Editorial Fraterna, 1990.

Cohen, Tom, Claire Colebrook, and J. Hillis Miller. *Theory and the Disappearing Future: On de Man, on Benjamin*. New York: Routledge, 2012.

Cohen Imach, Victoria. "Las máscaras o el pintor de paredes: Asunción de la periferia en 'Variaciones en rojo' de Rodolfo Walsh." *Hispamérica* 58 (1991): 3–15.

"Comunicado de la familia." N.d. (accessed 20 October 2017). http://www.santiagomaldonado.com/comunicado-la-familia-2010/.
Cortázar, Julio. *Cartas*, vol. 2. Edited by Aurora Bernárdez. Buenos Aires: Alfaguara, 2000.
———. *Cartas*, vol. 4. Edited by Aurora Bernárdez and Carles Álvarez Garriga. Buenos Aires: Alfaguara, 2012.
———. "Continuidad de los parques." In *Los relatos, 2: Juegos*. Madrid: Alianza, 2004. 7–8.
———. "Continuity of Parks." In *Blow-Up and Other Stories*, translated by Paul Blackburn. New York: Pantheon Books, 1967.
———. *Fantomas contra los vampiros multinacionales*. México D.F.: Excelsior, 1975.
———. *Fantomas versus the Multinational Vampires: An Attainable Utopia*. Translated by David Kurnick. Los Angeles: Semiotext(e), 2014.
———. "The Fellowship of Exile." Translated by John Incledon. *Review: Literature and Arts of the Americas* 15, no. 30 (1981): 14–16.
———. *Obra crítica*, vol. 3. Edited by Saúl Sosnowski. Madrid: Alfaguara, 1994.
Dandan, Alejandra. "No se sabe nada de lo que pasó con Pablo." *Página/12*. 11 October 2010 (accessed 18 March 2018). https://www.pagina12.com.ar/diario/elpais/1-154722-2010-10-11.html.
Davies, Lloyd Hughes. "Portraits of a Lady: Postmodern Readings of Tomás Eloy Martínez's *Santa Evita*." *Modern Language Review* 95, no. 2 (April 2000): 415–423.
———. *Projections of Peronism in Argentine Autobiography, Biography and Fiction*. Cardiff: University of Wales Press, 2007.
Dawes, James. "Human Rights in Literary Studies." *Human Rights Quarterly* 31 (2009): 394–409.
———. *The Novel of Human Rights*. Cambridge, MA: Harvard University Press, 2018.
———. *That the World May Know: Bearing Witness to Atrocity*. Cambridge, MA: Harvard University Press, 2007.
De Grandis, Rita. "Evita/Eva Perón: entre la Evita global y la local." *Revista Canadiense de Estudios Hispánicos* 23, no. 3 (Spring 1999): 521–528.
de Man, Paul. *Blindness and Insight: Essays in the Rhetoric of Contemporary Criticism*, 2nd ed. Minneapolis: University of Minnesota Press, 1983.
———. *The Resistance to Theory*. Minneapolis: University of Minnesota Press, 1986.
Draper, Susana. *Afterlives of Confinement: Spatial Transitions in Postdictatorship Latin America*. Pittsburgh: University of Pittsburgh Press, 2012.
Eco, Umberto. *The Limits of Interpretation*. Bloomington: Indiana University Press, 1991.
Feitlowitz, Marguerite. *A Lexicon of Terror: Argentina and the Legacies of Torture*. New York: Oxford University Press, 1998.
Fernández Vega, José. "De la teología a la política: El problema del mal en la literatura policial de Rodolfo Walsh." *Hispamérica: revista de literatura* 83 (1999): 5–15.

Fisher, Jo. *Mothers of the Disappeared*. Boston: South End Press, 1989.
Fletcher, Angus. *Allegory: The Theory of a Symbolic Mode*. Princeton: Princeton University Press, 2012.
Fontes, Claudia. "Reconstruction of the Portrait of Pablo Míguez." N.d. (accessed 18 March 2018). http://claudiafontes.com/project/reconstruction-of-the-portrait-of-pablo-miguez/.
Foucault, Michel. *The Order of Things: An Archaeology of the Human Sciences*. Vintage: New York, 1994.
Ford, Aníbal. "Walsh: la reconstrucción de los hechos." In *Nueva novela latinoamericana*, vol. 2, edited by Jorge Lafforgue, 272–322. Buenos Aires: Editorial Paidos, 1972.
Franco, Bridget V. "Floating Statues and Streams of Consciousness: Memory Work in Argentina's Río de la Plata and Río Salí." In *Written in the Water: The Image of the River in Latin/o American Literature*, edited by Jeanie Murphy and Elizabeth G. Rivero, 35–54. Lanham, MD: Lexington Books, 2018.
Franco, Jean. "Comic Stripping: Cortázar in the Age of Mechanical Reproduction." In *Julio Cortázar: New Readings*, edited by Carlos J. Alonso, 36–56. Cambridge: Cambridge University Press, 1998.
Fraser, Nicholas, and Marysa Navarro. *Evita: The Real Life of Eva Perón*. New York: W.W. Norton, 1996.
Freud, Sigmund. *The Interpretation of Dreams*. Translated by Joyce Crick. Oxford: Oxford University Press, 1999.
Gamerro, Carlos. "Rodolfo Walsh: Prólogo a una edición nonata de sus *Obras escogidas*." *Hispamérica* 123 (2012): 3–14.
Ganduglia, Silvia. "La representación de la historia en *La novela de Perón*." *Ideologies and Literature* 4, no. 1 (1989): 271–297.
Genette, Gérard. *Figures of Discourse*. Translated by Alan Sheridan. New York: Columbia University Press, 1982.
Girard, René. *Violence and the Sacred*. Translated by Patrick Gregory. Baltimore: Johns Hopkins University Press, 1977.
Gómez Carro, Carlos. "La amenaza elegante: *Fantomas*, Julio Cortázar y Gonzalo Martré." *Revista replicante*. 10 April 2011 (accessed 10 November 2017). http://revistareplicante.com/la-amenaza-elegante/.
Goñi, Uki. "Blaming the Victims: Dictator Denialism Is on the Rise in Argentina." *The Guardian*. 29 August 2016 (accessed 3 October 2016). https://www.theguardian.com/world/2016/aug/29/argentina-denial-dirty-war-genocide-mauricio-macri.
González Bermejo, Ernesto. *Conversaciones con Cortázar*. Barcelona: EDHASA, 1978.
Grosz, Elizabeth. "Architectures of Excess." In *Architecture from the Outside: Essays on Real and Virtual Space*, 151–166. Cambridge, MA: MIT Press, 2001.
Guest, Iain. *Behind the Disappearances: Argentina's Dirty War Against Human Rights and the United Nations*. Philadelphia: University of Pennsylvania Press, 1990.
Guillermoprieto, Alma. *Looking for History: Dispatches from Latin America*. New York: Pantheon Books, 2001.

Hill, Rebecca. *The Interval: Relation and Becoming in Irigaray, Aristotle, and Bergson.* New York: Fordham University Press, 2012.
Hillyer, Aaron. *The Disappearance of Literature: Blanchot, Agamben, and the Writers of the No.* New York: Bloomsbury, 2013.
Huyssen, Andreas. "Memory Sites in an Expanded Field: The Memory Park in Buenos Aires." In *Present Pasts: Urban Palimpsests and the Politics of Memory*, 94–109. Stanford: Stanford University Press, 2003.
Irigaray, Luce. *An Ethics of Sexual Difference.* Translated by Carolyn Burke and Gillian C. Gill. New York: Continuum, 2005.
Jakobson, Roman. "The Metaphoric and Metonymic Poles." In *Modern Criticism and Theory: A Reader*, 3rd ed., edited by David Lodge and Nigel Woods, 165–168. New York: Routledge, 2013.
Jameson, Fredric. *The Political Unconscious: Narrative as a Socially Symbolic Act.* New York: Routledge, 2002.
Kaiser, Susana. *Postmemories of Terror: A New Generation Copes with the Legacy of the "Dirty War."* New York: Palgrave Macmillan, 2005.
Katz, Paul Ryan. "A New 'Normal': Political Complicity, Exclusionary Violence and the Delegation of Argentine Jewish Associations during the Argentine Dirty War." *The International Journal of Transitional Justice* 5, no. 3 (November 2011): 366–389.
Koselleck, Reinhart. "History, Histories, and Formal Time Structures." In *Futures Past: On the Semantics of Historical Time*, translated by Keith Tribe, 93–104. Cambridge, MA: MIT Press.
——— . "Some Questions Regarding the Conceptual History of 'Crisis.'" In *The Practice of Conceptual History: Timing History, Spacing Concepts*, translated by Todd Samuel Presner et al., 236–247. Stanford. Stanford University Press, 2002.
——— . "The Unknown Future and the Art of Prognosis." In *The Practice of Conceptual History: Timing History, Spacing Concepts*, translated by Todd Samuel Presner et al., 131–147. Stanford: Stanford University Press, 2002.
Kurnick, David. "Three Booklets of 1975." In Julio Cortázar, *Fantomas versus the Multinational Vampires: An Attainable Utopia*, translated by David Kurnick, 81–87. Los Angeles: Semiotext(e), 2014.
Kusnetzoff, Juan Carlos. "Renegación, desmentida, desaparición y percepticido como técnicas psicopáticas de la salvación de la patria (Una visión psicoanalítica del informe de la CONADEP)." In *Psicoanálisis, represión, política*, edited by Oscar Abudara et al., 95–114. Buenos Aires: Ediciones Kargieman, 1986.
Lacan, Jacques. "Seminar on 'The Purloined Letter.'" In *The Poetics of Murder: Detective Fiction and Literary Theory*, edited by Glenn W. Most and William W. Stowe, 21–54. San Diego: Harcourt Brace Jovanovich, 1983.
Lafforgue, Jorge, ed. *Nuevo Texto Crítico* 12–13 (July 1993–June 1994).
Levine, Annette H. *Cry For Me, Argentina: The Performance of Trauma in the Short Narratives of Aída Bortnik, Griselda Gambaro, and Tununa Mercado.* Madison, NJ: Fairleigh Dickinson University Press, 2008.

Levine, Caroline. *Forms: Whole, Rhythm, Hierarchy, Network*. Princeton: Princeton University Press, 2015.

Levine, Michael G. *A Weak Messianic Power: Figures of a Time to Come in Benjamin, Derrida and Celan*. New York: Fordham University Press, 2014.

Lyotard, Jean-François. "The Other's Rights." In *The Politics of Human Rights*, edited by The Belgrade Circle, 181–188. London: Verso, 1999.

Gates-Madsen, Nancy J. *Trauma, Taboo, and Truth-Telling: Listening to Silences in Postdictatorship Argentina*. Madison: University of Wisconsin Press, 2016.

Mandelbaum, Juan. *Our Disappeared/Nuestros desaparecidos*. Newburgh: New Day Films, 2008.

Martin, Gerald. "Tomás Eloy Martínez, Biography and the Boom: *La novela de Perón* (1985) and *Santa Evita* (1995)." *Bulletin of Latin American Research* 31, no. 4 (2012): 460–472.

Martínez, Tomás Eloy. "Ficción e historia en *La novela de Perón*." *Hispamérica: revista de literatura* 17, no. 49 (April 1988): 41–49.

———. *Las memorias del general*. Buenos Aires: Planeta, 1996.

———. "Myth, History and Fiction in Latin America." Translated by Marguerite Feitlowitz. Lecture presented at the Inter-American Development Bank Cultural Center, Washington, DC, May 1999. Reprinted in *Encuentros* 32 (May 1999): 1–14.

———. *La novela de Perón*. New York: Vintage, 1985.

———. "La novela de Perón." *El Periodista de Buenos Aires*. September 1984.

———. *The Perón Novel*. Translated by Helen Lane. New York: Knopf, 1998.

———. *Santa Evita*. Buenos Aires: Editorial Planeta, 1995.

———. *Santa Evita*. Translated by Helen Lane. New York: Vintage, 1997.

Martínez-Richter, Marily, ed. *La caja de escritura: diálogos con narradores y críticos argentinos*. Madrid: Iberoamericana, 1997.

Massera, Emilio E. *El Camino a la democracia*. Caracas: El Cid Editor, 1979.

McCaughan, Michael. *True Crimes: Rodolfo Walsh, the Life and Times of a Radical Intellectual*. London: Latin American Bureau, 2002.

McClennen, Sophia A., and Joseph R. Slaughter. "Introducing Human Rights and Literary Forms; Or, The Vehicles and Vocabularies of Human Rights." *Comparative Literature Studies* 46, no. 1 (2009): 1–19.

McCloud, Scott. *Understanding Comics: The Invisible Art*. New York: HarperCollins, 1993.

McCracken, Ellen. "Hybridity and Postmodernity in the Argentine Meta-Comic: The Bridge Texts of Julio Cortázar and Ricardo Piglia." In *Latin American Literature and Mass Media*, edited by Edmundo Paz-Soldán and Debra A. Castillo, 139–151. New York: Garland, 2001.

———. "*Libro de Manuel* and *Fantomas contra los vampiros multinacionales*: Mass Culture, Art, and Politics." In *Literature and Popular Culture in the Hispanic World: A Symposium*, edited by Rose S. Minc, 69–77. Gaithersburg, MD: Hispamérica, 1981.

McDuffie, Keith. "*La novela de Perón*: historia, ficción, testimonio." In *La historia de la literatura iberoamericana*, compiled by Raquel Chang Rodríguez and Gabriella de Beer, 295–305. Hanover, NH: Ediciones del Norte, 1989.

McHale, Brian. *Postmodernist Fiction*. New York: Routledge, 1987.

"Las memorias del general." Fundación Tomás Eloy Martínez. 29 March 2016 (accessed 17 March 2018). http://fundaciontem.org/las-memorias-del-general.

Michelotti-Cristóbal, Graciela. "Eva Perón: Mujer, personaje, mito." *Confluencia* (Spring 1998): 135–144.

Miller, J. Hillis. *The Conflagration of Community: Fiction before and after Auschwitz*. Chicago: University of Chicago Press, 2011.

Nancy, Jean-Luc. *Le partage des voix*. Paris: Éditions Galilée, 1982.

Neyret, Juan Pablo. "Novela significa licencia para mentir." *Espéculo: Revista de estudios literarios* (2002): n.p., http://www.ucm.es/info/especulo/numero22/t_eloy.html.

Nunca Más: Informe de la Comisión Nacional sobre la Desaparición de Personas. Buenos Aires: EUDEBA, 1984.

Olivera, Héctor, dir. *La noche de los lápices*. New York: Latin American Video Archives, 1986.

Ortiz, Alicia Dujovne. *Eva Perón: La biografía*. Madrid: Santillana Ediciones Generales, 1996.

Parikh, Crystal. *Writing Human Rights: The Political Imaginaries of Writers of Color*. Minneapolis: University of Minnesota Press, 2017.

Parodi, Cristina. "Ficción y realidad en *La novela de Perón* de Tomás Eloy Martínez." *Nuevo Texto Crítico* 4, no. 8 (1991): 39–43.

Partnoy, Alicia. *The Little School: Tales of Disappearance and Survival*. Translated by Alicia Partnoy with Lois Athey and Sandra Braunstein. San Francisco: Cleis Press, 1986.

Pavel, Thomas. *Fictional Worlds*. Cambridge, MA: Harvard University Press, 1986.

Perloff, Marjorie. *21st-Century Modernism: The "New" Poetics*. Oxford: Wiley-Blackwell, 2002.

Phelan, James. *Narrative as Rhetoric: Techniques, Audiences, Ethics, Ideology*. Columbus: Ohio State University Press, 1996.

———. *Reading People, Reading Plots: Character, Progression, and the Interpretation of Narrative*. Chicago: University of Chicago Press, 1989.

Piglia, Ricardo. *Crítica y Ficción*. Madrid: Debolsillo, 2014.

———. *Por un relato futuro: Conversaciones con Juan José Saer*. Madrid: Anagrama, 2015.

Poe, Edgar Allan. "The Philosophy of Composition." In *The Norton Anthology of Theory and Criticism*, 739–750. New York: W.W. Norton & Co., 2001.

Premat, Julio. "Contratiempos. Literatura y época." *Revista de estudios hispánicos* 48, no. 1 (2014): 201–217.

———. *Non nova sed nove: inactualidades, anacronismos, resistencias en la literatura contemporánea*. Macerata: Quodlibet Elements, 2018.

Puenzo, Luis, dir. *La historia oficial*. Port Washington, NY: Koch Lorber Films, 1985.

Punte, María José. "Perón: Personaje de Novela." *RILCE: Revista de Filología Hispánica* 20, no. 2 (2004): 223–239.
Rajca, Andrew C. *Dissensual Subjects: Memory, Human Rights, and Postdictatorship in Argentina, Brazil, and Uruguay*. Evanston, IL: Northwestern University Press, 2018.
Rancière, Jacques. "Aesthetic Separation, Aesthetic Community: Scenes from the Aesthetic Regime of Art." Lecture delivered June 20, 2006, at the symposium Aesthetics and Politics: With and Around Jacques Rancière, University of Amsterdam. *Art and Research: A Journal of Ideas, Contexts, and Methods* 2, no. 1 (Summer 2008): http://www.artandresearch.org.uk/v2n1/pdfs/ranciere.pdf.
———. *The Emancipated Spectator*. Translated by Gregory Elliott. New York: Verso, 2011.
———. *The Politics of Aesthetics: The Distribution of the Sensible*. Translated by Gabriel Rockhill. London: Continuum, 2004.
Reati, Fernando. *Nombrar lo innombrable: Violencia política y representación literaria en la novela argentina, 1975–1985*. Buenos Aires: Editorial Legasa, 1992.
Richard, Nelly. *The Insubordination of Signs: Political Change, Cultural Transformation, and Poetics of the Crisis*. Translated by Alice A. Nelson and Silvia R. Tandeciarz. Durham, NC: Duke University Press, 2004.
Ricoeur, Paul. *The Rule of Metaphor: The Creation of Meaning in Language*. Translated by Robert Czerny. London: Routledge, 2003.
———. *Time and Narrative*, vol. 1. Translated by Kathleen McLaughlin and David Pellauer. Chicago: University of Chicago Press, 1984.
———. *Time and Narrative*, vol. 2. Translated by Kathleen McLaughlin and David Pellauer. Chicago: University of Chicago Press, 1985.
Rock, David. *Argentina 1516–1987: From Spanish Colonization to Alfonsín*. Berkeley: University of California Press, 1987.
Roitman, Janet. *Anti-Crisis*. Durham, NC: Duke University Press, 2014.
Rubin, Merle. Book review of *Fantomas*. *Los Angeles Times*. 10 August 1986 (accessed 10 November 2017). http://articles.latimes.com/1986-08-10/books/bk-2030_1_marcel-allain.
Sheinin, David M. K. *Consent of the Damned: Ordinary Argentinians in the Dirty War*. Gainesville: University of Florida Press, 2012.
Sherman, David. *In a Strange Room: Modernism's Corpses and Mortal Obligation*. Oxford: Oxford University Press, 2014.
Slaughter, Joseph R. *Human Rights, Inc.: The World Novel, Narrative Form, and International Law*. New York: Fordham University Press, 2007.
Stanton, Domna C., ed. "The Humanities in Human Rights: Critique, Language, Politics." *PMLA* 121, no. 5 (October 2006): 1518–1661.
Schulteis Moore, Alexandra, and Elizabeth Swanson Goldberg. *Teaching Human Rights in Literary and Cultural Studies*. New York: The Modern Language Association of America, 2015.

Standish, Peter. *Understanding Julio Cortázar*. Columbia: University of South Carolina Press, 2001.
Steimberg de Kaplán, Olga. "El problema de la verdad en la nueva novela histórica: la obra de Tomás Eloy Martínez." *Alba de América* 17, no. 32 (Spring 1999): 187–195.
Stern, Steve J., and Scott Strauss, ed. *The Human Rights Paradox: Universality and Its Discontents*. Madison: University of Wisconsin Press, 2014.
Swanson Goldberg, Elizabeth. *Beyond Terror: Gender, Narrative, Human Rights*. New Brunswick, NJ: Rutgers University Press, 2007.
Taylor, Diana. *Disappearing Acts: Spectacles of Gender and Nationalism in Argentina's "Dirty War."* Durham, NC: Duke University Press, 1998.
Timerman, Jacobo. *Prisoner without a Name, Cell without a Number*. Translated by Toby Talbot. Madison: University of Wisconsin Press, 2002.
Verbitsky, Horacio. *Ezeiza*. Buenos Aires: Editorial Contrapunto, 1985.
———. *El vuelo*. Buenos Aires: Planeta, 1995.
Vidler, Anthony. "X Marks the Spot: The Exhaustion of Space at the Scene of the Crime." In *Warped Space: Art, Architecture, and Anxiety in Modern Culture*, 123–132. Durham, NC: Duke University Press, 2000.
Vigueras-Fernández, Ricardo. "El regreso de Fantomas: la conspiración Cortázar-Martré contra el neoliberalismo." *Polifonía: Revista académica de estudios hispánicos* 4 (2014): 38–50.
Viñas, David. "Rodolfo Walsh, el ajedrez y la guerra." In *Literatura argentina y política: De Lugones a Walsh* II, edited by Laura Éstrin and Miguel A. Villafañe, 167–173. Buenos Aires: Editorial Sudamericana, 1996.
Villani, Mario, and Fernando Reati. *Desaparecido: Memorias de un cautiverio. Club Atlético, El Banco, El Olimpo, Pozo de Quilmes, y ESMA*. Buenos Aires: Editorial Biblos, 2011.
Vinelli, Natalia. *ANCLA: Una experiencia de comunicación clandestina orientada por Rodolfo Walsh*. Buenos Aires: La Rosa Blindada, 2000.
Walsh, Rodolfo. "Carta abierta de un escritor a la junta militar." Centro Cultural de la Memoria Haroldo Conti, 24 March 1977. http://conti.derhuman.jus.gov.ar/_pdf/serie_1_walsh.pdf, 8–13.
———. *El violento oficio de escribir: obra periodística, 1953–1977*. Edited by Daniel Link. Buenos Aires: Ediciones de la Flor, 2008.
———. *Ese hombre y otros escritos personales*. Edited by Daniel Link. Buenos Aires: Seix Barral, 1996.
———. *Un oscuro día de justicia/Zugzwang*. Buenos Aires: Ediciones de la Flor, 2006.
———. *Variaciones en rojo*. Madrid: Espasa Calpe, 2002.
Walsh, Rodolfo J., ed. *Diez cuentos policiales argentinos*. Buenos Aires: Libreria Hachette, 1953.
Walz, Robin. *Pulp Surrealism: Insolent Popular Culture in Early Twentieth-Century Paris*. Berkeley: University of California Press, 2000.

Weiser, Frans. "Lost Between Past and Future: Mario Benedetti's Geography of Return." In *Cartographies of Exile: A New Spatial* Literacy, edited by Karen Elizabeth Bishop, 173–190. New York: Routledge, 2016.

White, Hayden. *The Content of the Form: Narrative Discourse and Historical Representation*. Baltimore: Johns Hopkins University Press, 1987.

———. *Tropics of Discourse: Essays in Cultural Criticism*. Baltimore: Johns Hopkins University Press, 1978.

Index

Adorno, Theodor W., 19–20, 22, 212n13
Agamben, Giorgio, 135, 176, 194
Aira, César, 201
Allain, Marcel, 214–215n8
allegory, 11, 22–23
ANCLA, 211n1
Apollinaire, Guillaume, 214n8
Ara, Pedro, 160–161
Aramburu, Pedro Eugenio, 42–43, 161–162, 171, 222n1
Arendt, Hannah, 23, 29, 199
Argentina: Buenos Aires, 6, 39–40, 42, 46, 124, 161, 191; concentration camps, 5–6, 40; coup d'état of 1976, 3, 5, 11; death squads, 39–40, 101; falsified histories, 121–122; genocide, 2–3, 71; human rights abuses, reports of, 6, 72, 170; military dictatorship, 2, 4–5, 7–11, 15, 19, 31, 40, 71–72, 94, 101, 111, 117, 124, 127–128, 170; national cleansing, 6, 101; postdictatorship, 12, 19, 24, 35, 160; return to democratic rule, 2, 12, 129, 201; social blinding, 6–8, 170; state terrorism, 2, 4–5, 7, 41, 71, 79, 130, 170, 192, 198; torture and detention centers, 3, 5, 6, 79, 205n6

Aristotle, 174–175, 223n11
Arlt, Roberto, 46
Ashbery, John, 214–215n8
Auden, W. H., 47
Avelar, Idelber, 11, 22–23, 121–122, 147–148, 201, 206n19

Bakhtin, Mikhail, 12
Barthes, Roland, 40
Basso, Lelio, 83–84
Bataille, Georges, 175, 226n15
Baudrillard, Jean, 67, 135–137, 172, 174
Benedetti, Mario, 150, 221n47
Benjamin, Walter, 19, 103, 110, 128, 167, 194, 195, 221–222n50
Bioy Casares, Adolfo, 42, 137, 212n15
Blanchot, Maurice, 3, 29–31, 62, 160, 193–197, 199, 201, 207n29, 226n15
blind spots, 19–20, 103, 207n29
Borges, Jorge Luis, 37, 42, 48, 180; "El jardin de senderos que se bifurcan" (The Garden of Forking Paths), 46, 187–188; "La muerte y la brujula" (Death and the Compass), 46, 183–185, 187
Bortnik, Aida, 14
Brecht, Bertolt, 96–97
Bruzzone, Félix, 202

Buñuel, Luis, 107f, 108
Bustos Domecq, H., 42, 42, 60
Butler, Judith, 9, 206n17

CADA (Art Actions Collective), 19–20
Calvino, Italo, 40
Cámpora, Héctor, 123, 220n15
Camps, Ramón, 9
Capote, Truman, 42
Caruth, Cathy, 30, 209–210n56
Casey, Edward S., 175–176, 224n33
catastrophe: definition of, 95, 221–222n50; etymology of, 95; hermeneutics of, 71–117; recognizing of, 95, 102; reading, 30, 102, 111. *See also* crisis narratives; vision, stereoscopic
Catholic Church, 6
Char, René, 30, 195
Chejfec, Sergio, 201
Chile, 105, 201; National Stadium, 98; postdictatorship, 19–20
close reading, 12, 31–32
Cohen, Jean, 166
commons, narrative, 27–29, 37, 117, 122, 192, 198–202
community: disappearance and, 27–28, 199; dissensual, 28; exile and, 27–28, 199; narrative and, 37; new forms of, 176–177, 226n15
Confederación General de Trabajadores (CGT), 161
Cortázar, Julio, 10, 13–14, 18, 29, 30, 33–34, 69, 192, 195, 196, 198, 202; "Apocalipsis en Solentiname," 74; "Axolotl," 101; biography, 73–74; "Continuidad de los parques," 76, 89–90, 101; exile, 72–78; *Fantomas contra los vampiros*, 33–34, 71–117, 141, 174, 192, 199; "La boca noche arriba," 76, 89, 101; letter to Eduardo Jonquières, 84; letter to Lelio Basso, 83–84; letter to Roberto Fernández Retamar, 77, 85; *Libro de Manuel*, 105; politics and political activism, 77–87; "Segunda vez," 74; use of form, 111–117; on exile, 74–76
crisis narratives, 103. *See also* Roitman, Janet
Cruz Mota, Víctor, 80, 90, 103
Cuban Revolution, 77

Dawes, James, 26
De Man, Paul, 12, 20, 207n29
Delegation of Argentine Jewish Associations, 6
Deleuze, Gilles, 176
Derrida, Jacques, 12, 15, 147
disappearance: aesthetics of, 12, 18, 29, 51–52; community formed by, 27–28, 199; denial of, 8; displacement, 4, 13–14, 23, 30, 41, 170, 192, 199; dissimulation, 4, 13–14, 41, 67–69; doublespeak of, 71; doubling, 13, 34, 72–73, 78, 87, 94, 95–96, 103, 116; embodiment, remaindered, 4, 13–14, 30, 41, 199; enforced, 4–10, 71–72, 170–171, 208–209n42; epistemology of, 4, 10–11, 24; exile and, 28–29, 74; historical distortions regarding, 4–10; of literature, 3, 29–31, 191–202; as literary device, 3, 11, 25, 26, 69–70; narrative commons of, 27–29, 202; narrative modes of, 3, 10–15, 16, 18–19, 23, 26–27, 29, 69–70, 201; postmodern preoccupation with, 18; suspension, 13, 122–123, 125, 127–131, 156, 159, 192; as a tool of state terrorism, 4–10, 67–68, 71, 79, 125, 130, 162; withholding, 14, 15, 122–123, 125, 131, 145–146

displacement, 4, 13–14, 23, 30, 41, 170, 192, 199; *Fantomas contra los vampiros multinacionales*, 34, 72, 73, 78, 87, 94, 103, 114, 116
dissimulation, 4, 13–14, 20, 30, 31, 192; "Variaciones en rojo," 32–33, 40–41, 59–60, 66–69
Dorfman, Ariel, 207n27, 215n12
doubling, 4, 13–14, 30, 41, 192, 199; *Fantomas contra los vampiros multinacionales*, 34, 72–73, 78, 87, 94–96, 103, 116

Eco, Umberto, 60, 213n31, 217n43
Ediciones Novaro, 80
El Periodista de Buenos Aires, 218–219n9
emplotment, 188; definition of, 179–180; narrative, 180
embodiment, 4, 13–14, 30, 41, 199; *Santa Evita*, 171–177
Escuela Superior de Mecánica de la Armada (ESMA), 39–40, 170, 171, 209n42, 223n18
Euler, Leonhard, 63
excess: architectures of, 36, 175–177; of national imaginary, 162–163, 170, 174, 188, 189; structure of narrative, 160, 174, 188. *See also* woman-as-place
exile: alternate experiences of, 74–76; dis-exile, 150; disappearance as form of, 28; doubled state of, 73, 76; fellowship of, 73–78; forms of, 29; narrative commons and, 28–29
Ezeiza airport massacre, 123, 124, 220n15, 221–222n50

Facundo, 162
Fantomas contra los vampiros multinacionales (*Fantomas versus the Multinational Vampires*) (Cortázar), 33, 174; appendix, 95–96, 105–106, 113; bibliocide, 80, 90, 92–93, 96; Big Lie, 92–93, 100, 112–113; catastrophe, 34, 71–117; circulation, 86; copyright page, 95–96; cover art, 80, 81f, 82, 95, 99; disappearance in, 72, 88, 98, 100, 116–117, 141; displacement in, 34, 72–73, 78, 87, 94, 103, 114, 116; doubling in, 34, 72–73, 78, 87, 94–95, 96, 103, 116; duplication in, 72; embedded fictional worlds, 72, 78, 79, 90–92, 98, 100–101, 103–104, 106, 113, 192, 199; ending, 79, 104, 115–117; Fantomas, 34, 79–80, 81f, 86–87, 91f, 92, 96, 105, 110–111, 113–116; first print run, 83, 215n11; historical correlates, 95–96, 102–103, 105, 110, 114; *Inteligencia en llamas*, 79, 88–89, 90, 91f, 92, 96, 98, 100–101, 103, 104, 106–108, 113, 117; Julio Cortázar (narrator), 79, 88, 89, 91f, 92–93, 96–101, 103, 105–106, 110–111, 113, 114–116; marketing of, 82–85; multinational corporations in, 79, 82, 110, 113; narrative techniques, 72, 79, 87, 94–95, 100, 110, 113–114, 117; opening scene, 88–89, 104, 116; telephone call, 113–117; political message of, 73, 85–88, 94, 96, 97–99, 101–102, 110, 114–116; reader as participant/protagonist in, 89–90, 92, 101, 103–104, 106, 110, 114, 116; recursive ontologies in, 72; Russell Tribunal, 87, 88, 92–100, 105, 110, 112–113, 115; space and time, 104, 110; splicing in, 72; splitting in, 100–101, 103; supplemental/found materials, 99f, 105–106, 107f, 108, 109f, 110–111, 113; Susan Sontag, 90, 92–93, 111–113; utopia in, 99, 115–117

Fantomas, La amenaza elegante (Martré, Cruz Mota), 80, 90, 103; Cortázar's use of *Inteligencia en llamas*, 79, 88–92, 96, 98, 100–101, 103–104, 106, 108, 113, 117
Faulkner, William, 159, 179
Feitlowitz, Marguerite, 5–6, 8–9, 205n7, 222n3
Fernández Retamar, Roberto, 77, 85
Fletcher, Angus, 11
Fontes, Claudia, 1–2, 191, 203n2
formalism, 24–25
Foucault, Michel, 33, 39–40, 52–53, 135
Franco, Francisco, 135, 161
Frente Justicialista de Liberación, 123
Freud, Sigmund, 170, 223n17

Gambaro, Griselda, 14
García Márquez, Gabriel, 79
Gates-Madsen, Nancy J., 208n32, 210n59
Genette, Gérard, 15, 17
Geohumanities, 24
Girard, René, 135
González Bermejo, Ernesto, 82–83
Grosz, Elizabeth, 36, 175–176, 177, 189
Guattari, Félix, 176

Hamann, Johann Georg, 101–102, 110
Hegel, Georg Wilhelm Friedrich, 15
Heidegger, Martin, 176
Heker, Liliana, 14, 200
Hofstadter, Douglas, 141
Hölderlin, J. C. F., 30, 195
human rights: abuses, reports of, 6, 72, 79, 130, 204n4; discourse, 20, 22; evolution of international, 25; intervention, 22; Humanities and, 207–208n31; literary form and, 21–26; organizations, 2; paradoxes in, 20, 208n32; Western legal definitions of, 21

Inter-American Commission on Human Rights of the Organization of American States (OAS), 6
Irigaray, Luce, 175–176, 177, 223

Jakobson, Roman, 12, 36, 165, 170
Johnson, Barbara, 12
José Léon Suárez massacre, 42–43, 161
junta, military, 5, 6, 9–10, 39–40, 42, 70, 101, 130, 147, 170–171, 206n16, 222n3, 223n18

Kafka, Franz, 193
Kant, Immanuel, 21, 101–102
Kissinger, Henry, 92, 219n9
Klee, Paul, 128, 195
Koselleck, Reinhart, 30, 34, 101–104, 106, 116, 196
Kurnick, David, 86–87, 215n9, 217n57
Kusnetzoff, Juan Carlos, 205n11

La Nación, 40, 48
La novela de Perón (Martínez), 13, 34, 36, 119–158, 162; abeyance in, 123; absence in, 129, 134, 145–146, 148, 157; airplane, scene in, 125–132, 139–140, 142, 153; anticipation in, 155–156; countermemoirs, 142; disappearance in, 122, 125, 131, 139, 141; embedded worlds in, 141–142, 145, 199; ending, 136–137, 142; Evita, 142–143, 150, 152, 188–189; Ezeiza airport, 126–127, 129, 132–134, 137, 140, 142–143, 153–156; historical correlates, 124–125, 127–129, 131–132, 136, 139, 141, 143–144,

146–147, 154–158; *Horizonte*, 137, 142; inspiration for, 120–122, 130–131; Isabel de Perón, 128, 132, 142; López Rega, 132–133, 142–143, 149, 156, 188, 222n53; maps in, 153–154; narrative, 122, 124–126, 128–129, 143, 145, 149, 158, 166; opening scenes, 125–131; Perón in Madrid, 131, 149–152; Perón's death, 138, 142; Perón's mythic status, 134–137, 139, 148; Perón's return to Argentina, 123, 124–129, 132–134, 136, 139–140, 149, 152–154, 188–189; Montoneros, 131, 133–134, 136, 143, 155, 156; simulacrum and simulation in, 131–140; suspension in, 122–123, 125, 127–131, 156, 159, 192; televisions, 131, 133–134, 136–138; time and space in, 126, 128–129, 131, 145–146, 152, 156–157; withholding in, 122–123, 125, 131, 145–146
Lanusse, Alejandro Agustín, 123
Las Meninas (Velázquez), 33, 52, 53f
Lastiri, Raúl, 123
Lefebvre, Henri, 39
Leibniz, G. W., 159
Levine, Caroline, 24–25, 26
Link, Daniel, 212n16
Lonardi, Eduardo, 123, 135
López Rega, José, 92, 220n15
Lyotard, Jean-François, 23, 29, 199

Macri, Mauricio, 2, 204n4
Madres de Plaza de Mayo, 6, 7, 209n42
Maldonado, Santiago, 208–209n42
Mao Zedong, 135
Martí, José, 108
Martínez, Tomás Eloy, 10, 13, 14, 18, 29–30, 34, 69, 192, 196, 198, 202; interview with Juan Perón, 119–120, 124, 144–146; *La novela de Perón*, 34, 36, 119–158, 159, 162; *Santa Evita*, 13, 36–37, 116, 128, 142, 146–147, 150, 157, 159–190, 199
Martré, Gonzalo, 80, 90, 103
Massera, Emilio, 39, 170–171, 222n3, 223n18
McCloud, Scott, 104
McClennen, Sophia, 23, 25, 199
McCracken, Ellen, 85–86
McHale, Brian, 16–17, 141, 180, 221n36
Mercado, Tununa, 14, 200
metalepsis, 21, 144, 167
metaphor, 11, 152, 161, 165–166
metonymy, 11; definition of, 166; null intersection, 166; *Santa Evita*, 37, 160, 162, 165–167, 169, 171, 190, 223n17
Míguez, Pablo, 1–2, 191, 203n2
Miller, J. Hillis, 28, 209n46
modes of disappearance, definition of, 12–14. *See also* dissimulation; doubling; displacement; suspension; embodiment
Montoneros, 5, 161, 211n1, 220n15; fictional representations of, 142, 143, 153, 155–157
multinational corporations, 79; *Fantomas contra los vampiros multinacionales*, 79, 82, 110, 113

Nancy, Jean-Luc, 28, 176, 226n15
narrative: cipher, 167–168, 178, 185, 187, 190; colliding forms, 26; commons of disappearance, 27–29, 37, 117, 122, 192, 198–202; limits of, 15; modes of disappearance, 3, 10–15, 16, 18–19, 23, 16–27, 69–70, 201; strategies of disappearance, 16; suspension as a critical tool in, 130; true crime, 42

Neumann, Andrés, 202
New Critics, 31
Neyret, Juan Pablo, 124, 125
9/11, 21, 207n31

obliquity, 1–2, 4, 19–20, 31, 37, 41, 194–195, 200; as historical intervention, 19–20, 162; as literary strategy, 139–140, 160, 170; as reading strategy, 2, 20, 33, 41, 46, 69–70; of sight, 108, 198. *See also* blind spots
Osorio, Elsa, 201
otherness, 23

paradox, 19–20, 207n29; Zeno's, 184–187; human rights, 208n32
Pavel, Thomas, 114
Parque de la Memoria, 1, 191
Pauls, Alan, 201
percepticide, 7–8, 71, 108, 130, 205n11. *See also* social blinding
Perloff, Marjorie, 206n25
Perón, Eva "Evita" Duarte de, 120, 124, 137; body in life, 163, 167–168, 189; corpse of, 13, 161, 190, 222–223n7; corpse, damage to, 163, 222n5; corpse, hiding, 161, 162, 171–172, 177; death, 160; fictional portrayal in *La novela de Perón*, 142, 150, 152; fictional portrayal in *Santa Evita*, 128–129, 159–190; myths about and cult of memory, 161–162, 164, 167–168, 190; Spiritual Head of the Nation, 163; tour of Europe, 163. *See also* embodiment
Perón, Juan Domingo, 39–40, 160; exile, 73, 119, 123–124, 160–161; fictional portrayal in *La novela de Perón*, 13, 34, 36, 119–158; fictional portrayal in *Santa Evita*, 172; influence on Argentine history, 120–121; interview by Tomás Eloy Martínez, 119–120, 124, 145–146; memoirs, 35; mythic status, 134–135, 137, 162; official history, 35; return from exile, 34–35, 124
Perón, Isabel de, 5, 39, 74, 94, 101, 123, 124
Peronists/Peronism, 34–35, 123, 124; Frente Justicialista de Liberación, 123; historical significance of, 73–74; Montoneros, 5, 220n15; uprising against Aramburu, 42–43
personhood, altering definition of, 5, 9, 19, 130
Phelan, James, 221n39
Piglia, Ricardo, 14, 44–45, 94, 122, 147–148, 200, 212n5, 214n7
Pinochet, Augusto, 79
Plato, 174
Plaza de Mayo, 124
Poe, Edgar Allan, 41, 48, 211n4
postmodern literature, 17–18; experimentation, 25; ontological nature of, 16–17; politicization of, 18; refraction in, 17
precariousness: as constitutive of human life, 9; grievability, 9–10, 11
Premat, Julio, 206n25
Process of National Reorganization, 5–6, 101, 130

Quiroga, Horacio, 46

Rajca, Andrew C., 207n28
Rancière, Jacques, 27–28, 29, 176, 198–199, 207n29, 209n48
Reconstrucción del retrato de Pablo Míguez (Fontes), 1–2, 12, 191, 203n2
referral, 41, 52, 70
refraction, 15–20; in postmodern literature, 17

resistance, reading of/as, 15–20
Richard, Nelly, 19–20, 122, 127–128, 207n27
Ricoeur, Paul, 12, 36, 168, 170, 179–180, 187
Rilke, Rainer Maria, 195
Rio de la Plata, 1, 191
Robles, Raquel, 202
Rock, David, 123
Roitman, Janet, 103, 207n29, 217nn42–43
Russell, Bertrand, 79
Russell Tribunals, 33, 34, 79–80, 83, 85, 87, 94–96, 215n12; Russell Tribunal II in *Fantomas contra los vampiros multinacionales*, 87, 88, 92–100, 105, 110, 112–113, 115

Saer, Juan José, 14, 94, 147–148, 200, 212n5, 212n13, 214n7
Santa Evita (Martínez), 13, 36–37, 116, 128, 142, 146–147, 150, 159–190; absence in, 157, 167, 174; Borges in, 183–185, 187–188; cassette tape recording, 181–183, 185; Colonel Moori Koenig, 165, 168–183, 185, 187–188, 224–225n4; disappearance in, 161, 164–165, 170–171, 185, 190, 192; Dr. Ara, 164, 169, 171–173, 222n6, 222–223n7; emplotment in, 179–180, 188; Evita's burial, corpse, and copies, 165, 170, 178–188, 224n, 225n; Evita's corpse, 36, 159, 161, 163, 165, 167, 169, 171–172, 174, 177, 182–188, 190, 199; Evita's corpse as narrative cipher, 167–168, 178, 185, 187, 190; Evita's corpse, copies of, 165, 171–174, 177, 181–188; Evita's corpse, damage done to, 186, 222n5; historical correlates, 164, 167–168, 182, 186, 188; inspiration for, 165; Juan Perón, 172; López Rega, 181; maps in, 180–182, 185, 188; metonym in, 37, 160, 162, 165–167, 169, 171, 190; narrative, 160, 166, 171, 180, 182; superabundance in, 176–177, 188; Tomás Eloy Martínez, 165, 183; time and space in, 157, 168; Videla government, 170–171. *See also* embodiment; metonymy
Sartre, Jean-Paul, 79
Sherman, David, 178, 224n37
simulacrum, 131–140, 171–174, 182
simulation, 131–140, 182, 223–224n23
Slaughter, Joseph, 23, 25, 199
social blinding, 6–7, 170–171. *See also* percepticide
Souvestre, Pierre, 214–215n8
state-sponsored terrorism, disappearance as a tool of, 4–10, 67–68, 71, 79, 125, 130, 162
Stern, Steve J., 208n32
Strauss, Scott, 208n32
superabundance/the superabundant, 36–37, 160, 162, 171–177, 188. *See also* embodiment; excess; *Santa Evita*
suspension, 4, 13–14, 30, 41, 192, 199; as aesthetic tool, 130; epistemological, 10; in *La novela de Perón*, 122–123, 125, 127–131, 156, 159, 192; as mode of disappearance, 13, 122–123, 125, 127–131, 156, 159, 192; states of, 14, 129–130

Taylor, Diana, 7, 9, 71, 130, 189–190
time: in Blanchot, 30; in detective fiction, 41; in *Fantomas contra los vampiros multinacionales*, 104, 110; in *La novela de Perón*, 126, 128–129, 131, 145–146, 152, 156–157; in *Santa Evita*, 157, 168

transnationalism, 18, 29

United Nations, 2
United States: foreign policy in Latin America, 33, 79; occupation of Vietnam, 79

Valéry, Paul, 193
Variaciones en rojo (Walsh), 32, 40, 45–46, 47; "Asesinato a distancia," 47; author-protagonist in, 48; author's note, 47–48; end of book, 68; "La Aventura de las pruebas de imprenta," 47, 50; opening, 47–48; proofreader, role of, 49–50; "Variaciones en rojo," 32–33, 40–41, 46, 47, 50–54, 173
"Variaciones en rojo" (Walsh), 32, 46, 50–54; absence in, 32, 67; art, role in, 51, 53–54, 56, 58–61, 66, 68, 69, 173–174; Chief Jiménez (detective), 50–51, 54–56, 61, 63–64; crime scene, 50–51, 54–55, 62–64; Daniel Hernández (proofreader), 50, 52, 55–56, 58–59, 61–66, 68; deferral in, 41, 52; dialogue in, 54–55; disappearance in, 32, 40–41, 46, 51–52, 65–67, 69; dissimulation in, 41, 67–69; graph theory, 63–64; "ideal painting," 32–33, 59–60; miniature cityscape, 51, 55–56, 63, 66–67; murder weapon, 55, 61–62, 64, 66, 68; narrative, 65, 68; painting of humanity on an abyss, 51–52, 56, 58; proofreader, role in, 50; reader, role of, 50, 52, 54, 69; solving the crime, 61–65, 68
Velázquez, Diego, 33, 52–53
Videla, Jorge Rafael, 5, 39, 72, 74, 94, 101, 124, 162, 170
Vietnam War, 79

vision, stereoscopic, 31, 87, 95, 101–102. *See also* catastrophe; *Fantomas contra los vampiros multinacionales*

Walsh, Patricia, 40
Walsh, Rodolfo, 11, 13–14, 18, 29, 30, 33, 108, 179, 192, 196, 198, 202, 211n; "Asesinato a distancia," 47; "Carta abierta de un escritor a la junta militar," 42, 70; *Caso Satanowsky*, 42, 43; "Cuento para Tahures," 42; *Diez cuentos policiales argentinos*, 42; "Dos mil quinientos años de literatura policial," 48; early detective fiction, 40–41, 45–47, 67, 70–71; identification of body, 40; interview with Ricardo Piglia, 44–45; investigative journalism, 40, 42–44; "La Aventura de las pruebas de imprenta," 47, 50; literary journalism, 42; *Los oficios terrestres*, 43; "Massacre del barrio Jose Leon Suarez: un libro sin editorial," 43; murder, 39–40, 70; *Operación masacre*, 42–43, 161; political writing, 43–44; proofreader, job as a, 42; pseudonymous writings, 46; *¿Quién mató a Rosendo?*, 42, 43; scholarship on, 212–213n16; *Variaciones en rojo*, 32, 40, 45–48; "Variaciones en rojo," 32–33, 39, 46, 50–54
war on terror, 18
White, Hayden, 12, 27, 121, 139
withholding, 14, 15; *La novela de Perón*, 122–123, 125, 131, 145–146
woman-as-place, 175–177. *See also* excess, architectures of
world-building, 4, 13, 16–17, 21, 72
World Soccer Championships, 6

Yates, Donald, 43

www.ingramcontent.com/pod-product-compliance
Lightning Source LLC
Chambersburg PA
CBHW030537230426
43665CB00010B/933